Yes Sister, No Sister

My Life as a Trainee Nurse in 1950s Yorkshire

JENNIFER CRAIG

EBURY
PRESS

1 3 5 7 9 10 8 6 4 2

Published in 2010 by Ebury Press, an imprint of Ebury Publishing
A Random House Group company
First published in the UK by The Breedon Books Publishing
Company in 2002

The Random House Group Limited Reg. No. 954009

Addresses for companies within the Random House Group can be
found at www.randomhouse.co.uk

A CIP catalogue record for this book is available from the British Library

The Random House Group Limited supports the Forest Stewardship
Council® (FSC®), the leading international forest certification
organisation. All our titles that are printed on Greenpeace approved
FSC® certified paper carry the FSC® logo. Our paper procurement
policy can be found at www.randomhouse.co.uk/environment

Printed and bound in the UK by CPI Mackays, Chatham ME5 8TD

ISBN 9780091943424

To buy books by your favourite authors and register for offers visit
www.randomhouse.co.uk

This book is dedicated to Registered Nurses everywhere

This book is a work of non-fiction based on the life, experiences and recollections of the author. In most cases names of people have been changed to protect their privacy. However, it is impossible to conceal that the author's matrons were Kathleen Raven and Grace Watts, and that her tutors were Mrs B.M. Morley, Miss A.H.K. Bird and Miss Amy Squibbs.

In my outdoor uniform, February 1953. Cotton dress, starched cap, purple-lined woollen cloak — to be worn in all weathers.

Preface

THIS STORY IS based on my experience of training as a nurse at Leeds General Infirmary between 1952 and 1956 and of subsequently working there as a staff nurse, a night sister and a ward sister.

The events I have described are true. I have tried to give an accurate picture of the nursing procedures we followed at that time before they are lost to history. The pantomimes, surgeons' behaviour, housemen's antics and patients are, I hope, faithfully portrayed. The dialogue is, of course, fictitious. I have tried to capture the way people talked rather than give verbatim records.

To all nurses and doctors who worked at the hospital during the 1950s: I hope you enjoy this account and accept it in the spirit in which it is offered – as a memorial to times we shall never see again. We were great, weren't we?

To all nurses and doctors of today: I hope you read this with interest as you discover some of your historical precedents. I trust your work is as interesting for you as it was for us and I hope you are having as much fun as we had.

To the general reader: I may have given away a few trade secrets of what went on behind the starched uniforms, but only to reveal the essential humour and humanity of a great Yorkshire hospital. You have to remember that the majority of doctors and nurses, who essentially ran the hospital, were under thirty. If their youthful shenanigans shock you, I assure you that their patients always, yes always, came first.

Chapter 1

A NURSE AT LAST! I see myself comforting those in pain; soothing fevered brows; saying, 'There, this will make you feel better'; carefully changing dressings and efficiently plumping pillows so that a patient lies back with a sigh of gratitude.

Requirements:
- three pairs of black stockings
- one pair of flat, black serviceable shoes
- a selection of safety pins and studs
- a packet of white kirby grips
- two plain silver tiepins
- one pocket watch with a second hand
- one pair regulation nurses' scissors
- five pounds, ten shillings and sixpence for text books
- six exercise books, pens and pencils
- two draw-string laundry bags clearly marked with name

A uniform, piled on my bed, consists of a short-sleeved, purple- and white-check cotton dress with pockets everywhere. As well as waist pockets it has breast pockets, plus slots for holding pens and scissors. A separate rigid, round white collar is held on the dress with a safety pin and fastens with a stud at the front. The starched apron has a bib held up by tiepins and a waistband that also fastens with studs. Black stockings and shoes complete the outfit. Stocking seams have to be straight. I twist to check before attaching them to my suspender belt.

I admire the reflection of a nurse in the mirror. Can this be me? I wish I was tall, slender and glamorous, like the images of young women presented to me in *Woman's Own*, but I am not. I look more at home in hiking boots and a rucksack than in a little black dress and pearls. 'She's a sturdy lass' is how I am described.

I straighten my back, turn from side to side and pirouette. 'Look at me,' I want to shout to the world. 'Look at me. I'm a nurse.' I re-read my letter of acceptance:

Dear Miss Ross,
The Board of Governors of the Leeds General Infirmary is pleased to inform you that you have been accepted as a student nurse in their three year programme leading to State Registration. Please report to 47–49 Hyde Terrace on December 3, 1952 in the afternoon. The uniform you were measured for will be in your room; please put it on when you arrive.

My long, navy woollen cloak with a purple lining has purple straps that cross at the front and fasten at the back. In it I look exactly like the war posters declaring 'Your Country Needs You', which show a nurse in such a cloak. No cap yet. Two oblongs of white cloth, the size of a nappy, starched to the consistency of plywood, lie there on the bed. The mysteries of their construction are yet to be revealed.

A chain fastens my brand-new pocket watch into one of my breast pockets and I stick the scissors and a pen in the other. Wearing a short-sleeved cotton dress in winter in an unheated room is like wearing a bathing costume in a windy bus station. Even the cloak does not keep me warm. I put on a cardigan, pick up one white, starched oblong, safety pins and kirby grips and go down the three flights of stairs to the main floor.

The living room holds a group of girls dressed like me, who huddle around a small coal fire in a large hearth. We sit or stand, looking uncomfortable, not knowing what to say. A girl, who would seem more at home in jodhpurs and a riding hat than she does in her uniform, sits alone on a sofa. She has an aquiline nose, which makes her seem sophisticated, and permanently raised eyebrows that give her a surprised, questioning look. I plonk myself next to her.

'This is as absurd as I thought it was going to be,' she says. 'Imagine dressing like this in winter – or in summer for that matter. This collar is already chafing my neck.' She runs a finger around her collar. 'What's your name? I'm Judith Horsfall.'

'Jennifer Ross. Where are you from?'

'A little village called Haxby, not far from York. How about you?'

'My parents live in Bombay and I have just come back from there so I can train here. I wanted to go to London but I have relatives here and my mother wanted me to be near her sisters so they can keep an eye on me.' I had had quite a battle with my mother over where I would train. I had lost.

My father was in the army in Burma during the war and away from England for five years. We lived in Leeds. When he returned, a complete stranger to my brother and me, he could not settle in Britain. After a stint in the occupation forces he took a job in India running a service department for a major car sales firm.

'What were you doing before this?' I ask Judith.

'I did orthopaedic training for a year because you can start when you are 17 and I didn't know what else to do when I left school. How exciting being in India! What did you do? Did you go to school there?'

'No, I went to Leeds Girls High School and, after School Certificate, I had to wait two years to get into training. So I lived with my parents. They wanted to send me to a finishing school in the Himalayas but when I saw that you had to wear combinations, those all-in-one underwear with a flap for your bottom, I refused absolutely. So I just swam all day for two years, waiting until I was old enough to start training.'

'You might get awfully homesick with your Mum away. You'll have to come home with me sometimes. That is, if you can put up with my stupid brother!'

I smile at Judith. She must like me if she asks me home so quickly. 'I'd love to. But I don't think I'll get homesick. I've been waiting for this moment for two whole years. What was orthopaedic training like?'

Before Judith can answer there is a stir at the door as a large woman in a blue, long-sleeved dress, with a mass of frilled starch on her head, walks in. She takes a commanding spot near the fire. An image of my head-mistress at school comes to mind, along with an old feeling that my bowels are dissolving.

She surveys us for a moment before announcing, 'I'm Sister Thornton, one of the Home Sisters. Although I will not be living here, I shall be supervising you.' She catches sight of me and stops talking. 'What is your name?' she asks, staring at me.

'Jennifer Ross.'

'Jennifer Ross, *Sister*. Well, Nurse Ross, you are dressed in the uniform of a nurse from the Leeds General Infirmary. Such a uniform is not worn with a cardigan. Take it off at once.'

'Yes Sister.' I can feel my face turn red.

'Nor, by the way, is any jewellery or make-up allowed

when you are in uniform. Now, as I was saying, I am not resident here so one of you must assume responsibility for the behaviour of the group. Who is the eldest?'

She looks around. No one says anything. 'How old are you?' she asks the girl on her right. 'Go round and state your age.'

Among the eighteens and nineteens there is suddenly a twenty-seven. We all turn to stare at the elder among us. She is a lively looking girl with freckles and brown eyes with a hint of mischief in them.

'Is there anyone older than twenty-seven?' Silence. 'What is your name?' Sister asks the older nurse.

'Sheila Dawson.'

'Sheila Dawson, *Sister*.' She speaks sharply. 'Well, Nurse Dawson, I am putting you in charge. I will explain what you all have to do and Nurse Dawson will see that you do it.' Sheila seems as if she is having trouble keeping a straight face.

'As you know, Roundhay Hall is where you will be going through Preliminary Training School and you will be going there each day by bus.'

She pauses to stare first at one girl and then at another. I am not sure whether we are meant to meet her eyes or whether we are to lower ours in submission.

'Eventually, the PTS will sleep there but the rooms are not ready yet. You will get dinner there each day but you will have breakfast and supper at the Infirmary.' She stands to attention with her hands in front of her like a fig leaf. 'You will walk to the Infirmary each morning leaving here at 7am, have breakfast and then be in the bus by 8am so you will be ready to start classes at 8.30am. The bus will take you back to the Infirmary for supper at 6pm. Then you will walk back here.'

Sister Thornton allows herself to assume an 'at ease' position with her hands behind her back, but the change does little to dispel my growing discomfort. 'As you walk through the streets in uniform, you must behave with decorum as befits a LGI nurse. You will walk in pairs, keep together and talk in subdued tones. There is to be no laughter. Is that understood?'

'Yes Sister,' we chorus.

'We're in the army now,' Judith sings under her breath.

'The reasons you chose nursing are many and varied but what you must understand is that we require girls with dedication and strength of character and who can obey orders. Mistakes can cause the death of a patient.' Sister Thornton looks around at our upturned faces and sighs. 'Most of you will prove to be unsuitable. I doubt if even half of you will finish training.'

She looks around again and her eyes light on me. She regards me contemplatively as if thinking that here is one unsuitable girl; anyone who wears a cardigan with her uniform is destined to fail. 'You must make many sacrifices for your patients and be prepared to make nursing your whole life. If you do not possess these qualities, you will be asked to leave.'

Am I prepared to make nursing my whole life? I look around me. How many of us are? How many of us will finish? What if I kill someone by doing the wrong thing? I might give the wrong medicine and poison someone, or pull out a tube or … what else could I possibly do wrong that would harm a patient? These ideas had not crossed my mind before and now I am full of misgivings.

Will I be one of those who gives up, or, perish the thought, be asked to leave? If I am, what will I do instead? At one time I yearned to be a vet but I had been informed that women are not strong enough to be vets. When I said I wanted to be a nurse, my family smiled and told me that it is a wonderful career: I would never be short of a job and the training is ideal preparation for marriage. At school I took the courses listed under 'Nursing as a Career', so along with physics and chemistry, I had struggled with Latin.

Sister Thornton's voice invades my consciousness. 'All lights must be out by 10.30pm and the door is to be locked at 10 sharp by Nurse Dawson. There will be no late passes while you are in PTS. Now I will show you how to make a cap. Gather round this table. Can someone please give me their cap?' Sister Thornton takes one of the proffered white boards and folds it to produce a cap that fits the head above the ears, soars upwards, folds in a neat line and then hangs down at the back.

'There, that's easy isn't it?' she says. 'The head band is plain but when you have finished your probationary period, and if you succeed, you will be given a cap with the LGI emblem on the band. Now everyone is to make up a cap, put it on, and then it will be time for you to walk to the Infirmary for supper.'

'Why do we need to wear uniform if we are only going there for supper, Sister?' Judith asks. There is silence as Sister Thornton recovers from the question.

'Nurse, you are now a nurse of the Leeds General Infirmary and as such you will appear clean and neat at all times. You will be making your first appearance in the dining room and will be looked at by the rest of the staff. We do not want them to think that this PTS is sloppy, do we?'

'No Sister.'

'I shall leave you now. Make up your caps and then Nurse Dawson will see that you are properly assembled before you walk down the hill to the Infirmary.'

'How will we know where to go, Sister?' asks Sheila.

'Go in through the front door and ask the hall porter to direct you. I will call in tomorrow evening to see how you are doing.' She leaves and Sheila flops on a sofa, doubles up her knees and howls with laughter.

'Oh, my God! Me in charge! Wait till my brothers hear about this! Now then you lot, pay attention! Nurse Ross, stand up. Say "Yes Nurse Dawson" when I speak to you and curtsy.' She stands up to imitate the voice and posture of Sister Thornton.

'Nurse Ross, you are not behaving with decorum. Pulling that face does not befit the uniform of a LGI nurse. We will walk to the Infirmary two by two, by the left, quick march a-n-d left, right, left, ouch!' Someone has thrown a cushion at her.

Feeling more cheerful we all make up something that can be called a cap, put them on and hold them in place with white kirby grips. We fetch our cloaks and prepare to leave. It is raining. No one is sure whether an umbrella detracts from the dignity of the uniform so we leave them behind. Our cloak hoods do not fully cover our beautiful starched caps so we arrive for the first time at the Infirmary with pieces of limp cloth hanging from our heads like nun's veils.

We enter the front door of the Infirmary. The panelled hall with its marble floor ends in an elegant staircase in the distance. It begins as one wide set of steps that divide into two graciously curved flights leading upwards. The panels of the hall hold boards on which are painted, in gold, the names of the medical consultants and which announce whether they are in the house or not. One board is for physicians with the title of 'Doctor' and the other for surgeons with the title of 'Mister'.

A glassed-off room at the entrance holds a switchboard, hanging clipboards, several dirty mugs and Jim. Jim, the senior hall porter, is part of the institution, and rumour has it that he was hired when the foundation stone was laid. As this was in 1868, he would be over 80 years old, which he clearly is not. His job is to answer those internal calls that seek someone such as a doctor or a sister, buzz the beeper of that person, and then tell them where they are needed when they phone him back. He is also in charge of a small army of porters who manoeuvre patients on trolleys, oxygen tanks, food canteens and equipment around the hospital.

Jim directs us to the dining room. 'Go up them stairs and turn right onto the main corridor and then you'll see an arrer pointing to t'dining room at t'other end. Aye, it's grand to see such bright young lasses and I hopes tha'll be right happy.'

The main corridor of the hospital is about a quarter of a mile long. Its linoleum surface stretches into the horizon, and with hardly any people in it at this time of the evening, it reminds me of the yellow brick road in the *Wizard of Oz*. There is a distinctive smell about the place, a warm smell with a mixture of boiled cabbage, furniture polish and disinfectant.

We find the dining room without difficulty. It is the size of a gymnasium and filled with tables for eight. The chatter ceases as we enter. Everyone stares at us, and no doubt, at our limp caps. The room is full of young women, most in uniform like ours, but one or two are in mufti. A mass of purple at one end of the room attracts my attention. Three tables are for permanent staff nurses – perms – who wear purple dresses with long sleeves ending in stiff cuffs, small purple capes like army nurses and caps like ours.

We are surprised to find that we are served by waitresses rather than having to line up at a counter. If this first supper is a sample of the meals we are to be given, we will certainly not go hungry. Three courses, beef barley soup, sausages, baked potatoes and peas, followed by steamed pudding and custard arrive quickly, one after the other. Although most foods that were rationed during the war are now freely available, we still need coupons for butter and sugar and we have to carry these around with us in small tin containers.

Everyone in the room seems to be eating hurriedly and they barely finish before they are scraping back their chairs to leave.

'We will only get 20 minutes to eat by the time we've walked to and from our wards,' Judith says. 'That's why we learn to eat so fast.'

'The food's good anyway,' I say.

'They have to keep the slave labour going or we'll collapse and so will the hospital,' Judith says.

I sit between Judith and a girl called Marie Chart. Marie seems a serious type who doesn't smile much. Attractive dark eyes and olive skin give a hint of her Italian ancestry. She tells me that her childhood sweetheart is a medical student in another city and, after completing their respective training, they plan to marry and become missionaries.

'We want to start a hospital or a medical clinic in a country where there is a lot of leprosy,' she says. 'Both Charles and I believe that we have been called by God to serve lepers.' I hear Judith draw in her breath but she doesn't say anything. 'Do you feel you have a calling?' Marie asks me.

'No, I can't say I do. I really wanted to be a vet but at school we were told women aren't strong enough. In fact, the three choices for us were teaching, nursing or secretarial work.'

'Not strong enough to be vets but strong enough to hoof 20-stone patients around,' Judith says. 'Amazing isn't it? You see pictures of women from other countries carrying huge loads on their backs but we are not strong enough to do what we want to do.'

'Well, after all, a woman's place is in the home beside her husband,' Marie says.

'Don't be so bloody silly,' Judith snaps. 'I suppose all you want out of life is to have lots of snotty babies and bake cakes.'

Marie is indignant. 'Babies are not snotty, they are beautiful. They are God's gift to us.'

'Canting fool,' I hear Judith mutter as I quickly ask Marie how many brothers and sisters she has.

'I am one of nine but Charles is an only child so we will be a real family for him. In fact, that's how I got to know him. My brother Paul used to bring him home from school as both his parents work and he was on his own.' She holds her knife and fork correctly, cuts her food into delicate pieces and chews the prescribed 20 times.

'When will you marry?' I ask, as in contrast, I stuff large pieces of baked potato into my mouth and talk with my mouth full.

'When we've both finished training, which will be in 1956. Charles is two years older than me so he's started medical school.' I am tired of asking Marie questions and as she doesn't respond by asking me about my life, I turn to Judith.

'What are you going to do when you've finished training?'

'God knows. And if today is anything to go by, I may not finish. If all sisters are like that Thornton woman, I will never survive. Did you see her face when I asked her why we have to wear uniform to come here just to eat?'

I laugh. 'She looked as though she was going to have a fit! "Nurse, you are now a nurse of the Leeds General Infirmary and as such you will appear clean and neat at all times"' I say, imitating Sister Thornton.

'Completely irrational. She didn't even answer the question. I wanted to ask why we can't be clean and neat in our own clothes, but I didn't dare. Look around; there's lots of people in mufti. And I don't see why we should wear cotton dresses when it's freezing. It's warm here but there we are walking in the streets and sitting in rooms with no heat…'

She doesn't finish but takes a gulp of tea. 'Not only that, she had no business frightening us all by saying we could kill a patient. Most of what we will be doing is routine menial jobs if it's anything like orthopaedic training.'

'What was it like in orthopaedic training?'

'Much more relaxed. Has to be. The patients are there for months at a time. Poor little kiddies in casts and splints to correct congenital deformities. Some of them have to lie in body casts for weeks and weeks.'

'Did you learn much that will help here?'

'Well, we had to know the skeleton pretty well and I expect a lot of the ward procedures are the same. Bed making, bedbaths, that sort of thing. But we didn't get any acutes or emergencies. And most of the patients who weren't children were young. So this will be very different.'

'Come on, Sheila's getting us all up to go.' I say. 'This is a damn nuisance – having to carry tins of butter and sugar everywhere we go.'

'I think it will be easier to give up sweetened tea and buttered bread, don't you?' replies Judith.

Despite the rain and cold we endure as we walk back up the hill to Hyde Terrace, I am so happy I could sing. I am with a group of girls my own age and we are going to be nurses. I feel proud in my uniform. Even though the stiff collar and starched apron are uncomfortable, I love them. They fulfil my image of a nurse – competent, caring, a figure to be relied upon in any emergency.

Yet I have an unfamiliar sense of unease as Sister Thornton's words come back to me. I had been so excited about starting training and the thought of failure had never crossed my mind. Judith said she might never finish if the sisters were like Thornton. Surely they couldn't be? Sisters must be the most skilled, the most kind, the most caring of nurses, or they wouldn't be sisters. They will be eager to help us become like them and will show patience as we struggle to learn.

I know the work is hard but everyone says it is very rewarding and worthwhile. No, I am not going to be put off by Thornton; I am going to be a really good nurse and, one day, I will be a sister.

Chapter 2

NTHE BUS to Roundhay Hall I sit next to a goofy-looking girl with the unlikely name of Hermione Blinkr. She tells me this apologetically and says that she is usually known as Blinks. Large glasses that distort her eyes above her slightly buck teeth give her a gormless look; but when she smiles she has that certain attraction some ugly people possess. I am drawn to her as one who is drawn to a sad-eyed spaniel. I feel protective as I sense she cannot stand up for herself.

'I live in Newcastle,' Blinks tells me, 'but I came to Leeds to get away from my mother and sisters. They tell me all the time that I will never survive nurses' training. I'm determined to show them.' She takes off her glasses to polish them with her handkerchief and gives me a big grin. 'According to them I'm not good for anything except serving fish and chips in a lorry driver's caff. I don't want to go home on my days off to that.'

'What did you do before this?'

'I stayed at school in the sixth form.'

'Did you like it?' Going into the sixth form had been an option for me but I could hardly wait to leave the boredom of school.

'Well, I didn't have much choice.' Blinks paused for a minute. 'I'm the youngest of four girls. My older sisters went to university, one's still there, but I didn't get high enough marks.' She turns to smile at me. 'So here I am, the dumbo of the family.'

'Marks don't mean everything,' I say. 'One girl in my form never did well and now she runs a dance academy even though she's only 19. Did you really want to go to university?'

'To he truthful, I don't know what I want to do. This is the lesser of several awful choices. I was told that nursing is great preparation for marriage.'

We both laugh. 'I was told that too.'

'I can't see myself getting married whether I become a nurse or not. Who would propose to someone like me?' Blinks laughs as she says this; I can see that she has no self-confidence.

'I don't see why not,' I say. 'I'm sure you'd make a wonderful wife.'

Blinks pulls my arm from under my cloak and holds her own alongside it. 'Look at that,' she says. 'Look how strong you are and how scrawny I am. My sister says I would blow over in a breeze.'

'Men don't marry women because of the size of their arms,' I say, laughing. 'They like to be mothered.'

'They also like to look at a nice smile like yours.'

'Ah yes, but I'm not the sort to pander to a man. My mother said I should never beat a man at sports because they don't like it. Well, tough tatties I say.'

The bus turns through a gateway of stone columns supporting lions rampant that look lonely without their wrought iron gates. I expect these were removed in the war effort. Roundhay Hall had been a minor stately home before it was donated to the Infirmary. A square, grey stone building set within several acres of lawn and trees, that, to me, seems far too dignified to house a preliminary training school for nurses. At this time of the year the trees are bare and the grass gleams with ice. A chill wind lifts my cloak as I descend from the bus and nearly whips my cap off. Are we going to freeze in unheated rooms here? I will never survive. I have been cold ever since I arrived back in England from India.

Two Sister Tutors meet us. They wear grey dresses and straight caps like American nurses but with a frill across the top. Sister Uprichard and Sister Downes are to be prominent figures in our lives for the next three months so we examine them carefully. Sister Uprichard is plump, with a large bosom and a round, cheerful face. Sister Downes is small, bird-like, with a walk like a penguin. This particular walk propels her along at a tremendous rate – soundless and efficient.

Up and Down, as they are naturally dubbed, show us

round. The main floor holds a lounge, classrooms, a practical room, kitchens, including one where we will learn to cook, and a large, cheerful dining room. Upstairs are to be the bedrooms where future generations of probationers will sleep. There is central heating, thank heaven.

Our first instruction is how we are to address sisters. We are to stand when spoken to and stand when they enter a room. We are to say 'Yes Sister' or 'No Sister.' We are to realise that, in comparison to them, we are on the same level of the biological scale as an amoeba.

When Up and Down finally leave the room we all relax and carry on with getting to know each other. Suddenly Sister Downes re-enters. Well-trained at Leeds Girls High School, I stand up along with about two others. Down looks around and leaves the room, only to enter once more seconds later. Again only I and one or two others stand. Everyone else continues to lounge in her seat and chat. With a frozen face, Down leaves again. She returns with the same result as before, but this time she claps her hands and says 'Obviously we have a group here who cannot follow directions. You have only been here ten minutes and you have already demonstrated that you are incapable of listening and learning. I fear for the future of nursing.' With this, she leaves the room, re-enters and the entire class springs to its feet.

'Be seated. Now I will explain your timetable for the time you are here. You were late this morning but in future we expect you here promptly at 8.30am.' She stands at the front of the class holding a sheaf of papers. 'You will have classes until one o'clock, an hour for lunch and then leave at six o'clock. There will be two short tea breaks, one in the morning and one in the afternoon. Some afternoons you will be out, either on the wards or on a field trip. I will now hand out individual timetables as you are not always together.'

She passes out sheets of paper. We are together for lectures on anatomy and physiology, nutrition, hygiene and care of patients with a variety of diseases. We split up for cooking, time in the practical room and experience on the wards. There are also several field trips planned.

All this time, Up has been sitting to one side. When Down has finished she comes to the front of the class. 'Now, Sister Downes and I would like to know your names. I want you each to stand up, tell us your name and where you are from. We will be writing down your names as you go round.'

There are 32 of us. The previous evening there had been 33 but one girl was so homesick she left this morning. 'How ridiculous!' I said to Judith when we heard. 'Can you believe that someone would apply, go through an interview, arrive here and then leave because they miss their mummy?' I feel contemptuous. I am the one whose parents are far away while this girl lives nearby. If I leave it will be for a reason far more important than homesickness.

After the introductions we are led into the practical room. It is set up as a small ward with eight beds, a sterilising room and a sluice room which houses urinals, bedpans and a bedpan hopper that washes bedpans and urine testing equipment. At one end is a cupboard containing numerous enamel bowls, instruments and linen. Dummies occupy two of the beds. A skeleton hangs in one corner, metal poles on wheels and with hooks on them are clustered in another corner, and in another are stainless steel, two-tier trolleys. Large, colourful anatomical maps decorate the walls.

'Now nurses, I want you to watch carefully while Sister Downes and I make a bed. Afterwards I will ask you what you observed. Nurse Horsfall, would you please time us? Start counting from when I say "go".'

Up takes two chairs and places them back to back at the foot of one of the beds. 'Go,' she says, and she and Down move as though they have suddenly been switched on. In unison, like professional ballroom dancers, they strip the bed, one sheet and blanket at a time. Each piece of bedding is folded in three and laid over the two chairs. Then they make up the bed again.

'How long was that, Nurse Horsfall?'

'Two minutes, 45 seconds, Sister.' We are awed.

'What did you notice?'

'That you moved together as a team,' says one girl.

'Yes, you are to strive to work exactly together. It is faster for one thing but also much easier on your back. What else?'

'The counterpane hangs with the same amount on each side and the corners are an exact triangle,' replies another.

Down strokes the counterpane of the bed they have made. 'The ward looks neater when the beds are well-made and a neat ward is a sign of good nursing. What else?'

'The bottom sheet is as taut as a drum.'

'Yes. Wrinkled sheets are one of the main causes of bedsores.' Down takes on a grim tone. 'Bedsores are due to poor nursing care – nothing else, despite what you may hear to the contrary. What else?'

No one answers.

'We shook the blankets and sheets as little as possible to avoid creating dust in the air and so spreading infection. We will make it again more slowly and point out some of the things to watch for. Then you will work in pairs to make a bed.'

I work with a girl called Wendy Sandstone, or Sandy. We are hopeless. When she is at the top of the bed, I am at the bottom. It takes us a good ten minutes to strip and make the bed and the result is lop-sided and the bottom sheet has wrinkles in it.

Up comes over. 'Never mind, nurses, try again. You will soon get the hang of it. Start at the top of the bed then you'll have enough sheet to make good corners. Here, Nurse Sandstone, let me show you.'

We try again with a slightly better result but still the

counterpane is crooked. This time we have Down check us. 'You obviously have no sense of balance. Nurse Ross, can't you tell when one of you has more counterpane than the other? Do it again.'

Finally we make a presentable bed and are allowed to go for dinner. Sandy loves to chat. She prattles on about whether the peas are cooked properly, have I seen someone or other's cap and isn't it funny folded that way, whether it is the number six bus that stops outside the front door of the hospital or the number eight, aren't the flowers in the front hall pretty, will her shoes last a year, and so on. She has a crush on June Allyson, the film star, and writes to her asking for autographed photographs which she pins up on the inside of her wardrobe.

Her mother died when Sandy was 12. After that she was expected to, and did, run the house for her father and two older brothers. Only when the brothers left home was she allowed to contemplate a career for herself. Her days off are to be spent cleaning the house and leaving a week's meals ready for her father, as these are the conditions under which she was allowed to leave home.

After dinner and a walk around the grounds, we have the first of many lectures. It is firmly implanted into us that the control of disease and the way to health lies through clean water, treatment of sewerage, hygiene and fresh air. The first hygiene lecture includes personal hygiene, which Down approaches head-on with little or no regard for our sensibilities. We are told that we are to bathe daily with particular attention to our underarms.

'Patients are sick enough without having to smell a nurse's armpits as she bends over them,' Down says. 'You must constantly check that you do not smell and if any of you realise that one of your colleagues smells, you must inform her. It is difficult to smell your own breath so you must ask a colleague to check for you.'

From then on we exhale vigorously at each other to do the breath test and begin a life-long habit of surreptitiously sniffing our armpits.

I go out for a day with a district nurse and see for myself the appalling conditions in which some people live. I have seen abject poverty in India but I did not realise it is also prevalent in my own country. Many people live in 'one-up one-downs', as the rows of small houses built in the Industrial Revolution are called. They are literally two rooms, one on top of the other. There are no bathrooms. Six houses share an outside toilet and each house has one cold-water tap. Despite the lack of running hot water the steps of most of the houses are well scrubbed and the lace curtains at the windows gleam white against the grimy brick walls. All except for the one house that we enter.

The district nurse knocks on the door and I can hear shuffling inside. Finally the door opens.

'Coom in, coom in,' an old man says.

After we step straight from the pavement into the living

room, I am met by an unpleasant rancid smell. When my eyes are accustomed to the dim light, I see a large, square table that takes up most of the space. On it stands a medley of unwashed empty milk bottles, chipped mugs, dirty plates precariously balanced on each other, greasy cutlery, a box of sugar cubes, a stale loaf, several slices of old toast and a collection of tins.

A coal fire burns in the hearth beneath a cluttered mantelpiece. Drawn up to this is a plush-covered easy chair with a cushion holding down the protruding springs. Under the window, a stone sink with one leaking tap has a wooden draining board covered with more dirty dishes. In the sink, a pan, containing what looks like burnt porridge, is filled with greasy water and the plop, plop of water dripping into it is an irritating background sound.

Against one wall stands a cabinet with a crocheted runner covering its uncluttered surface. On it sits a framed photograph of a woman wearing a fur collar and a cloche hat of the 1920s.

'Good morning, Mr Harrop,' the district nurse says. 'This is a student nurse from the Infirmary who is spending the day with me. How are you?'

'Nicely, thank you,' says the old man. He has been tall but is now lean and bent. He wears a collarless shirt, a stained grey woollen cardigan and pyjama bottoms. 'Would you like a cuppa?'

I am relieved to hear the district nurse say, 'No thank

you, Mr Harrop. We're running a bit late today. How's your leg?'

He sits on the easy chair, extends one leg and rolls up the pyjamas to uncover a bandage around his calf. The district nurse kneels down to unroll the bandage and I promptly feel sick when a huge ulcer, taking up most of his calf, is revealed.

'It's looking a wee bit better,' she says. 'There's signs of granulation down this edge, look.'

Looking better? How much worse can it be than this? I stare at the cavernous wound. It looks as if an animal has taken a bite out of him and then sprayed it with green pus. The district nurse pulls a dressing tray out of her bag. She washes her hands with her own soap and dries them on her own towel. Then she throws the old dressing on the fire before starting to clean the ulcer. I can hardly look. Will I ever be able to attend such a horrible wound without vomiting? My image of myself efficiently changing dressings quickly vanishes. Instead I see a dithering twerp who has to swallow hard and smile through clenched teeth.

Desperately needing something to do or say, I pick up the photo of the young woman and say, 'Was this your wife? She was very beautiful.'

'Ay, she were that. Allus was, even to the end. I never fancied another woman, only her. She died three year since.' Mr Harrop takes the photograph from me and strokes the glass. 'I still miss her. T'house wouldn't be this mess if she was here.'

'When is your niece coming again, Mr Harrop?' the district nurse asks.

'She couldn't come last week but she should be here today. She'll clean up and bring me some bread and tea. I'll be alright.'

'I'm a bit worried that you're not eating properly,' the district nurse says as she packs her bag.

'Oh, I'm alright. Neighbour brings me a Sunday dinner and my niece will bring me some fish'n'chips and mushy peas. Tha' don't need much to eat at my age.'

We leave and as we retrieve our bicycles I say, 'That's terrible. How can we leave an old man like that? He should be in a home.'

The district nurse is attaching her bag to her pannier when she looks at me and says, 'What makes you think he would he better off in a home?'

'Well, he'd get regular meals for one thing and he wouldn't be so dirty. His clothes are filthy and did you see the state of the sink and dishes? It was disgusting!'

'You're making a lot of judgements about how people should live. The most valuable thing for old people is their independence and that's what he has. Does it really matter if his clothes and house are dirty? Does it?' She stops to look straight at me with her clear grey eyes.

I don't know how to answer. We have just had lectures on hygiene and here is a nurse who does not seem to think it matters. I had seen filth in India, but nevertheless, people

YES SISTER, NO S

did cope and even seemed cheerful. But
we should just walk away from an old ma
look after himself.

'The most important thing for you to learn, la
stop thinking you can change the world. Nurses can
do so much. If Mr Harrop wants to go into a home, I wi
arrange it, but he doesn't.'

My mentor mounts her bike and as we pedal off she says,
'When you get dirty patients coming into the hospital,
remember they often have only cold water and no proper
bathrooms. It's a wonder they manage at all.'

I will appreciate the difficulties people live under, and I
will value independence, but I will not stop thinking I can
change the world because I know I can.

STER
I still don't think
n who cannot
ss, is to
only

ter 3

...edral with immensely high ceilings. Tall windows, wanting only stained glass to support the illusion, rise up to finish in an arch. Rows of beds, each with a white counterpane, stretch to infinity down either side. An untidy line down the centre of the ward consists of Sister's desk first, followed by a sink, oxygen tanks, a medicine cabinet on wheels, an emergency trolley, easy chairs, and eventually, a long wooden table covered with vases of yellow and rust chrysanthemums. Beyond that is a low built-in set of cupboards topped with a work surface.

'Come along Nurse Ross, don't stand there gawking!' Sister Downes says as we first enter Ward 21. I feel like a newborn lamb that first confronts the enormity of a moor.

'Sister Curtis, this is Nurse Ross who will be here until 6pm. She is to go to first supper and is then off duty.' Down leaves me to my fate.

Sister Curtis is an immense woman who seems truly formidable in her sister's uniform. Her appearance is deceptive however, for she has a gentle voice and her first words are 'Yes, the first sight of a ward is overwhelming. It will shrink in time.' She leads me to her desk. 'I'm glad you're here as you can be very useful to us. Perhaps you can begin by taking these TPRs for me.' She writes eight bed numbers on a piece of paper. I must be looking blank as she says, 'You know, temperature, pulse and respirations. The thermometer tray is on the cabinet at the end of the ward. Have you been shown how to chart TPRs?'

'Yes Sister.'

I try not to draw attention to myself by letting my feet clop on the polished wooden floor but I am sure all eyes are on me. I wonder if my stocking seams are straight. I hope a patient won't call me. A man does call out but to his neighbour. 'Jack, has tha' got a pencil?' His neighbour nods. 'Nurse, can you pass t'pencil this way?' Thank goodness for a request I can readily meet. 'Thanks luv,' he says as I hand him the unpainted wooden pencil.

The thermometer tray lies on the cabinet as promised and I am relieved to see that it looks just like the one in PTS. Bed eight is the first on the list. The occupant is asleep. Not wanting to wake him up, I move to the next on the list. This time a pair of suspicious eyes glare at me from a sallow, drawn face.

'Just going to take your temperature, Mr Greenside,' I say, noting his name on the temperature chart that hangs above his bed. Glass thermometers rest in a container of pink fluid in a tray holding cotton wool balls. I wipe one and attempt to shake it down with that flick of the wrist expert nurses have mastered but I have not. My shakings are to no avail: the mercury remains where it is at 99 degrees. Frustrated, I use my whole arm but even this windmill approach will not shift the mercury. I look for another thermometer and am relieved to find one registering 96 degrees.

'Can you put this under your tongue please.' Mr Greenside's toothless mouth opens for me to place the thermometer under his tongue. My pocket watch is ready, his wrist is held out, but he has no pulse! In a panic, I feel around his thin, bony wrist, pressing gently on various parts, but there is no pulse. My first task, a simple one of counting a pulse and I can't do it. Any remaining images of competence vanish.

I try the other wrist. Oh joy – there is a pulse. I carefully count it for a full minute and then surreptitiously count his respirations. We had been told not to let patients see us counting respirations because if they do, they tend to breathe differently. After taking the thermometer out of his mouth, I read it and replace it in the container. I record the numbers on the temperature chart as we had been shown, making neat dots on the appropriate graph line, joining them to previous dots with a straight line, not a curved line. 'Some nurses get sloppy and use curved lines, which do not give a true picture of the variations in TPR, and this PTS is not going to be sloppy, is it?' echoes in my mind.

After 45 minutes I take my list of the eight TPRs to Sister Curtis. She receives it graciously and thanks me as though I have performed some special service. She refrains from telling me that the average time for taking TPRs on the entire ward of 34 patients is 30 minutes.

'Now perhaps you can help Nurse Watkins with the teas.'

Watkins is wheeling round a trolley of cups and saucers and a giant metal teapot. 'Oh good,' she says when I come up to her, 'you can do the feeds. Go to everyone with a feeding cup and help them drink their tea. Be careful it's not too hot for them.'

I find the first bed with a white china feeding cup, a bowl-like vessel with a curved spout like a teapot, and stand holding it to the patient's lips.

Watkins comes over and hisses, 'You have to sit down to feed patients. Makes them think you aren't hurrying them. Only time you're allowed to sit down!'

Sitting holding cups to lips gives me a chance to look around. The influence of Florence Nightingale, who designed these wards, accounts for the high ceilings and tall windows. Because of her emphasis on fresh air, each patient is allocated a certain cubic footage of space. Despite it being an open ward, each patient has considerable privacy. From my position at the head of a bed I cannot see the adjacent beds because of the bunch of drawn back curtains, and the beds opposite are so far away I need binoculars to see them. Besides, all the paraphernalia in the centre of the ward obstructs the view.

I can see the comings and goings of the nurses, which means that a patient has a nurse in view at all times but, more importantly, the nurses can see the patients as they walk up and down. Sister Uprichard's words come back to me: 'Wards should never be without a nurse in sight. If you go out of the ward, into the sluice room for example, you are to ensure that there is another nurse on the ward before doing so.'

It is remarkably quiet given the presence of so many people. There is the occasional cough and the murmur of distant voices but the general atmosphere is one of drowsiness, particularly as it is the afternoon and treatments, physician's visits and various tests have been done. A warm stuffiness adds to the drowsy feeling as, despite the many windows, they are all firmly closed. I am almost too warm, even in my cotton dress, but I notice that many patients have their bedclothes drawn up to their chins. Some even hug a 'chest blanket' as we call the small blankets used for covering body parts during procedures and bed baths.

Sister Curtis is making notes in a book she carries as she talks to some of the patients. Her dress is a pretty blue with long sleeves that usually end in solid, white removable cuffs, but now she has the sleeves rolled up and secured with soft, white, voile cuffs. I wonder what I will look like in one. Her apron is the same as mine but the bonnet she wears is a mass of starched white frill that looks more like a bridal bouquet than a nurse's uniform.

I have to feed a patient in an oxygen tent but I am baffled about how to gain entry. These tents are made of a sort of perspex, which hang from a frame to envelop the patient and the head of the bed. A man-sized, green-painted oxygen cylinder, with a dial and a handle like those in submarines, delivers oxygen into the canopy. A 'No Smoking' sign dangles from it. The tent is firmly tucked into the bed all around, secured by a folded sheet across the patient's hips. Am I supposed to remove the sheet? Eventually I notice a large zip running across the front that I undo to reach the patient.

He is a large, florid man with red cheeks and bluish lips. 'Your tea is here,' I say, holding the feeding cup to his lips. He takes one sip, coughs, chokes and gasps for air. Oh my god, I've choked him. I can feel sweat break out on my forehead. What do I do? I stand dithering until Sister Curtis comes over, leans the man forward, takes an oxygen mask that is hanging from the cylinder and places it over his face. He gradually returns to normal.

'Don't worry, Nurse Ross,' Sister says. 'Just carry on with the others.' I feel too nervous to feed anyone else. Surely feeding people is a task anyone can do without choking them? I want the floor to swallow me up until it's time to go.

Watkins and I collect the dirty cups and saucers that we leave in the kitchen for the orderly to wash. I want to know what it is like to drink out of a feeding cup so I grab an opportunity to go into the kitchen, pour some tea into a clean feeding cup, and hide behind the door to drink. The tea tastes like it does when it's been in a thermos and I don't like the sensation of a stream of fluid being poured into me without my control.

Next is a bottle round. Wearing pink gowns over our uniforms, Watkins and I offer glass urinals from a crate to all the men who are bedridden. After a few minutes we collect the full ones. Watkins shows me how to measure the urine of the bottles on Intake and Output and record the amount on the I & O chart.

'Once in a while you get a dirty old man who wants you to put his thingy into the bottle for him. When that happens, use a pair of rat-toothed forceps. He won't ask again!' With this sage advice we go for tea.

When we return we prepare for the patients' supper. 'You have to watch Kitchen,' Watkins says as she plugs in the large, wheeled, metal canteen and starts stacking plates in it. 'They'll be here soon to bring the hot containers but if it's Walls' ice-cream for pudding, they put it in the hot canteen too and then it drips all over the floor.'

Pointing to a wide staircase with a wrought iron handrail on one side of the foyer I ask, 'What's up there?'

'Ward 22, the female medical ward,' Watkins says. 'Most

of the wards in the old part have the men's and women's wards together so the consultants don't have to walk far.'

We set all the bed tables with cutlery, find each patient's serviette and fill up the water glasses. Finally, as time for supper draws near, we go round to sit everyone up. Some patients prefer to sit at the big table in the centre so we clear the flowers onto the work table, set places for them and help them out of bed if necessary. Just as supper is to be served by Sister, it is time for me to go. I ask to be excused. She says, 'Thank you so much, nurse, you have been a great help. I look forward to seeing you next week.'

I practically skip to the dining room. I have actually looked after patients. I am a real nurse.

As she cuts up a sausage, Sandy greets me with, 'Well, did you kill anyone?'

'Don't talk like that,' Judith says, eyeing a forkful of cabbage suspiciously. 'The chances of killing a patient are nil and all that stupid Thornton woman has done is make us nervous. How did you get on, Jen?'

'Alright. Except I had to take eight TPRs and it took me 45 minutes. Sister didn't say anything though. How did you get on?'

'Guess what ward I'm on?' Judith rolls her eyes. 'Orthopaedics!'

'Just the experience you need. Is it anything like before?'

'Not really. Mostly fractures and surgeries, not congenital deformities. But anyway, all I did was help with teas and supper plates and do a bedpan round.'

Sandy is listening intently. She hasn't been on a ward yet. 'Tell me what it was like? Were you scared? What did you do?'

'I was scared when I first went on,' I say. 'The ward seemed to stretch for ever and ever.' I explain to her that I'd had to walk to the far end of the ward to get the thermometers and how I feared that a patient would call me. 'Working with someone else wasn't so bad, but I still felt silly walking up and down in front of all the patients.'

Sister Thornton comes to the dining room, stands in the entrance, and beckons to Sheila. Do we stand up when we're in the middle of a meal? She motions to us to sit down with an impatient wave of her hand. She talks to Sheila for a few minutes, then she leaves. I am bursting with curiosity.

Sheila comes over. 'Another one down. Moyra Asquith just left. A patient vomited all down her apron and she said she couldn't stand it.'

Would I leave if someone vomited over me? Or rather, *when* someone vomits over me? I have never really thought about the more sordid side of nursing. Emptying urinals was neither smelly nor repulsive and the only time a man had wanted a bedpan this afternoon, Watkins had seen to it. My baby brother puked a few times but it was curdled milk that smelled of baby. What about all the other things people discharge? What's the word? Excreta.

'Judith, what's it like dealing with bowel movements and other, um excreta?' I ask, drawing out the last word.

'You have to get used to it. If you don't, you may as well give up, because it's there alright!'

Will I get used to it? Perhaps my image of nursing is a bit too rosy.

Chapter 4

LIFE IN HYDE TERRACE is a continual fight against cold. Three terraced houses have been converted into one building which had been used as quarters for Canadian forces during the war and is now a temporary nurses' home until Roundhay Hall is ready. Two of the original doors are boarded up, giving the building an abandoned look. The main door, that we use, opens into a tiny hall and then another door gives entry to the main hall. Despite the double doors, a draught whistles through the hall, up the stairs and straight into my room. At least it seems so to me.

We had been allocated rooms in alphabetical order and my room is in what had been an attic. The lower floors have radiators but the attics are unheated on the principle that heat rises, but, of course, there has to be heat in the first place if the principle is to be demonstrated. When the terrace was built, servants lived in the attic rooms and heat for servants was considered an unnecessary luxury.

I have a room of my own as there is barely room for one bed in it let alone two, as in most rooms. Next to me are

Sandy and another girl, next to them, Jess Talbot, with two others in a three-bedded room. We huddle in our quilts in the biggest room to plan a survival strategy.

'The first thing we need is hot-water bottles,' Sandy says. 'We can fill them in the kitchen downstairs. If we do it as soon as we come in, our beds will be warm when we go to bed.'

'Can anyone bring some electric fires?' someone asks.

'We have an old paraffin stove at home that we used in the air-raid shelter,' another girl says, 'That will do for one room or even on the landing. It will be better than electric fires as I don't think there are any plugs.'

We look around. There is one double plug on the landing but none in anyone's room.

'I'll see if my aunts have a paraffin stove too. If we can get one for each room, and the landing, that should help,' I say.

Jess Talbot starts to giggle. She is a tiny girl, not much more than four feet tall. She has such a dainty look about her that I am reminded of a pixie in the Flower Fairies books. Her upper lip is strangely formed in an attractive way and she talks with a cross between a lisp and a whistle.

'My uncle wath in the commandoth. I'll ask him how they thurvived in the cold.'

After our first day off we return with blankets, wool hats, gloves, hot-water bottles and wonder of wonders, three paraffin stoves, so our rooms are frost-free when we go to bed. My bed is so heavy with blankets I can hardly turn over but I am warm in it.

Because Blinks is in a main floor room with two radiators and two empty beds, we tend to congregate there, as it is warmer than the sitting room. We can draw the beds up to the radiators and lean against them. She started with two roommates but they have both left. She is remarkably good-natured about her room being always full of people and she carries on as though we are not there. Most of the time she joins in the chatter but if she is tired, she simply goes to bed, seemingly oblivious to the noise.

There is not much time for gossip and fun as we have so much studying to do. Blinks's room takes on the appearance of a refugee camp with figures swathed in quilts lining the walls, and books and papers strewn in the middle. Conversation is in the form of questions:

'What's the lining of the knee joint called?'

'Does the superior vena cava go into the right or the left auricle?'

'Damn, who's taken my rubber?'

'What's that supposed to be?' Gazing at someone's diagram.

I am amazed to find Marie kneeling beside her bed one evening and I realise how important her religion is to her. She has joined the Nurse's Christian Fellowship and spends hours in the crypt of the Anglican church next door to the Infirmary, tending to the feet of tramps who seek refuge there.

'Why aren't you a Catholic?' I ask her.

'Most of my family is but my father is not, and he wouldn't hear of us being brought up Catholic, so we became High Anglican which is the next best thing. What religion are you?'

'I was brought up Church of England. In fact, I spent the war years in a vicarage, but I've been reading Bertrand Russell's essay, "Why I Am Not a Christian", and I agree with his views.'

Marie quickly changes the subject, as does everyone I have tried to discuss the essay with. Everyone but Judith, that is. One night we sit up debating whether there is a god or not and decide we agree with Russell who says that the only reason people think there is a god is that they have been taught that there is. We aren't so sure that we agree with him that when we die we rot; we believe our flesh will rot, but we think there is some sort of spirit or energy that dissipates and is used again.

Judith is somewhat aloof from the rest of us. She always has the top marks on our weekly tests and although she is always reading, it is not textbooks. She is the most well-read person of my age I have met and I enjoy our conversations about all sorts of topics. Her example encourages me to join the city library. One of the first books I take out is *The Scourge of the Swastika* by Lord Russell of Liverpool. He was one of the judges at the Nuremberg trials and has published his book at his own expense, as he does not think that the events in Nazi Germany should go unremembered by the general public. I read the book with a horror I am unable to express and I cannot look at the dreadful pictures of piles of skeleton-like bodies without crying.

'How can anyone do anything like this?' I say to Judith, showing her the pictures. 'Can you imagine being herded into freight trains and being packed so tightly that you can't sit down? Or go to the toilet? It was so cold that some people's skin stuck to the side of the cars and was torn off when they left.' Tears roll down my face as my imagination runs away with me.

'That's why we fought the war, Jen.'

'The Germans must be monstrous people. And to think, we nursed them with our own men when they were wounded.'

'The Germans are just like us. You surely don't think the same thing can't happen here?'

'Of course not! The British wouldn't do things like that.'

Judith rolls off her bed to sit in a chair. 'The same thing can happen anywhere if the wrong people get into power. Look at the number of thugs we have in this country – those who knock down old ladies for their purses – that sort of thing. If those types get control of government, then we'd be just the same.'

'But why did the German people allow it to happen? Why didn't they do something to stop this?' I say pointing to the atrocious pictures.

'A lot of them didn't know such things were happening and if they did, what could they do about it? What would you do if you knew you'd be shot if you said anything? Not much. The important thing is to learn from this and make sure that the thugs don't get control.'

Such conversations with Judith provide a mental stimulation that PTS does not. There is so much ritual, so much rote learning, so much unquestioned policy, that my mind feels numb. I would like more debate, more discussion, more critical analysis, but the general view of the institution, as of all adults in my life, is that such young people cannot possibly know anything worth listening to, nor hold a valid opinion. PTS is just like school. We have to sit and listen and make notes. To question anything was seen as impertinence.

We are in Blinks's room when the subject of sexual intercourse comes up. 'Hey, look at this.' Wee Jess points to a diagram of a disembodied penis in an equally disembodied vagina.

'What book's that? It's not in my anatomy book.'

'No, thith is one I bought in the medical book shop. I think it has better illuthrations,' Jess says.

'Let me see,' I say. Jess passes the book over. I know that a man inserts his penis into a woman to do 'It', but I have never been sure how he gets such a floppy thing in. It must be like pushing toothpaste back into the tube. The diagram shows a very stiff penis, not floppy at all. I pass the book to

Sandy hoping someone else will ask the questions that I dare not.

'Wow,' she says. 'They don't often show pictures of erections.' She reads, 'Under conditions of erotic excitement the arteries in the penis dilate and the veins constrict. The resulting high blood pressure causes the penis to become erect. Erection makes possible the transmission of semen into the body of the female.'

Ah, so that's how 'It's' done.

'My brother once had a hard-on at the swimming pool at school,' someone says. 'His trunks gave him away and everyone teased him like crazy.'

'Mine did the same thing,' Sandy says, 'only it was during gym and he pushed out his shorts which were too small anyway. They don't seem to have any control over it.'

I have a brother. Why didn't he tell me about this? I know I must not allow myself to be alone with a boy because 'you never know what might happen.' At school we were once unexpectedly assembled to be informed of a dreadful misdeed – a Leeds Girls High School girl had been seen talking to a Grammar School boy at the school gates! I was also taught that girls who did 'It' before marriage were in for a fate worse than death, though I am not sure what that fate is.

'Has anyone here gone all the way?' someone asks.

Blinks turns red. Surely she hasn't? She must be embarrassed by the question, as I am. 'You don't think we'd own up to it if we had,' Sandy says. 'Come on, let's get on with studying the pancreas.'

One evening begins much as usual. Sheila Dawson, the only one with a boyfriend, and a key, is out. Some girls are listening to *Hancock's Half-Hour* on the wireless in the sitting room while the more solitary are in their rooms. The rest of us are gathered in Blinks's room with the intention of studying the anatomy and physiology of the stomach and large intestine. I am pleased that Judith has joined us for a change.

We start off amicably enough. 'What are the enzymes in the stomach?' Blinks asks.

'Lazy Amy trips in and lies on a – I can't think what a 'pays' is,' I say. Blinks laughs. 'What on earth are you talking about?' Marie asks. She has no imagination.

'Trypsin, amylase and lipase. I remember them by making up sentences about them.'

'They're not in the stomach; they're in the duodenum,' Judith says. 'The enzymes of the stomach are pepsin and rennin.'

'Right, so they are. What do rennin and pepsin do? Amylase breaks down starch, trypsin breaks down proteins and lipase breaks down fats.'

'You'll have to make up a sentence like Lennin, alias rennin, coagulates milk and then peeps into a short polypeptide chain hanging ... where would it hang?' Judith asks me.

'It could be a bicycle chain,' I say.

'Did Lenin ride a bicycle?'

'Not if he was rennin!' I quip.

Marie has had enough. 'Would you two please stop being silly and let's get on with studying for the test tomorrow.' She has not been doing well on the weekly tests and is clearly worried.

'OK,' says Blinks, 'What's the anatomy of the stomach?'

'Come on, Marie, you answer,' Judith says. 'You're the one that wants to know.'

'Don't you want to know too?'

'I already do,' Judith says.

'Oh, you're such a clever clogs,' Marie sneers. 'Miss Know-it-all!'

'Now, now, children,' Wee Jess says. 'Let's juth thtick with the anatomy of the thtomach. The thtomach is a large, muscular thac connected at its opening to the oethophagus and at its end to the duodenum. Two thphincters act as valves. What is the one called at the oethophagus end?'

'The pylorus,' Marie says.

Judith corrects her. 'No, that's at the duodenal end. It's the cardiac sphincter at the oesophagus end.'

Marie jumps up and stamps one foot. 'Who do you think you are?' she demands of Judith.

'Oh, for goodness sake, Marie, Judith is only giving the right answer.' I am beginning to feel uncomfortable. 'Let's pack it in if we can't get on.'

'If she knows so much, why is she here?' Marie is beside herself.

'Oh, you pompous, prissy prig, I'll go.' Judith gets to her feet and gathers up her books.

'No, don't go,' I say hastily. 'I'm sure Marie didn't mean it. She's just worried about the test like we all are, aren't you Marie?'

'I don't care if she does go. She can boil her head for all I care.' Marie is almost crying.

'If Judith goes, I go,' I say.

'Me too,' from Wee Jess.

Blinks is walking up and down polishing her glasses furiously. 'Look,' she says, 'I love having you all here but if you're going to row, I want you to leave.' Her face goes red as she speaks and I know it has been an effort for her to be so forthright.

'I think we'd better pack it in for tonight anyway,' I say, as I pick up my books. 'We're all obviously tired.'

I wonder if things will ever be the same again. I had thought that as we are all going through a difficult training together, we'd automatically be friends. I had imagined us as comrades-in-arms with an *esprit de corps* and the sort of camaraderie we had learned as we grew up during the war: don't let the side down; wait your turn or the Nazis will win; share and share alike; chin up; play up, play up, and play the game. I hadn't reckoned with two such different characters as Marie and Judith who clash every time they speak to each other. Marie's rigid outlook, her strict adherence to rules, and her blind acceptance of all that is taught is too much for Judith's intelligence. I love Judith's quick comprehension and her ability to see through nonsense. Yet I like Marie too, for dull though she is, she has a warm heart. I look hard for her good qualities, as I so badly want us to be one big happy family.

Chapter 5

Rules for Bandaging:

- *Select a bandage of the right width: 1–1½in are used for the fingers, 2–2½in for the head, 2½–3in for the limbs and 3½–4in for the hip, trunk or shoulders.*
- *Bandage from within outwards and from below upwards on the trunk and limbs and from the uninjured part to the injured part.*
- *Stand in front of the patient except for a capelline (head) bandage or one for the back of the neck.*
- *Cover two-thirds of the preceding layer of bandage leaving one-third exposed.*
- *Fasten the bandage firmly with a knot or safety pin, but not where the patient is likely to lie on it.*
- *When removing a bandage, pass it from hand to hand, not pulling it off with one hand.*

M Y GRANDMOTHER'S HOUSE, a terraced house in Leeds, similar to Hyde Terrace, but warm, is my home for the Christmas holidays. As a child I had always loved visiting Amma's house. I would sit in the kitchen as

she made bread, my mouth watering in anticipation of the tiny loaf she made especially for me and each of the other children. She would give me a piece of dough to knead and shape into any form I liked; sometimes I made dough men with raisins for eyes and I was always disappointed when the shape blurred and the eyes sank into the dough as it rose.

The house was alive with people and activity. While the men were away at war, the daughters, except for my mother, with their children, moved in. How everyone squeezed in I never knew, but beds were shared and they managed somehow. The family considers itself fortunate as, despite the fact that all sons and sons-in-law were in the armed forces, no one was killed.

It is a demonstrative family. Everyone present greets everyone who arrives with a hug and a kiss as if there has been a long absence. As each person leaves the same hugs and kisses are exchanged with as much enthusiasm as for the arrival. During the war, Canadian service men were billeted in the same street. There were always at least two having supper and joining in the evening singsong. All my aunts can sit down at the piano and hammer out 'A Nightingale Sang in Berkeley Square', 'It's a Long Way to Tipperary', Noel Coward's songs, and my favourite, 'Alice Blue Gown'.

For Christmas, each room of the house is festooned with homemade paper chains and paper bells that concertina to fold flat for storage. A live tree is dug up from the garden and re-planted after it has been decorated with carefully preserved pre-war baubles. A silver monkey wearing a fez is my favourite. It hangs there as it has done for many Christmases. Candles, in clip-on candleholders, are dotted around the tree waiting to be lit on Christmas day for a brief period of wonder.

Amma greets me with pleasure. 'Oh, Jennifer, I am so glad you can get Christmas off. We've got you a seat for the pantomime on Boxing Day and the Sunshine Girls are in it again. Come into the kitchen and tell me all about it,' she says after a giant hug. 'We are all so proud of you. Is it very hard?'

I tell her all about PTS and my friends as I stuff myself with the rich, moist fruitcake covered with marzipan and icing that Amma makes every year.

'We go on the wards for one afternoon a week and look after real, live patients and one of them told me how much better he felt when I'd washed his face and hands and sat him up and he says I brought joy to his old soul with my smile and that I'm going to make a wonderful nurse.'

'How nice,' Amma murmurs as she peels boiled chestnuts for stuffing. 'Go on.'

I talk on, encouraged by her receptive noises, and eventually tell her about the row between Marie and Judith.

'People get crotchety when they're tired,' Amma says, 'and then they get on each other's nerves. Don't take it too seriously. They will probably learn to tolerate each other but if they don't, don't let it worry you. Keep being friends with them both and don't get involved.'

'I'll try. Oh,' I say suddenly, 'I've got some presents to wrap but I haven't any paper.'

'There's some in the press. Help yourself. I'll put the iron on to heat.'

Amma lifts up one lid of the Aga cooker and places a flat iron on the hot plate, as I go to the press to find some Christmas paper and string. Each piece of paper, used many times, is ironed for the next use, then carefully folded after the present is unwrapped.

'I've got something to show you,' Amma says as she unfolds a newspaper. There is a spread about the Leeds General Infirmary with photos of the hospital from the air. These clearly show the original Victorian three-storey blocks, which, held together by small, low connecting wings, look like a giant bird in flight. The red brick has been blackened by decades of industrial smoke so that the Infirmary stands as a dirty monument to the Industrial Revolution. A journalist has compared the place to St Pancras station in London. The slanted cone-shaped roofs are similar, but the station does not have the enormous windows running along each side of each wing.

'It looks huge, doesn't it?' I say.

Behind the main building are numerous extensions. Insertions of temporary huts into every available space give the impression of a town built without a planning department. On the outer perimeter lies the Nurses' Home, which is also of blackened brick and has three wings, though not as tall as those of the hospital. Around this building is a high brick wall. I point to it.

'This is where we'll be living when we finish PTS.'

'They're going to make sure people can't get in, aren't they?' Amma says and laughs. 'Or out!'

Christmas Day follows the family tradition of a walk by all those not involved in dinner preparation, greeting of non-residents' arrival for dinner, pulling of crackers, feasting on turkey with roast potatoes and Brussels sprouts and eating plum pudding with the hope of finding one of the sixpences in it. Those who did not prepare dinner wash up while others walk. When all is clean and tidy, we gather in the drawing room to listen to the Queen's speech, drink tea and open presents in the light of the tree candles. I do not have time to miss my own family until I go to bed. Once there I hide my tears, as I do not want to seem ungrateful.

On the bus back to Hyde Terrace I bask in the residual warmth of my mother's family and in the excitement I feel about going back. I do not realise that it will be 12 years before I have a Christmas off duty again.

Up and Down greet us in Roundhay Hall as though we have not been away and the routine continues from where we left off. In the kitchen we learn to make beef tea, Benger's food (from a partially digested fortified milk powder), custard, scrambled eggs and other dishes suitable for patients on a light diet. We have to explain the nutritional value and the calorie count of every dish we prepare to Up, who in a large, white chef's apron, demonstrates how to make each dish before she supervises our efforts. She shows us how to set a tray.

'Appearance is all important in a meal for the sick,' she says. 'Do not serve white fish, mashed potatoes, cauliflower with white sauce, on a white plate. Think about colour.' She places a pale blue tray cloth on the tray and sets out cutlery. 'Each piece of silver must be clean – no egg on the tines of the fork, no smears on the knife. Choose cheerful crockery and make the tray look attractive.'

The kitchen is stocked with a large selection of cloths, serviettes and patterned crockery in a variety of shapes and sizes.

'If a patient has a small appetite, present a small serving on a small plate. Do not overwhelm him with food nor serve tiny helpings on a large plate.' She places a small vase of flowers on the tray, 'There, doesn't that look nice?'

Judith and I are in the same session for cookery. 'God knows why we're learning all this,' she says, 'We're never going to use it. Unless we become private nurses for the wealthy, of course.'

We visit the waterworks, the sewerage plant, the salvage department and a block of flats that has been built to replace some of the slums. At the sewerage plant we have to be able to describe exactly what happens to the results of a visit to the lavatory from the moment it is flushed to the final emission of pure water. We are assured that the final product is pure water but as no one takes up the offer to sip it, the attendant drinks a glassful. 'Tha' shouldn't be so squeamish,' he says. He chuckles. 'Especially if tha's going to be nurses.'

At the Leeds Salvage Department we watch how rubbish is sieved and separated into reusable piles. The smell makes me gag. We all hold handkerchiefs to our noses.

'Good grief,' I say to Judith, 'How can anyone stand this stench long enough to work here? It's making me feel sick.'

'You wait,' Judith says, 'This is like roses compared with what we're going to put up with if orthopaedics is anything to judge by.'

Down takes us for bandaging, which she considers to be an art. We learn not only how to apply a 'many-tailed bandage' to an abdomen, but how to make one. For an average adult, strips of flannel, about four inches wide and a yard long, are overlapped then sewn together in the centre with a feather-stitch, to make a pad about 12 inches square. This pad is placed under the patient and the loose ends are then brought across the abdomen alternately. The last one is secured with a safety pin.

Down loves to see a well-applied bandage. Parallel edges and even spaces between the overlaps seem to satisfy her need for order and neatness.

'Come and look at this, nurses,' she says when Sandy,

who seems to have an aptitude for this task, does a beautiful job on my arm. 'Here is a nurse with a sense of balance and order.' Down has the beatific expression of one who has seen the Sistine Chapel for the first time. 'See how perfectly parallel the edges are, and how neat this is. Not too tight and not too loose. Well done, Nurse Sandstone.'

'She should come and see your room, Sandy,' I say. 'Not much sense of balance and order there, unless you call the heap of dirty clothes balanced.'

'Oh, shut up!' is all Sandy can say.

The most difficult bandage is a cappeline, or head bandage. Two bandages are used. One circles the head to secure the other that criss-crosses it. We are all dreading being asked to demonstrate one in our exams.

We face three days of exams at the end of PTS. Roundhay Hall develops an atmosphere of hushed tension in contrast to the relative tranquillity we have enjoyed until now. Up and Down behave as though they are mothers entering their offspring in a Bonny Baby competition.

'Nurse Talbot, please arrive for your examination with a cap that properly covers your hair,' Down says to Jess.

'Everyone bring a clean apron in case of accidents,' says Up.

'Four ward sisters will be here to examine you in the practical room and the kitchen on the first day and to take orals on the second. We want you to look as if you have learned something while you are here.'

'Do try and behave like nurses, not like a pack of giggling school-girls.'

Shortly after we arrive on the first day of exams, a taxi bearing four uniformed ward sisters draws up. Up and Down greet them as if they are royalty, then escort three into the practical room and one into the kitchen. I can't understand why they seem so nervous. Surely it is we, we who are to be examined, who should be tense.

We sit in the classroom trying to study for the written exams. We do not have to wait long before three people are called into the practical room and four into the kitchen. I am one of the four. I have an hour to prepare a meal for a patient on a Sippy Two diet.

First I make a beef consommé, which I leave simmering on a low light while I purée vegetables and put a junket to set. Then comes the moment to set a tray and serve my delicacies. I find a soup bowl and go to get my pan of consommé only to find, to my horror, that someone has turned up the light and it has boiled down to about a table-spoonful. I add boiling water to it and hope for the best. The examiner either does not notice how watery the soup is or else she has tasted so much that her palate is dulled.

As either Up or Down are in the classroom we cannot compare notes until dinner time. Before we go into the dining room, Down calls me over and asks if I brought a spare apron. I tell her I have. She says, 'Could I please borrow it? One of the sisters has had an accident.'

I fetch the apron and go to the dining room. Everyone is there except Marie.

'Marie is in the cloakroom blubbering,' Wee Jess tells us. 'She was my partner in the practical and she managed to thoak the thister with enema tholution.'

We are all grinning. 'What happened?'

Wee Jess fills her mouth with sausage and says, 'Marie had to thet an enema tray. Then she had to make up the thoap tholution and demonstrate how she would give it. So she holds up the enema can to expel air from the tube and before she could pinch off the tube, she'd thquirted the thister from head to toe.'

Before we could give vent to our amusement, Down comes in with a sister, my size, in a clean apron, followed by Up with a red-eyed Marie. Marie collects her dinner and comes to sit down. No one knows what to say.

'I've failed,' she says. 'Did Jess tell you what happened? I'll have to do PTS all over again and then I won't be trained when Charles is.' She pushes away her plate.

'What did Up say to you?' Wee Jess asks. 'I thaw her talking to you.'

'She said I hadn't to worry – it could happen to anyone. But I know I've failed. How can they pass someone who covers a sister with enema solution?' She starts to cry again.

Judith is choking on something and leaves suddenly. I can feel my abdomen tighten as I try not to laugh. If only Marie wasn't so deadly serious, she could perhaps see the funny side of it, though, I admit, I might not think it funny if it had happened to me.

The lengthy written exams are essay type with the use of English taken into consideration. We are asked such questions as:

- Describe the anatomy and physiology of the liver; illustrate with a diagram.
- How would you sterilise a) record syringe, b) artery forceps, c) gum elastic catheter, d) cotton balls.
- If you have a supply of morphia grains ¼, how would you prepare an injection of morphia grains ⅙?

On our final day we are each interviewed by Up and Down, who give us our results. We all pass, including Marie. As usual, Judith is top. I do well in anatomy and about average in everything else. I am thrilled with my report that says, 'Nurse Ross's enthusiasm for nursing is only exceeded by her sense of vocation.'

Up and Down come out to wave the bus goodbye as we make our last journey between Roundhay Hall and the Infirmary. We are to pack our trunks in Rothwell Terrace where they will be transported to the Nurses' Home, and after two days off we are to report to the Nurses' Home to start three months as 'peaks'. At one time, probationers wore peaked caps and although the caps have long gone, the name remains. Our caps are the same throughout our training, though after peaking, we will be given caps with the LGI emblem embroidered on the brim. As in the army, our passage through the various stages of training is marked by additions to our uniform.

'Well Blinks,' I say on the bus. 'So far so good. I wonder what is in store for us now.'

Chapter 6

SISTER O'DONNELLY, COMMONLY known as the Sod, not, we are to discover, without justification, meets us in the Nurses' Home in her position as head Home Sister. We are assembled in the large hall off the entrance foyer when she appears. She is a tall, thin woman whose top half does not articulate with her bottom half. It is as if her hinges are loose so that she leans back slightly without the compensation of an abdominal thrust. Her right hand dangles down from her wrist and when she walks, this arm swings from the elbow across her body.

'Good afternoon, narrses,' she says. 'It is my duty to welcome ye to the Narrses Home and to explain to ye the rules for living in it. Ye will be on the second floor of the north wing. I have here a list of the rooms ye have been allocated.' Her thin, bony hands hold a clipboard that shakes slightly. 'Yorr trunks are in yorr rooms. This afternoon yorr to unpack and leave yorr trunks outside yorr doors then they will be removed to the basement. Ye will not be needing them again until ye leave here for good, as in future, when ye move yorr room, ye will move yorr things in your drawers.'

I bite my lips and clamp my hand to my mouth but unfortunately I meet Sheila's eye. She lets out a snort of laughter and the rest of us, unable to hold it in, crumple into hysterical mirth.

The Sod turns a shade of purple, stands up and shouts, 'Indeed, ye are the rudest set of narrses it has been my misfortune to meet! I trust yorr training will teach ye some manners. I am going to leave. I shall return in five minutes and when I return I expect ye to have controlled yourselves.' She marches out, her floppy right arm in furious motion.

'I've wet my knickers,' Wee Jess gasps. We dissolve again.

Marie, the only one not in a state of hysteria, says 'Oh for goodness sake, stop it! She'll be back in a minute and I for one don't want to get on the wrong side of her on our first day.'

A few minutes later the Sod returns. By this time we have assumed some semblance of seriousness. 'Now I will explain to ye the rules. Lights out is at 10.30. There is to be no noise after that time and everyone is to be in her own room. The doors are locked at 10pm. Ye may have one late pass a week until 11pm and one until 1am every month. No men are allowed in the building beyond the front foyer.'

'We're obviously not here to enjoy ourselves,' mutters Judith.

'Did ye say something, narrse?' The Sod glowers.

'I said, I should think not, Sister,' Judith says quickly.

The Sod looks suspicious but carries on. 'Each corridor has a kitchen where ye may make yorrselves a hot drink. Milk is provided but ye must supply yorr own tea, cocoa, etc. Yorr to leave the kitchens clean and tidy.'

Her voice, with its distinct Irish accent, drones on while I look around me. We are seated in rows taking up a small portion of a large room with a stage at one end boasting a grand piano. As windows are on both sides of the room I realise we are on the lower floor of one of the bedroom wings. I am gazing at the pattern of the parquet floor when the Sod's voice comes back into my consciousness.

'… day off, ye may have breakfast in bed as long as ye write the order in the book in time. This is a great privilege which can be denied for misbehaviour.' She pauses as if to ensure that the message has sunk in. 'Laundry: each Tuesday yorr to strip yorr beds and leave them to air with the window open. Put yorr sheets and towel into the dirty pillowcase and take it to the end of the corridor. Personal laundry is to be put in yorr bags and left at the end of the corridor on Mondays and Thursdays. Are there any questions?' Her expression does not invite questions but some brave soul asks one.

'What if we are having a day off on Tuesdays, Sister?'

'The laundry is not collected until the afternoon so ye

have until noon to strip yorr bed. Clean laundry is returned at that time.' She looks around.

'Yorr all on duty tomorrow at 7.30 on the wards ye were on in PTS. At the end of yorr first year ye may live out but we discourage it as narrses who live out always seem very tired. Are there any more questions?'

Silence. 'Very well, ye may go.'

'They don't want us to live out as then they can't control our lives,' Judith says as we walk up to the second floor. 'And have you seen a nurse who doesn't look tired? It's because we have to work like slaves that makes us tired, not living out.'

Our rooms are identical but comfortable. Each has a radiator, so no more getting up shivering. A built-in wardrobe, with a cupboard at the top and drawers at the bottom, serves as the bed end. In addition there is a desk, a bedside table, an easy chair and a washbasin. Communal bathrooms are at each end of the corridor.

We wander round from room to room to find out where our friends are before tackling our unpacking. Blinks is in the room opposite mine and after I've unpacked I go to visit her.

'How are you doing, Blinks?' I ask. She does not seem to have made much progress as her trunk is still almost full. 'Can I give you a hand?'

'Thanks.' She grins at me. 'I started to look at my photograph album and lost track of time. Here, you look at it while I finish.'

I look through her album. The photos are neatly pasted in and each is labelled in white ink on the black paper. There are many of family groups taken in a large garden.

'Is this your house?' I ask Blinks. She glances at the album and nods.

'It looks wonderful,' I say, admiring the gabled stone house with roses climbing around the door. 'These must be your sisters. They look nice.'

'No, they're a pain. Let me show you my favourite photo of my father. Here, dressed in cricket whites. Isn't he hand-some?'

'What does he do?'

'He's a doctor. A gynaecologist and obstetrician. All his patients love him, he's so gentle and kind.'

'So that's where you get it from,' I say. Blinks blushes.

At six o'clock we go for supper. As the Sod said nothing about wearing uniform, all but Marie go in mufti.

'Let's go to the pictures,' Sandy says. 'It's probably the last evening we'll ever have off together. *The Quiet Man is* playing at the Odeon. I heard it's really good.'

'What's it about?'

'An American ex-boxer goes to Ireland where he was born. John Wayne's in it and I love him. That chunky look – mmmmm!'

We all go to the Odeon where the long evening of entertainment starts at 7pm. After 'God Save the Queen' there is a 'B' picture, news, a cartoon and then an interval, during which an organist plays on an organ that rises up out of the floor. We buy ice-creams from an usherette who walks round with a tray hanging from her neck displaying sweets, chocolate and choc ices. Then comes the main picture. We are all so engrossed, we completely forget the time and the fact that we need a late pass to be back after 10pm. It is after 11pm when we reach the Nurses' Home. The three wings of it are almost in darkness with only one or two windows still with lights shining through.

'What are we going to do now?' someone asks. There is silence.

'We can go round to the front door of the hospital and ask to be let in,' Marie says, 'Let's just own up and take the consequences.'

'Don't be so daft! Get into a row on our first day here? Not likely! Let's see if we can get in before we have to do that,' Sheila says. A high wall surrounds the whole of the Nurses' Home. We skirt round it but cannot find a gate or any way in.

'Give me a leg up.' This is Judith reaching up to the top of the wall. I bend down and cup my hands for her foot. She is astride the wall in a second.

'What can you see?'

'Not much. But if someone else comes up here we can both jump down and do a recce,' Judith whispers.

'How will you get back out again?'

Suddenly a window above us opens and a head appears.

We fall silent. Judith, still balanced on the top of the wall, freezes. She stands out like a sore thumb, silhouetted against the sky.

'What are you doing?' the head whispers.

'Trying to get in,' Judith replies. 'We're the new peaks and we haven't got late passes.'

'Can you all get over the wall?' the silhouette asks. If you can, I will let down a rope ladder.'

'I've just paid two and six for new nylons and I'm not ruining them by climbing a wall,' someone says.

'Take them off then.'

'Good idea.' We all lift our skirts to undo our suspenders just as a motor bike roars up the street. Its headlight reflects a group of young women with their shoes off, bending down to take off their stockings.

'What's this then, t'Folies Bergere?' a male voice asks.

'Nay, they think it's the seaside and they're goin' paddling!' His friend laughs.

'Come on – give us a dance.' He starts to sing, 'Knees up Mother Brown, knees up Mother…'

'Shhshhh – you'll have us fired. Instead of making daft remarks make yourselves useful by giving us a hand up the wall,' Sandy says to them.

'Right you are luv, anything to oblige.'

We are all hoisted up to the top of the wall, jump down the other side and end up in a privet hedge. We scramble through that to find the foot of the rope ladder. It is not easy to climb an unanchored rope ladder but we all manage somehow. As it is dark, we cannot see who our rescuer is but we thank her profusely.

'Where are we?' someone asks.

'You're on the second floor of the east wing. Where are your rooms?'

'The second floor of the north wing,' I reply.

'Go out in twos and threes, turn left, then right, go up a short flight of stairs, through a double door and you're there. And be quiet! The night sisters go to sick bay about now,' our unknown friend says.

We creep out in small groups and make our way back to our rooms without incident. We never did find out who our saviour was but Sheila goes to an outdoors shop on her next day off to buy a rope ladder that we all chip in for. She calls a meeting to discuss how to arrange for unexpected and emergency entry into the 'Virgin's Retreat', as it is known.

'Pam and I walked all round the Nurses' Home in daylight. We found a place where you don't have to climb the wall. There's a low wall that used to have railings in it that I expect were taken out during the war. It's on Curzon Street and it looks as if you are going into the building where the Lady Almoners are, but if you go round their building, you are in the grounds of the Nurses' Home.'

She draws a map on the back of an envelope. 'There's a hedge here,' she says, pointing to her map, 'but there's a gap

in it so you go through that and then you're outside the
north wing. We have to use a window on the west side or
else we're opposite where the sisters sleep. You all better
find the way while it's light. Now, we need to arrange how
to get in when no one knows you're out there. Any ideas?'

'We can throw stones at a window.'

'We can get the front hall porter to wake someone up,'
Marie suggests.

'Don't be silly.' Judith is scornful.

'Can we hide the ladder somewhere?'

'Then how would we get it up to the second floor
window, stupid?'

'It isn't going to work. The only way it will work is if we
know we are going to be late and make sure someone is
awake to let us in,' Sheila says. 'All the people on the west
side will have to take it in turns, set an alarm to wake up at
an arranged time, and let down the ladder.'

'Why can't we just let down the ladder before we go to
bed and then it doesn't matter what time we come in,' I say.

'Brilliant!' Sheila says. 'That's it. If you know you're going
to be late, you have to arrange with someone on the west
side to let the ladder down before they go to bed, after it's
dark. Then you climb in, pull up the ladder and hide it in
your room until the next time.'

'What if more than one person is going to be late?'

'Then you'll have to leave the ladder until the last person
is in. You'll just have to arrange that with each other. There's

nothing we can do if you are locked out in an emergency – we were just lucky to find that person awake.'

Having made these elaborate arrangements, we never use them, as at that time we have no idea how exhausted we are going to be after a day on the wards when a bath and bed are the only things we want.

Chapter 7

Urine Testing

- *Note the colour and appearance.*

- *Dip litmus paper into specimen to see whether it is acid or alkaline. It must be acid for further tests. Measure the specific gravity. The result should be 1008. Dilute if necessary.*

- *Test for blood. Put 4cc of urine into a test tube. Add 3–4 drops of Tincture of Guaiacum, shake the tube and then pour in about half an inch of ozonic ether. If blood is present, a blue ring appears at the junction of the two fluids.*

- *Test for sugar. Light a Bunsen burner, pour 5cc of Benedict's Solution into a test tube, add 10 drops of urine with a dropper and boil the result. Urine with no sugar does not change colour when boiling, but the presence of sugar makes it change from blue to green to yellow to red, depending on the amount of sugar.*

- *Test for albumin. Boil a test tube three parts full of urine, and add a few drops of acetic acid. A cloudy result means that albumin is present.*

I REPORT ON DUTY at 7.30am to begin my probationary period on Sister Curtis's ward. The most senior
of the student nurses organises us to make beds or to get
ready for breakfast or to test urines. I am relieved to see that
Watkins is still there and she is instructed to show me how
to test urine.

We are in the freezing sluice room for this task. A row
of glass containers, which look like long drink glasses, hold
yellow liquid with an almost enticing resemblance to
cider. Bunsen burners, a crate of test tubes and bottles of
testing solution lie on a workbench. Watkins produces
matches from her pocket. 'You can never find any matches
around here, so I bring my own,' she says as she lights the
Bunsen burners. 'You do all the tests for albumin and I'll
do the sugars.'

She looks behind her as if a sister might pop out from
behind the bedpans before saying, 'You're not supposed to
do this but I take a sample from each urine and then test
the whole lot for sugar. If there's none, that's OK. If there
is sugar I have to test them one at a time to find out whose
it is. I make a game of it. Guess the patient. Sometimes I'm
right first time.'

'Can I do the same thing with the albumins?' I ask as I
wave a test tube in and out of the burner flame.

'No. Doesn't work because you need a nearly full test
tube of urine. It works for sugar because you only need a
few drops.'

'This is going to take ages,' I say as finally my first sample boils and I add acetic acid.

'Yes, it's a heckuva job to get this done by eight,' Watkins says, 'and usually I'm still stuck in the sluice room during prayers.'

Promptly at 8am Sister Curtis and the permanent staff nurses (perms) enter the ward. We all gather round the central table.

'Good morning, nurses,' says Sister. 'Let us pray.'

We kneel while Sister reads out a prayer. Then we say the Lord's Prayer in unison and many patients do the same.

Sister and the perms receive the report from the night charge nurse while we serve breakfast. Then comes a bottle round, followed by the first of several rounds of 'lockers'. The job of lockers involves setting a trolley with a basin of carbolic (a disinfectant), a cloth, a small pail for rubbish and a large jug of fresh water. Each locker top is wiped with carbolic, which means manoevering around bottles of Lucozade, glasses of water and get well cards. Sweet papers, old newspapers and other rubbish are removed, ashtrays emptied and wiped. Finally the drinking glasses are topped up with water. Our visit is an opportunity for patients to ask us to do small things such as find something in their locker or take a letter to put in the post.

Half of us go to first coffee while the other half begins the morning tasks. Sister has made out a work list. I am down to do 'beds and backs' with a third year nurse called Tomson. Two others are also doing beds and backs, one is doing treatments and a staff nurse is giving out medicines.

Tomson sets a trolley with piles of clean linen, a basin, a jug of warm water, soap, small towels, methylated spirits and talcum powder. We are to do one side of the ward while the other pair does the other. Some of the patients have been designated to get a bedbath.

'We'll start with those who have to be turned every two hours,' says Tomson, wheeling the trolley to one of the beds. 'What's your off duty?'

'I don't know,' I answer.

'You don't know!' She looks incredulous. 'Don't you know where the book is?' I shake my head. 'The most important book on the ward and you don't know where it is! Here, I'll show you.'

We go to Sister's desk. She takes a hard-covered exercise book from a drawer, opens it at the current week and shows me a hand-drawn calendar with the names of all the nurses down one side. My name is at the bottom of the list.

'You're a two-five today and tomorrow, then you have your half-day and day off, then a five-to, then a ten-one, then a two-five.'

I hardly know what she is talking about and say so.

'A two-five means you go to second dinner at 1.30 and come back at five. A half-day, you go to second dinner and then you're off.' She pauses to say 'Just a minute, Mr Forbes,' to a patient who has called her.

'A five-to means you go to first dinner and work until five, and a ten-one means you go to second coffee and come back on at one having had dinner. That's the worst because you still have to get up in the morning and you only work two hours before being off. Sister Curtis is pretty good about off duty. If you want a particular evening or day off, you write it here,' she says pointing to a page. 'You have to keep checking the book and remember when you are off as no one will tell you.'

We go back to the trolley and start beds and backs. Each patient has his sacrum, heels and elbows washed with soap and water, then rubbed with methylated spirits to harden the skin, and finally dusted with talcum powder. Each time I open the bottle of meths, the fumes settle in my throat and make me choke and the smell seems to linger long after the bottle is closed.

Some patients wash themselves, some sit in an easy chair for an hour or two and some we bedbath. I like bed bathing patients. There is an intimacy about the procedure that leads to confidences that we otherwise would not hear. Instead of the patient in bed six, he becomes Albert Jones who takes his grandsons fishing in the canal and breeds racing pigeons.

Bedbaths are an opportunity to examine patients. Tomson shows me how to test for pitting oedema. 'You press the skin over the ankle like this, not too hard, hold it for a few seconds and then release your finger. If a dent remains, that's pitting oedema and you need to tell Sister.'

The mouths of helpless patients are cleaned with glycerine and lemon after we remove their dentures. I have never had to deal with false teeth before and holding slimy plates and brushing congealed food from between teeth is revolting. I keep thinking of my grandfather's ill-fitting teeth, which clicked as he ate so every meal was accompanied by a sound like castanets.

We come to one bed where the patient is lying in what looks like a cowpat but without the sweet odour of hay. The sight and smell are appalling. I want to pull the bedclothes back over him and walk away. Tomson appears unmoved but I can feel my stomach heaving. 'I want to be sick,' I whisper to her.

'Nurse Ross, would you go and get me some more tow (a type of cotton wool), and fill this jug with hot water,' she says, glaring at me. She hands me an enamel jug.

I leave with relief and go to the sluice room. For once I am glad that it has only mesh-covered windows as I take big gulps of fresh air. I do not want to go back. If I wait long enough Tomson will have cleaned up the horrible mess. Then I feel guilty. 'Pull yourself together,' I say to myself and go back. I will never become a nurse if I can't learn to control the repulsion I was taught as a child about bowel movements.

When we have finished and the old man is looking clean and comfortable, Tomson says, 'You'll soon get used to it. The important thing is to keep your respect for the patient. They can't help it and would be just as revolted if they knew.'

'Never talk to each other over patients,' is another instruction from Tomson. 'It's rude for one thing, but don't assume they can't hear even when they seem unconscious. So *if* you're turning an unconscious patient, tell him what you are doing and also tell him what day it is, what the weather is like – that sort of thing.'

Noon is time for the patients' dinner. The big, heated trolley is wheeled into the middle of the ward and plugged into a floor plug. Sister and the perm put on their cuffs to serve each meal, as we stand with trays ready to deliver them. Sister seems to know how much each patient can eat and what sort of diet is required. Helpless patients, who need to be fed, are served last. Then we go round with a trolley to collect and stack the dirty plates and cutlery. While half the nurses go for their own dinner, the other half do a bottle round, followed by yet another round of wiping lockers.

The evening routine is much the same. As the most junior nurse I get the supper dishes ready, wipe lockers, serve suppers, feed helpless patients, do a bottle round and help turn the patients who have to be turned every two hours. During visiting hour, which is actually half an hour,

I wash rubber draw sheets with carbolic and clean the sluice room. When the night staff comes on at nine o'clock, we can go off duty if our tasks are completed.

Judith, Jess, Blinks, Sandy and I meet in Sandy's room to compare notes but we are all so tired, no one says much. We go to bed as soon as we've finished our cocoa. No one has done anything that I have not and it sounds as if the routines on every ward are the same.

The days that follow are much like the first, though one day Sister Curtis stops me while I am wiping a locker to ask if I have given an intramuscular injection yet. I tell her I haven't.

'Well, I have just the patient for your first injection. He is very, very fat and won't feel a thing!'

We go into the sterilising room to take a glass syringe and some needles out of the small steriliser with forceps and put them into a sterile kidney basin. At the worktable, Sister hands me a glass bottle, about two inches tall, filled with thick white fluid and with a rubber stopper in the cap.

'This is penicillin,' Sister says. 'You can see how thick it is, so what size needle will you need?' I point to a two-inch needle with a wide bore.

'That is the right size of bore but as he is so large, I think a three-inch will be better. Now show me how you will draw up 2cc of penicillin.'

I put the syringe together being careful not to handle the inside part of the plunger, and attach the needle to the outer part. Then I wipe the top of the phial with a cotton ball moistened with alcohol, insert the needle into the rubber stopper, hold the bottle upside-down, withdraw 2cc of the white fluid and push out air with the plunger. I lay the syringe in the kidney basin with the needle resting on an alcohol swab.

'Now, before we approach the patient, what are you going to do?' Sister asks in her usual gentle way.

'I'm going to tell him it is time for him to have his penicillin, draw the curtains, and ask him to roll over and pull down his pyjama bottoms. Then I will swab his skin with an alcohol swab and holding the syringe perpendicular to his skin, I will, I will...' I indicate the motion rather than try to explain it.

'Very good. But what part of him will you inject?'

'The upper, outer quadrant of his buttock.'

'Why that part?'

'Because the sciatic nerve runs down through the inner part of the buttock and you can damage it if you hit it with a needle.'

'Yes, come on then. I think you know what you're doing. Don't tell him you have never done it before. Just go to the bed with as much confidence as you can.'

I am nervous but excited. My first injection! We go to the bed and I draw the curtains and the patient obligingly gets ready, as he knows what to expect. He is certainly an enormous man with a huge bottom. I swab the skin and aim the syringe. Not quite hard enough, but it goes in and I push down the plunger. As the fluid is so dense, I have to push really hard. I withdraw the needle and swab the area again, giving it a good rub to help the penicillin disperse into the tissues.

'Didn't feel a thing, nurse,' the patient says. He gives me a wink. I am sure he knows I have not done it before. I pull the curtains back and Sister Curtis and I go back to the sterilising room to wash the syringe and needle before putting them in the steriliser.

'Well done, Nurse Ross. I must make sure that you have many opportunities to do this again before you go on nights as you will have to give lots of injections then. I must also see that you have the chance to give some subcutaneous injections too. If you have your GNC record here I will sign it.'

State registration requirements include three years training in an accredited training school, a Preliminary Examination after one year, a Final Examination and completion of a Record of Practical Instruction and Experience for the Certificate of General Nursing. Sister Curtis is referring to the latter.

I produce my plain, brown cardboard-bound booklet for Sister Curtis to mark one stroke in the appropriate column to signify that I have been instructed in the giving of injections. A cross will indicate that I am proficient. Curtis tells me to show her my record before I change wards so that she can fill in other columns.

I go back to wiping lockers feeling that I am, at last, getting somewhere. The next day I give a subcutaneous injection of morphia. To prepare it, I am shown how to light a spirit lamp and place a tablet of morphia in 1.5cc of water in a teaspoon, which I then hold over the flame until the tablet dissolves.

'This tablet is a quarter of a grain,' Sister Curtis says, 'and it is dissolved in 1.5cc of water. So how many ccs will you need to give a sixth of a grain, which is what this man needs?'

I take a piece of paper out of my pocket and write out the calculation. 'One cc,' I say.

'Yes, that's right. Morphia is listed under the Dangerous Drug Act, or DDA, and these drugs are kept in this locked cupboard, and I, or whoever is in charge, must carry the key on our person.' She pulls a bunch of keys out of her pocket to show me the DDA cupboard key. 'Now I will watch you give it to him.'

I inject the morphia into the patient's upper arm and he receives it with a sigh of relief. Curtis shows me how to record the narcotic in the DDA register and how to record it, in red ink, on the patient's chart.

'These drugs are addictive so we must be careful how often they are given. But do use some common sense! If someone is dying it doesn't really matter if they become addicted to narcotics – it's more important that they're free of pain.'

When I compare notes with my friends, I am the only one to have given both types of injection so far. I strut around the room until someone throws a pillow at me.

We spend a lot of time grumbling about the Sod. She has the habit of going into our rooms and stripping our beds if she thinks they are not made properly.

'Look at this!' Judith says when she opens her door after coming off duty. 'That bloody woman's been in and stripped my bed again. In future I'm just leaving it as what's the point of making it twice. And it's none of her damned business how I leave my bed anyway.'

'And to think she goes to Mass every day,' says Marie who happens to pass by.

'Fat lot of good it does her,' Judith says.

'Ah, but think how much worse she'd be if she didn't go,' Marie says.

Can she be developing a sense of humour?

One evening, after nine o'clock, when most of us are in the Nurses' Home, there is a fire drill. The Sod had warned us this would happen and told us to read the instructions, but, of course, none of us but Marie had done so. Fortunately, Marie is in and tells us we are to check the rooms on either side of us, gather in the passage and then leave the building.

Most of us are in pyjamas and dressing gowns as we wait outside. The Sod comes out with a list and we are to answer

'Here' when our name is called. She goes through the names.

'Narrse Talbot.' Silence. Again, 'Narrse Talbot. Has anyone seen Narrse Talbot?'

'Yes Sister, I walked over with her when we came off duty,' Sandy says.

The Sod finishes the list and says, 'Everyone stay here except Narrse Ross and Narrse Chart. Come with me.' Marie and I follow the Sod as she runs up to our corridor. 'Ye two take a side each and I will look in the bathrooms.'

I run down one side, opening doors and looking in rooms as Marie runs down the other. We reach the end of the corridor in time to hear the Sod saying, 'Narrse Talbot, what in the name o' mercy arre ye doing lying in a bath during fire drill?'

I cringe for her as Wee Jess says, 'I thought that being in water ith the thafest place to he during a fire, Thister.'

My first death occurs one evening during visiting hours. I am alone on the ward with another peak. Madson is serving a second term of probation as she has not measured up to the mysterious, unexplained expectations we are to meet in order to get our permanent caps and move out of probation. I find the patient in bed 20 looking faintly green and not breathing. Madson comes over.

'I think he's dead,' I whisper. We gaze at him in horror, not having the first idea what to do. I recall, from some movie, that one is supposed to close the eyes with a cupped hand, but this man's are already closed.

Both the perms, thinking the ward was quiet and with nothing to do during visiting time, had gone to supper at the same time. 'Put screens round him,' I say to Madson, 'and I'll run to the dining room.'

The dining room is a long way from the ward. I forget such directions as 'Always walk in a stately manner' as I pelt along the main corridor. Breathless, I hurl myself into the staff nurses' section of the dining room and search the surprised faces for one of my staff nurses. I don't have to look for long as they see me, and the three of us hurry back to the ward.

The staff nurses lay out the body but they do not volunteer to show either Madson or me how to do this. I think they feel guilty about leaving us alone but they don't ask us anything about the experience or reassure us that we had done the right thing. I feel shaken and guilty. Was there something we could have done? Perhaps the man would be alive if I was more competent.

I miserably go off duty and find Judith to tell her about the incident.

'There's nothing you could have done, Jen. He was dead when you found him, wasn't he? At least you realised that he was dead and went for help. And you pulled the screens around so visitors couldn't see. What more could you have done?'

'I don't know,' I say. 'That's just it.'

'Look, you've been in the hospital for four weeks – how can you be expected to know what to do? The staff nurses should never have gone to supper together and left two peaks alone.'

'He died peacefully, that's a blessing,' I say, feeling comforted. 'I expected death to be revolting, but it wasn't. In fact he looked just the same except for the greenish colour and not breathing. Next time I won't be so scared.'

Chapter 8

ALTHOUGH WE ARE supposed to peak for three months, our set is put on night duty after only six weeks. I report for duty at 9pm on a male orthopaedic ward with a third-year nurse called Collins. After the report from the day sister, I am to go around with a trolley of hot drinks. 'What would you like?' I ask the patient in the first bed.

'What have you got?' he returns.

'Hot milk, cold milk, Horlicks, Ovaltine or tea,' I recite.

'Horlicks please,' he says.

Damn – Horlicks takes forever to mix, but I spoon some into a beaker, mix it with cold water, add hot milk and move the trolley three feet to the end of the next bed. 'What would you like?' I ask.

'What have you got?' comes the reply.

'Hot milk, cold milk, Horlicks, Ovaltine or tea,' I chant again.

'Tea, please.'

At the next bed I have learned and ask the patient,

'Would you like hot milk, cold milk, Horlicks, Ovaltine or tea?'

Many of the patients are young men with fractured femurs who lie on their backs with the broken leg resting in a Thomas's splint suspended from a Balkan frame. These splints resemble metal tomato plant holders with the bigger circle padded with leather. The extended metal rods, when fitted with a cloth, act as a sling for the leg. Tapes running down each side of the leg finish in cords that wind through pulleys in the Balkan frame to support a hanging weight. Thus both support and traction are achieved.

All the young men are together at one end of the ward and the legs in the splints look like an army with legs raised in a Nazi salute. As they feel well, but have to lie in more or less one position for six weeks, they become extremely bored. A new nurse is just what they need to liven up their day.

'Come and 'ave a look at this nurse,' one says as I go round with the drinks, 'it needs some attention.'

I innocently go to his bed as he lifts up the top sheet. Howls of laughter from all round as all the young men lift up their sheets and say, 'Come an' look at mine too.'

I dread the bottle round but having learned from Watkins, I go into the sterilising room and put a pair of rat-toothed forceps in my pocket. Sure enough, one of the young men lies back weakly and groans, 'I can't manage, nurse, you'll have to put it in for me.'

'Certainly,' I say, and approach with the forceps held menacingly.

He cringes. 'No, no, I can manage after all. My strength has returned.' No one else tries the same trick.

Collins and I do beds and backs to get everyone settled for the night. These patients not only need back care but we have to lubricate the ring of the Thomas's splints with Vaseline or else the leather becomes hard and cuts into the skin. It is like being in a stable and looking after the tack.

One young man, Tom, has been there for nearly three months with a fracture that refuses to heal. After several operations he is now in a cast from groin to ankle.

'Lift your bottom up,' I order and he hoists himself by holding onto his pull bar so I can give the sacral area a good rub.

'Give us a goodnight kiss, nurse,' he says, puckering up his mouth.

'How do I know if you've been a good boy?' I respond.

'Oh, I have, I have. Even Sister says I'm a good boy.'

I look at his head sheet then say, 'Sorry, it says here that goodnight kisses are forbidden.'

The night sister comes to give out the o.n. drugs (sleeping pills) with the charge nurse and I follow behind them. After they check the medicine and the dose between them they leave the pill in a teaspoon. I then help the patient swallow it.

Eventually the ward settles down and the lights are

turned out. In the dim glow of a few night-lights the ward looks even more like a cathedral as vast, dark shadows replace the uniformity of the rows of beds. When at midnight Collins goes for dinner, I am left alone. I am thrilled! I am in charge of all these sleeping forms, ready to minister to their every need. It doesn't occur to me that if anything goes wrong, I have no idea what to do. I pick up a torch and walk quietly round the ward feeling immensely important – all these men look to me for succour and …

the entrance of the night sister breaks my reverie.

'I will do a round, Nurse Ross,' she says.

We go to the first bed. She looks at me expectantly. I don't know what to say. 'Who is this patient?' she finally asks.

'I don't know,' I reply.

'Didn't you take report?'

'Yes Sister.'

'Nurse Ross, when you do a round with a night sister, you are to know every patient's name, their religion, their diagnosis and their investigations and treatment. As this is your first night, I will say no more, but tomorrow night, I shall expect a proper round.' She walks round while I trail miserably behind her.

When Collins comes back, she sees my panic and wants to know what has happened. She thinks one of the patients must have collapsed but when I tell her that Sister has visited and I am to know all 32 names, diagnoses and treatments by tomorrow, she says, 'Oh is that all! The sisters do that to all the new first-year nurses. Don't worry; we'll make a list out when you come back from dinner. You'll soon learn it.'

'But I'll never learn all that by tomorrow night and she says she'll be back tomorrow to do a round.'

'She won't. She's off and Busby is back. She's our regular night sister.'

'What's she like?'

'Oh, she's OK. Used to be in the QAs (Queen Alexandra's Royal Army Nursing Corps) and knows how to talk to these men. They practically salute when she comes round. You'd better go for dinner.'

Thus began the training for quick memorisation of a ward full of patients and I understand why Up and Down learned our names so quickly. At first we can hardly say some of the diagnoses, especially the surgical ones such as gastro-jejunostomy. We have no idea what Addison's Disease is or what CHF (Congestive Heart Failure) stands for, but we soon learn. Until now, the patients have been bodies that need to be fed, watered and bedpanned but on nights they become people with things wrong with them that we have to know about.

The first night wears on. One of my duties is to pack the drums with dressings I have made. From rolls of cotton wool I make small balls, and from rolls of gauze I cut and fold strips into squares. Then I stuff the drums. Drums are round metal containers that actually do resemble drums.

Circling the side is a sliding metal plate, which, in one position covers holes in the drum, and in another, leaves the holes open. When they are filled with dressings I put the drums out to be autoclaved. Before being put in the autoclave, the holes are open and when the drums are 'cooked', so to speak, the holes are covered with the sliding plate.

I also clean and boil syringes in the steriliser, make sure the needles are not blocked, wash down the trolleys with carbolic and collect the urines to be tested by the day staff. In the kitchen, I have to set the trolley for the day staff to give out the breakfast cutlery, put on an enormous pot of porridge, make sure it doesn't burn, cut mounds of bread and butter and cover them with damp cloths. In between these tasks, we go round turning patients who have to be turned frequently, give out urinals, make sleepless patients a warm drink, and do the various treatments that need to be done.

Around three o'clock I am dying to go to bed. I have to struggle to keep my eyes open and my body feels so heavy, I can hardly move. All I want to do is lie down and go to sleep. At four o'clock I go for tea and find the rest of my set in the same condition.

'Oh God, I'm never going to survive this,' Sandy says, laying her head on the table. 'Come and get me in the morning.'

'I had no idea this was going to be so awful,' says Marie who is on a female medical ward. 'I thought nights would be quiet and that we can sit down and take it easy but so far I've been rushed off my feet. Half the patients have gone dotty and keep calling out for a dead relative or something. If they're not incontinent, they want a bedpan all the time.'

Judith says, 'Be a nurse – a distinguished career for women!'

Only Blinks seems to be wide-awake. She is on a children's ward.

'My patients sleep OK,' she says. 'In fact they were fast asleep when we went on. There isn't much to do except clean things. But there is one poor little thing with steatorrhoea and we have to collect all his stool, and seeing that he has constant diarrhoea, it's not easy.'

'What's steatorrhoea?'

'It's when they can't absorb fat so it all comes out in the stool and makes it white. We have to keep him on a sort of frame to raise his bottom so he doesn't sit in it.'

'Do you have many babies?'

'No, they're nursed on Princess Mary ward. Babies up to a year go there then we have them until they're 14.'

'I don't want to go on a children's ward very much. I don't know how to talk to them,' I say.

'Oh, they're easy to talk to. I love children. Not that we have much chance to talk to them in the night but I'm looking forward to six when they wake up.'

I can imagine that Blinks is really good with children. She would be sweet but firm with them and remain unruffled no matter what they did.

I get a second wind about five o'clock and anyway, we are so busy that I forget how I feel. Before the ward sister comes on we have to bedbath the sickest patients, do a bottle round, hand out wash bowls to everyone, collect them, give out cups of tea, take everyone's temperature, pulse and respiration, give out medicines, do dressings and other treatments, and deal with any unexpected event. In addition, there are always the two hourly turns, patients to feed with drinks and mouths to clean, all of which are a constant throughout the 24 hours.

Compared to the day staff that arrive at 7.30 looking fresh with sleep and with clean aprons, Collins and I present a worn, bedraggled appearance. Sister and the perms come on at eight and, after prayers, I am free to go while Collins has to stay to give report. To the dining room for breakfast, then a bath, then at last, fall into bed. One of my aunts told me how nice it must be to be on nights, as I would have all day to do things in. She didn't seem to realise that we still need a good eight hours sleep and that night duty does not entail sitting reading or knitting. In fact, it is 11 hours of hard labour relieved only by two half-hour breaks.

One night my ward is very quiet and Sister Busby, our regular night sister, comes in to tell Collins that she is borrowing me for Ward 12 as they are very busy with a death.

'Have you laid anyone out before?' she asks.

'No Sister.'

'Well, I will help you and you will see that it is not too bad.' Such concern is rare in sisters. 'It is your last service for your patient. Always treat a body with the same respect you gave when it was alive.'

'Yes Sister.'

Busby rolls up her sleeves and together we wash the body and comb the hair. The body feels cold and as we roll it from side to side I can see the skin is blue and mottled. Busby still covers the part of the body that we are not washing, to preserve modesty, in the same way we do with live patients.

We pack the rectum with tow, tie the big toes together, put on a clean nightie and finally try to tie up the jaw with a piece of gauze bandage. There is a slit in it for the chin and the other ends are knotted above the head.

Busby says, 'This is an inadequate way of keeping the chin up but we do it anyway. To send a body to the morgue without the traditional gauze bandage around the head is sure to bring trouble from the mortuary attendants.' She rolls her eyes. 'To question the ritual will bring even more.'

I'm amazed that she talks to me like, well, like a colleague. Finally we attach a name-tag to the toe bandage, wrap the body in a clean sheet and slide it on to a trolley. An orderly from the morgue comes to fetch it as we close the curtains round all the beds in the vain hope of concealing the death from the other patients.

Not everyone in my set is introduced to death as gently

as I was. Jean Smith was on the neurosurgical ward. They admitted a young man who had flown off his motor bike and was virtually dead on arrival. His head injuries were so terrible that brain tissue was oozing out of the numerous lacerations. He was declared dead as soon as the houseman arrived, then Jean had to lay him out. She and the senior nurse attempted to pack the wounds as best as they could but the oozing continued. In the morgue, the attendant complained about the discharge to the night sister, who went straight to the ward to tell off the nurses.

'The way you laid out that patient was simply awful; his head wrappings are soaked already. Nurse Smith, take some fresh packing, go to the morgue and re-pack the head'.

Jean Smith, 18 years old, picked up the dressings and left the ward, but instead of going to a morgue in the middle of the night, went to her room, and instead of packing a dead man's head, she packed her suitcase and left for home. She was the seventh in our set of 33 to do so.

Chapter 9

SISTER BUSBY IS tall and dark. If she had been a man, she would have had a moustache, worn tweeds and been addressed as 'Major'. She holds herself erect as she walks round the ward, with her hands behind her back. Her hospital badge holds up the bib of her apron on one side, and a bar of military ribbons the other. She is older than the other night sisters as they are only doing nights until a ward comes free and they can become a ward sister. Busby, however, has chosen to be on nights permanently.

I am rubbing a patient's back when he tells me that she had been in France, had escaped at Dunkirk and then was in North Africa.

'How do you know that?' I ask him.

'Coz I was there too and she told me one night. You can tell from t'ribbons any road. She got the MBE tha' knows.'

'What's that?'

'Member of the British Empire. It's the medal given to nurses for gallantry as they weren't eligible for the DSO.'

'What did she get it for?'

'I don't know – she wouldn't tell me. But she's a grand lass tha' knows.'

She is a 'grand lass' and I adore her. I never did find out what she did to earn the MBE but I did learn that 12,000 State Registered Nurses served in the war and 235 were killed in action. Although our training often focuses on tradition, we are never informed of the part that nurses played in the war, nor indeed is the general public.

After a few nights Busby asks to do a round with me. 'You can use your list if you like, Nurse Ross. I know how hard it is to remember everything at first.'

We stand at the bottom of the first bed. I say in a low voice, 'Mr Headingly, age 42, repair of comminuted fracture of radius and ulna, fourth day. He's up and about and due to go home when his stitches come out.'

'What does "comminuted" mean?' Busby asks.

'It means the bone broke into fragments so that just putting on a splint won't heal it. The fragments have to be put back into place.'

'Why does he have a splint on rather than a cast?'

'Well, he's got stitches in so I expect it's so they can be taken out and the wound dressed.'

'Yes. So he's got a splint held on with an elastic bandage. What do you have to watch out for?'

'That the bandage isn't too tight.'

'Yes, that it wasn't put on too tight but also so that his

arm doesn't swell so the bandage becomes too tight. So what do you check?'

I think for a moment. 'That his fingers aren't blue or swollen and that they are warm and that he can feel me touching them.'

'Very good. Suppose you do find his fingers swollen, cold and insensitive to touch, what would you do?'

'Tell Collins or call you.'

Busby laughs. 'Suppose we're not here and you have to make a decision, what would you do?' She seems to be enjoying herself. So am I.

'I would take off the bandage being careful to leave the arm in the splint, and examine the wound. Then I would put the bandage back on more loosely and check his hand frequently. I would also make sure his arm is elevated on a pillow.'

'Good. Now, what would be the signs of an infected wound?'

'Redness, swelling, hot to the touch and a purulent discharge.'

'What would you do if the wound was like that?'

'If you or Collins weren't here I would notify the houseman.'

'Before you notified anyone, what else would you do?' I shake my head. 'You would take his temperature, wouldn't you? Now when we next do a round, I want you to be able to explain to me why the temperature rises when there's an infection.'

YES SISTER, NO SISTER

We move round the ward in a similar way – Busby asking questions and me trying to answer them. It is clear that she is trying to teach, not humiliate, and I feel so stimulated when she has finished that the menial tasks do not seem so boring. When I'm a sister, I'm going to teach like she does.

As I become confident about the names and diagnoses, she will start the round at the last bed on the ward and go backwards, to make sure I really know the patients. One night she starts walking round and suddenly stops at one bed to ask, 'Who's that?' I don't know, but I make up a name and diagnosis and say them with assurance. Our eyes meet. I know she knows I am bluffing but she doesn't say anything.

Just after we come on one night, Collins sends for her because a new patient is in considerable pain. He has a fractured femur and numerous cuts and bruises after a fall down a quarry on his bike. His leg is in a Thomas's splint. When Busby arrives she asks who put it on.

'I think the houseman did, Sister,' Collins says.

'It is not the right size nor are the cords wound through the pulleys correctly,' Busby says. 'Let's give him some morphia and I will find a more suitable splint. Do you have a tape measure?'

She measures the good leg and the width of the thigh at the groin. She leaves, to return 20 minutes later with two splints she has ferreted out from some storeroom in the basement. She sizes up the splints with the patient and chooses one. Then she makes a sling to support the leg with pieces of flannel and safety pins.

'Start lubricating the pad will you Nurse Ross, and then I will explain exactly what I want you both to do.'

Collins has to maintain traction on the tapes while I have to stand ready to take the old splint and hand her the new one.

'Right, pull,' she orders Collins as she lifts the leg and extracts the splint. She puts on the new one. The ring now fits snugly in the groin instead of on the thigh as the previous one had been. She adroitly manoevres the cords through the pulleys and finally hangs a weight on the end. All this time the young man has hardly said a word as the morphia has quelled the pain, but after the splint is fitted, he sighs and goes to sleep.

The houseman comes on the next night to find out what had happened to his splint. I thought he would be angry but instead he says, 'I got full marks for that splint on rounds this morning and I knew it wasn't the one I put on. Mr Wetherby showed the students how well it fitted and how the traction worked. He praised me to the hilt. Who did put it on?'

'Sister Busby.'

'I thought so. I must thank her. She saved my bacon.'

This incident is my first hint of the relationship between the night sisters and the housemen. They work as a team supporting each other through thick and thin. Housemen are recent graduates from the medical school who live in the hospital and who are on call 24 hours a day. A decent night's sleep depends on the ability of the night sisters to handle medical matters and make decisions. Dressers, who are final-year medical students, assist housemen. They work a few hours a week performing such tasks as withdrawing blood for analysis by the lab, shaving and catheterising male patients and assisting in theatre during the night.

I return from dinner one night as the phone in the foyer is ringing. We are getting an emergency. Before I have time to even enter the ward to let Collins know, the trolley arrives accompanied by a dresser, Busby and a porter. They wheel the trolley beside an empty bed but we do not put the young man into it. Huge eyes stare from an ashen face, his breath comes in short pants. His skin is icy cold.

Air hunger, I think, he must be in shock.

'He's been run over by a train,' the porter tells me, 'he works on the railways.'

'Cut off his trousers, Nurse Ross,' Busby orders as she administers oxygen.

I hold the cuff of one leg of his thick, navy, wool trousers and set to work with my nurses' regulation scissors. I need shears for this job, not inadequate scissors. As I work, I notice that the hollow of the trolley made by his body is slopping with blood, which seems to increase by the minute. I decide to start at the calf by making a cut across the leg so I hold his foot to gain purchase. The foot seems to move very easily from side to side. Suddenly I realise that his whole leg is coming towards me as I pull on the foot.

'Oh my God,' I say, 'his legs have been cut off!'

'Quick, wheel him straight to theatre, I think the RSO (Resident Surgical Officer) is still there.' Busby's voice is calm but authoritative. 'Nurse Collins, phone them to warn them we are coming and to have some O negative blood ready.'

They all rush out leaving me holding my little pair of scissors and trembling with shock.

Sister Busby returns later to say that we are to expect Bill Stokes back from theatre within an hour or two and to make up an amputation bed.

'He has had a bilateral amputation and is in shock, so put the bed up on blocks. Also get an IV pole and oxygen ready.' She turns to me and says, 'You did very well, Nurse Ross. You kept calm – that's important in an emergency. He was lucky – it was a crush injury. That's why he didn't bleed to death.'

'Why didn't they treat him in casualty, Sister?' asks Collins.

'Big flap on. Car accident. I should have examined him better and taken him straight to theatre. My fault. I didn't know the extent of his injuries.'

Bill struggles for his life for several days. He is barely conscious. I finally get a chance to soothe a fevered brow as he runs a temperature for days and we are frequently giving him cool sponge downs. When he begins to recover a little, the agony sets in. People who have amputations still feel pain and sensation in the part that is not there and he is particularly bothered by an intense itch in one foot that he always wants us to scratch. He has only been married for a year. His pregnant wife loyally visits him every day but her visits seem to make him more, not less, depressed.

'How can I ever be a husband again?' he cries as tears flow down his cheeks. 'What will my baby think of a father with no legs?'

We try to assure him that he is still a man and still love-able but he cannot be consoled.

Bill goes to a convalescent hospital in due course, to be fitted with artificial limbs and to learn to walk with them. We hear news of him from time to time but the news is not good. He suffers from severe depression until one day he has a visit from Douglas Bader, the legless airman who flew in the Battle of Britain. Doug took him in a wheelchair to the local pub where they both got thoroughly drunk. After that, Bill began to see a future for himself and his family. Two years later I heard that he visited the ward looking very chipper in a smart suit, showing off how well he could walk on his artificial legs, and proud that he had a prom-ising office job with the railways.

Chapter 10

AFTER BREAKFAST (it is still breakfast even though we have done a night's work), we drag ourselves to the Nurses' Home, have a bath, make a drink and meet in one person's room to relate the night's events. Usually we end up screaming with hysterical laughter. A psychologist would tell us we are releasing pent-up tension because we are unable to discuss our feelings of inadequacy or describe the impact of the continual exposure to sights, sounds and smells that are beyond our experience or imagination. We revel in humour, the cruder the better.

One morning Sandy asks, 'Did you hear what happened to Wee Jess last night?'

We wait expectantly. Jess works on a male surgical ward. She has gone home for nights off but not before telling Sandy her story.

'They had an acute appendix in and Mr Sedgewick was in theatre waiting to do an emergency appendicectomy. Jess sent for the dresser to come to shave the patient but he didn't come. The phone rang and a voice said, "Where the hell is that appendix patient? I can't wait all night."

'Jess told him that she had sent for the dresser to shave the patient and that the patient would be there as soon as he was prepped. Well, a few minutes later the phone rings. Mr Sedgewick again. "What the bloody hell are you doing – get that patient here at once nurse, or I'll tell the night sister how bloody inefficient you are."

'Jess didn't know what to do. Should she just send the patient unprepped or what? The charge nurse was at dinner. Jess stood there dithering when suddenly a man in a white coat came barging in. She rushed up to him, thrust a shaving tray into his hands, told him which patient it was and to hurry up because a horrible man kept phoning to shout at her.' Sandy starts to laugh and roll about on the bed.

'Oh come on Sandy,' Blinks says. 'What happened?'

Sandy regains control and carries on with her story. 'A few minutes later a dresser walked in and said he'd come to shave the patient for theatre. Jess told him another dresser was already there. "What other dresser? I'm the only one on." "The one that's shaving the patient," Jess said. Then the charge nurse came back, goes to see what was going on and says to Jess, "What's Mr Sedgewick doing shaving a patient?" Jess nearly died! Well, he and the dresser got the man on a trolley and as they passed Jess, Mr Sedgewick winked at her and said, "Next time a horrible man shouts at you on the phone, tell him to bugger off!"'

★

After Jean Smith left, Judith was moved to the neurosurgical ward. A few nights later she tells this story. She was alone on the ward, sitting at the desk when a bald-headed figure, vulnerable in a too-short hospital gown, loomed up out of the dark. She knew by the look in his eye and the way he walked towards her that something was wrong, so she hurried out of the ward to the phone. Before she could get to it, the man came out of the ward, grabbed her by the neck and started to bang her head against the wall.

'I thought I was going to choke to death. I couldn't get his hands off. I've never been so scared in my life. Just then Sister came in and the man let go. And do you know what she said?' At this, Judith starts to laugh. 'Do you know what she said? She said...' Judith can hardly get the words out. 'She said, "Really nurse, you shouldn't have let him get as bad as this."' We all collapse with mirth at the sheer inanity of the scene.

Judith does not often join us. One morning I go into her room to urge her to come and sit with us all. She is lying on her bed with her eyes closed, listening to a Mozart piano concerto being played on her portable, wind-up gramophone.

'It was bad enough living through last night without talking about it,' she says. 'I am trying to remember that there is a more sane life outside LGI. Though one good thing happened.'

'What was that?'

'Marie got her comeuppance! Silly twit was kneeling beside the bed of a dying patient praying for her soul when Sister Busby found her. Tore a strip off her. Said she had no business imposing her religious beliefs on others and that praying beside a bed did not fall within the duties of a nurse. Besides which,' Judith starts to laugh. 'The patient was Jewish!'

Judith missed my telling the story of when I was sent to help on her ward. We were very quiet and I was told to go and help on Judith's ward for an hour as they had had a death and an emergency admission. I laid out the body with Judith and then she asked me to check up on a patient in bed ten.

'He smells and I think he's had a BM, but watch out because he puts it in his locker,' Judith said.

I approached the bed, shining a torch on it and the locker. There was certainly a smell but I could not see the source of it. All of a sudden I skidded in something, fell flat on my back and shot under the bed. I didn't have to guess what I had slipped in as it was all over my shoe. Judith came to help me up.

'Oh shit,' I said.

'You're absolutely right.'

'It's all over my shoe,' I said as I took it off.

Judith started to laugh. We were both doubled up when the night sister came in.

'What are you doing with only one shoe on, nurse?' She had the expression of a Queen Victoria who is not amused.

'I stepped in something, Sister. I'm just going to wash my shoe.' I told her.

'What did you step in?'

'Oh just something the patient dropped on the floor, Sister.'

Sheila Dawson comes into the room where we are all gathered one morning, flops on the bed and says, 'Whew! What a night! We had a man who died with an erection.'

'Go on, I don't believe you,' Wee Jess says. We all nod in agreement.

'No, I'm not kidding. He had the most enormous dick you have *ever* seen and when he died it stood straight up.' Everyone's face is registering astonishment.

'What did you do?'

'We tried putting ice packs on it, then hot water bottles, but it still was as hard as a rock. In the end we just had to wrap him up in the sheet. It looked really peculiar – made the corpse look like a tent!'

'Well at least you can tell his wife that he died thinking of her,' I say.

'He's going to need a special coffin if it doesn't go down, one that looks like a submarine with an up periscope. How do you explain that to an undertaker?'

We are all laughing except Marie, who says, 'Was he young or can this happen at any age?'

'He was quite old but had a reputation for being a randy bugger all his life,' Sheila answers, grinning.

'Well he should have a good time in heaven – ready for anything,' Sandy says.

'Oh really, God doesn't allow that sort of thing in heaven.' Once again Marie is serious.

We get into an argument about whether sex is allowed in heaven. Marie goes to bed in a huff.

Some mornings we have the energy to walk into town, do some shopping and go for coffee at Schofields. They serve it in elegant silver coffeepots accompanied by a tiered tray of fancy cakes. You take the ones you want and then pay later. I am there with Sandy one day. I like going shopping with her as she has a dress sense that I do not. She is able to spot something that I would not even consider and I am amazed how much it suits me. Today she points out a blue, cashmere twinset on sale that I look really nice in. I am delighted with my purchase as we make for the cafe.

'I can stand most things,' says Sandy, after we have been served. 'Emptying bedpans, wiping bums, vomit, patients who blow off in your face, but it's sputum mugs that get to me. When it sticks on the sides – urrgh.'

'Do you mind,' I say, helping myself to another cake, 'I'm trying to enjoy these.'

'A man spilt his sputum mug all down the radiator and I had to clean it up. I thought I was going to be sick.'

'Sandy, will you shut up. It gets to me too and I don't want to feel sick right now. Talk about something else.' I take another cake.

'What else? OK. Have you thought of a way of boiling 32 eggs at once so they're not hard?'

'Collins told me to put them all in a pillow case and stick it into the pot when the water's boiling. But they still come out hard.'

We make the patients' breakfast at night. It is the same thing every day – porridge, boiled eggs and bread and butter. We put the porridge on at midnight and it is served at 8 am. As letting the porridge burn is a crime as heinous as murder we are neurotic about checking the water in the double boiler every hour.

'Have you ever thought that we're more like maids than nurses?' Sandy asks me. I'm surprised, as she is not given to introspection. 'Do you ever regret going into this?'

'Sometimes, but not often. Why? Do you?'

'Anyone can do what we do. I can't see why we need School Certificate to get in.'

'Only teaching hospitals do. Other hospitals take anything that walks,' I say. 'Cheer up Sandy, it gets better in second year and soon there'll be three sets junior to us so we won't be doing bedpans and lockers so much.'

'Yes, but it isn't much of a challenge to the old brain, is

YES SISTER, NO SISTER

it? I mean, we learn all this stuff, then all we do is maid's work.'

'When we're more senior, we'll be doing more. Next night duty we might be in charge.' Second-year night duty means that some of us will be the senior nurse on the ward, at least some of the time, though others will still have to be the junior. 'And we'll be in block soon. That will be a challenge to your brain! Stop moaning and tell me something funny.'

Sandy thinks for a minute. 'Well, this didn't happen to me but to Jones on the ward above me. A man peed in his fruit bowl. Jones decided to sterilise it but she didn't realise it wasn't glass – it was a sort of Perspex – and it came out like a gramophone record. It was his own fruit bowl and his wife was furious. She wanted to know what we were doing putting it in a steriliser in the first place. No one wanted to tell her.' She paused. 'Not very funny. You tell me one.'

'We have this man who complains the whole time. The patient next to him got fed up and said to him, "Will you put a sock in it you miserable old bugger. If it was Florence Nightingale herself, you'd complain her bloody light was too bright."' I say, using the long vowels of a Yorkshire accent.

Sandy laughs, and then says, 'Did you hear about Mr Lambert? He was consulting on a patient on Ward 11 when another patient called out at the top of his voice, "Don't let that butcher get near thee, luv. He right buggered me up, he did." He must have felt so embarrassed!'

'Never! Surgeons don't get embarrassed.'

The waitress comes up holding a pad of bills. 'How many cakes?'

'Well, um, ten,' I say.

'Ee luv, tha' must have been hungry,' the waitress says putting the bill on the table. She walks away sniggering and we leave laughing.

I have my first run in with the Sod while on night duty. We had all moved to rooms on a floor designated for night nurses where the original blackout curtains remain and where quiet is maintained during the day. The cleaner for the floor starts work at 6am so she can finish by the time we are going to bed. She is deaf and dumb but still manages to communicate very well by effective, though sometimes grotesque, body language. She pointed at my photos one day. I told her about my brothers and offered her a chocolate. From then on we have been on amicable terms.

I have had a dreadful night with two emergencies from a car accident. We are late off duty, breakfast is cold, and all I want is a bath and my bed. I am lucky to find a free bathroom straight away and manage to relax a little in the tub of hot water. I put on my dressing gown and return to my room. It is locked. I can't understand it as I know I left it open. The cleaner appears and parodies a figure walking down the corridor.

'Sister O'Donnelly?' I ask.

She nods. Then she pretends to open a door, produces some keys, locks the door, and puts the keys in her pocket.

'Sister O'Donnelly went into my room, took my keys, locked the door and walked away with my keys?'

The cleaner nods vigorously, then walks away from my room in a fair imitation of the Sod's gait.

I am furious. Still in my dressing gown and clutching my towel and sponge bag, I stride down to sick bay, walk into the outer office and without knocking, storm into the inner office. The Sod is sitting at her desk with two Home Sisters in the other chairs. I march up to her desk, thump the flat of my hand down upon it and say loudly, 'Give me my keys.'

In her astonishment the Sod simply hands me the keys but recovers enough to say, 'Ye should knock before entering,' as I march out.

She doesn't bother me again. Her favourite prey is Blinks. She will walk into her room while she is asleep, wake her up and say, 'Narrse Blinker, do ye not know ye should stand up when a sister comes into the room?'

Blinks will get out of her bed in her pyjamas and stand until the Sod leaves.

Judith tells Blinks she is a fool to be bullied. 'Didn't you read *Tom Brown's Schooldays?* It shows you that the only way to deal with bullies is to stand up to them. Now, let's rehearse.' She leaves the room, walks in and says in an Irish accent, 'Do you not know you should stand up when a sister comes into the room. Now, Blinks, what are you going to say?'

Blinks stares at her helplessly and mutters something inaudible.

'Blinks, all you have to say is that you are off duty and you don't have to stand up when off duty. Now, say it.'

Blinks repeats the words but without assurance. We know that she will simply stand up and that the Sod will continue to bully her.

After the rehearsal, Judith says, 'You know, that woman should be fired. She's an alcoholic for one thing and completely incompetent. What I hate about this hospital is the way some sisters get away with murder. You know the saying – power tends to corrupt, absolute power corrupts absolutely. Who said that, I wonder. They were right.'

Chapter 11

'NURSE, CAN I have a bedpan?'
'Why didn't you have one during the bedpan round?' I ask through gritted teeth.

'Didn't need one then, luv, but I do now.'

I am on yet another medical ward, a female one. Female wards are harder to work on than male ones because it is so much more difficult to give out bedpans than urinals. A bedpan requires screening the bed, lifting the patient both on and off it, handing out toilet paper and a small wash-basin. The two most junior nurses put pink gowns on over their uniforms and prepare for the ordeal several times a day. Each stainless steel bedpan has to be warmed under a hot tap, as, stored where they are in the freezing sluice room, their introduction straight from there would add to the heart attack rate. They are then piled on a trolley to be wheeled around the ward.

For the few yards from the trolley to the patient, a bedpan must be covered with a cloth because its naked form might prove an embarrassment. Two nurses lift a large body onto a bedpan, move to the next person and so on around the ward.

Once everyone is enthroned, we begin again by lifting the bodies off. If a woman has had a bowel movement, we will wipe her clean as this task requires the agility of an athlete to perform at the best of times and most of the women are too sick or too large to do it themselves. We then empty the bedpans, measure the contents of those on Intake and Output, stack them, wash down the trolley with carbolic, take off the pink gowns and go back on the ward. No wonder that we long to be senior enough to rarely do this chore.

At first, wiping someone else's bottom was appalling. For so long, since toddler-hood, such attention is strictly personal. To be doing this for adults old enough to be my parents or grandparents seems somehow obscene. But after a short time, one bottom begins to look like any other; looking at one is the same as looking at a face. It takes longer to get used to the smell and I still gag sometimes.

The sister on the ward is known as the Dragon. She is on holiday when I first start there and the two weeks of her absence are peaceful and uneventful. Then at 8 o'clock one morning in she marches to take prayers. One look at that frozen face and I know I am in for trouble. I hate her at first sight. I suspect the feeling is mutual as her eyes are upon me from the moment she walks in. It is a face that never smiles. Her mother's prediction that if you pull a face like that and the wind changes, you will look like that forever, must have come true; she has been caught with the permanent expression of one who has a particularly odious smell under the nose.

On her first day, she appears between the curtains as I am doing beds and backs. 'There is a right side and wrong side to a draw sheet, nurse, and that is the wrong side.' The only way I can detect a difference in sides is from the narrow seam. Later, she appears again. 'Didn't they teach you in PTS to change the draw sheet to get rid of the crumbs?'

'There weren't any crumbs in PTS Sister,' I say. I swear she snorts and I swear smoke comes out of her nostrils.

She seems to be behind me all the time and always has a complaint to make. Whatever I am doing, I am doing it wrong. 'Why are you setting up that enema tray like that? Didn't they teach you what size enema tubes to use?' 'Don't you know to clean a mouth properly? This one looks as if it hasn't been cleaned for days.' 'Nurse Ross, how many times do I have to tell you to be careful not to break a thermometer? Do you realise how much they cost?' 'Nurse Ross, did you get talcum powder all over the floor? Sweep it up at once.'

She does not allow us to go for meals or breaks until the bed wheels are straight and the bed-tables lined up at the foot of the beds where the patients can't reach them. One day she sends for the junior night nurse, who is in bed, makes her get dressed in uniform and come back to the ward. The trolleys were not cleaned to her satisfaction.

I long for the times when she is off. She has only been back a week when I find out that I am getting three ten-ones in one week. The best off duty, apart from a day off of course, is a five-to. I have none of those. Two ten-ones in one week sometimes happens but three or four are unheard of.

The Dragon's blue-eyed girl is Ann Milbury. She came on the same day the Dragon returned from holiday. When the Dragon asked her which set she is in, Milbury told her that she takes finals when I do. This is true but Milbury is in the set below me, and is therefore my junior. State Registration exams are held three times a year whereas sets of nurses commence four times a year, so every year two sets of nurses take finals together. As a result of Milbury's deceit I am always placed junior to her on the work lists and so do more menial tasks.

Milbury is my first encounter with the sort of person who gains recognition by ingratiating herself with her superiors and by subtle put-downs of others. One evening she and I are on with one of the perms, Sutcliffe, who is far too nice to perm for the Dragon. Sutcliffe comes into the bathroom where I am washing rubber sheets with carbolic and hanging them on the pulley-type drying racks.

'Nurse Ross,' she says, 'I am very disappointed with you. You were supposed to clean up Mrs Potts ready for her visitors and she's soaking wet.'

'I changed her bed about half an hour ago, just before visitors,' I mutter, carrying on with what I am doing.

'Nurse Milbury told me you haven't been near her since before supper.'

'Then Milbury is lying,' I shout, slapping a wet rubber

draw sheet against the side of the bath, 'and not for the first time. She told you she is in the same set as me; she is not, she is in the set below me. I'm sick to death of this ward and sick to death of nursing. Do you realise that I have four ten-ones next week? Four! And Milbury doesn't have one. When I'm trained, I shall never be as unfair as you lot. That is, if I stay here and finish.' I am nearly in tears.

Sutcliffe looks thoughtful after this outburst. Although the Dragon is still breathing down my neck, the number of ten-ones is reduced to two and Milbury is placed below me on the work lists.

One morning I wake up feeling dreadful but go on duty anyway. The morning drags on. My legs feel wobbly and barely able to hold me up. I feel so woozy that I don't care what the Dragon says. Finally dinnertime comes but instead of going to the dining room, I go to sick bay.

'I don't feel very well,' I tell the Home Sister. She takes my temperature. It is 104 degrees, which puts me out of the classification of those who simply do not want to work into those who are Truly Sick. I am put to bed and I lie in a fever of unknown origin for three days. A commode is placed in my room, which I am too embarrassed to use. How can I expect a sister to empty my urine, or worse?

'You'll have to use it eventually, you know,' the Home Sister says smiling.

I do.

During the night and next day I am delirious but not so

far gone that I cannot appreciate the nursing care I receive. The Sod does not appear so I can't judge if she is different with nurses who are sick. The other Home Sisters are attentive and concerned. They give me cool sponge baths and fresh sheets every few hours and then leave me to sleep. Cold drinks and delightfully enticing light meals are put in front of me. There are even flowers on my tray. It is hard to believe that these Keepers of the Morality of the Virgin's Retreat can be so kind.

Eventually I recover. I am sent home for a few days with instructions to report to sick bay on my first day back before I go on duty. I spend a few days being spoiled by Amma before I return, and after being checked by the physician, I go on duty. It is about 10.30am. The Dragon greets me with, 'Ah Nurse Ross, you're back. I believe you are a ten-one.' She looks in the off duty book to check. 'Yes you are, so come back at one.'

'But it's 10.30 now Sister.'

'Yes, come back at one o'clock,' she orders as she turns her back on me.

I've had it! I can bear the hard work and the exhaustion. Smells, vomit and bowel movements no longer make me gag. I am not homesick. But I cannot, and will not tolerate injustice. I never imagined that this is what would make me give up. I no longer care. My desire to finish at all costs seems to have flown out of the window; instead, I am relieved at the thought of leaving. I shall miss Judith, Sandy,

Blinks and Wee Jess and I know they will be surprised when they hear I have gone. They seem to think that I love nursing.

I go to Matron's office. 'I want to give in my notice,' I say to Miss Darcy, the Deputy Matron.

'Oh dear,' she says, 'What's happened?'

I tell her about all the ten-ones, about being ill, about going back on duty to be told that I am to return at one to work a straight eight hours when I have just been in sick bay. 'And I cannot work with that sister. People in India treat their coolies better than she treats me.'

'Will you stay if you are put on another ward?'

I think for a while. 'Alright,' I say. I really have no plans. I don't know where to go or what other job to do. Our other choices at school had been the Leeds Teacher's College or the Yorkshire Ladies' Secretarial College but neither of these appeals to me.

'Just a minute, I need to check the allocation,' Miss Darcy says and leaves the room. As I sit waiting for her I become dimly aware that I have some power, that leaving is an option. 'They' do not want us to leave, as the place would collapse without us. I do not have to put up with injustice and contempt.

Miss Darcy returns. 'You are to go to Ward A of the private patient's wing. It is a quiet ward and as you have been ill, you need a bit of a rest.'

The Dragon sends for me a few days later to sign my

report. All the ticks are in the Poor column. The overall assessment is Poor. She has written, 'Nurse Ross has no promise as a nurse. She is surly and unwilling to accept direction. She has no team spirit and is reluctant to help other nurses or to take on additional work.'

I take the piece of paper and where it calls for my signature I write, 'Over.' On the back of the page I write, 'This report is as unjust as my treatment on this ward was. This Sister is a *despot* and is not suited to be in charge of either patients or student nurses.' In the background I can hear her asking me what I think I am doing. I sign beneath my writing, pick up the report and prepare to go to Matron's office with it. I am not going to leave it with the Dragon as she can easily re-write it and leave off what I have written.

'Where do you think you are going with that?' she screams.

'To Matron's office.'

'How dare you, give it to me, come back at once.' I can hear her shouting as I triumphantly march out of her ward.

I expect a call to see Matron but it doesn't come and I forget about it. I don't know what happened to the report or whether Matron saw the Dragon rather than me. All I know is that I am not going to put up with that sort of treatment again. Nor will I be like that when I am a sister.

Chapter 12

The following articles would be prepared on a tray
for a medical fomentation:

- *Chest blanket*
- *Jug of boiling water*
- *Fomentation wringer*
- *Large bowl*
- *Bandages*
- *Safety pins*
- *A square of flannel cut to the appropriate size*
- *A square of oiled paper slightly larger than the*
  flannel
- *A square of brown wool larger than the oiled*
  paper
- *Cover for the tray*

The patient's bed is screened and he is told what is
going to happen. The part is exposed and the patient
kept warm with the chest blanket. The nurse then
fetches her prepared tray and the jug of boiling
water. The square of flannel is wrapped in the
fomentation wringer and placed in the bowl with the
ends of the fomentation wringer hanging outside the

bowl. The boiling water is then poured into the bowl. The fomentation wringer is wrung tightly to squeeze out as much water as possible. It is opened and the hot square of flannel placed on the part. Before putting it on the patient it should be tested on the back of the hand or the patient may be burned. The oiled paper is then placed over the flannel, the brown wool over the oiled paper and the whole lot is firmly bandaged on. If the fomentation is not prepared at the bedside, it should be taken to the patient between two heated plates.

'I FEEL AS IF we should put up a memorial plaque,' Judith says as she looks around the classroom on the first day of a block of classes. 'We can list all those who fell while answering the call of duty.'

'No. It should be a monument to those with enough savvy to leave,' I say.

Of the 33 who started, 17 remain. Although some of those at the starting gate were not cut out to be nurses, some have left as the direct result of the actions of sisters. Jean Smith, for example, should never have been sent to a mortuary in the middle of the night when she had only been in the hospital for three months. Barbara Young left in the first two weeks. She had been found sitting in the kitchen by the Sister, who asked her why she was sitting down and why she was not on the ward. Barbara said her feet ached. She received such a hail of invective that she got up and walked out. Neither of these two girls handed in their notice but simply packed and departed. Others had gone to Matron's office, as I had done, but where I had been persuaded to stay, the others had not.

The education, for which we labour 58 hours a week, consists of three months in Preliminary Training School and six weeks in each of the three years. These six-week periods, known as 'blocks', are held in that part of the Nurses' Home which houses classrooms, practical rooms and a library. Classes run from 9.30am to 4.30pm, but so that we will not think that a day's work is for seven hours, we go on the wards from 7.30am to 9am and from 5pm to 6pm every weekday and on Saturday mornings.

We look forward to our first block as a relief from what is becoming a relentless routine of menial tasks and also because we have weekends off. It is a time when we will be all together again for a change. We rarely see each other even though our rooms are in the same corridor. By the time we have come off duty, often late, walked over to the Nurses' Home and had a bath, we have no energy left to do anything but flop into bed.

The senior Sister Tutor, Agatha Japp, walks in. We all stand. So does she. From the front of the class she gazes at each one of us but as she is smiling, we do not feel intimidated, merely puzzled. It is a warm smile, which exposes extraordinarily large front teeth with a gap between them.

In her bonnet, with strings tied beneath her chin, she reminds me of Jemima Puddleduck.

'Please sit down,' she says. We sit. She continues to gaze at us and I realise that her classes will be held at a much slower pace than our usual rushed routine.

'Who is Jennifer Ross?' she asks. I stand. I can feel my face redden. What on earth have I done?

'Are you related to Wendy Ross?'

'Yes, Sister, she's my aunt.' My father's youngest sister had trained at LGI just in time to be propelled into the war.

'And are you going to be as good a nurse as she was?'

Inwardly I curse Wendy as I say, 'I hope so, Sister.'

Her gaze continues but finally she says, 'Good. Please sit down.' She then outlines our timetable, which, except for the absence of field trips and cookery, is much the same as in PTS with one major exception. Medical staff give many of the lectures. As they take pride in being asked to lecture us, they also take the trouble to prepare well and, generally speaking, we find their lectures enjoyable and informative.

When surgeons are introduced to us, we are told to always address them as 'Mister' if they are Fellows of the Royal College of Surgeons, not as 'Doctor'. To become an FRCS is an arduous business; recognition of this feat with the title of 'Mister' acknowledges that the noble art of surgery began in barber's shops.

AJ, as Sister Japp is known, gives us lectures on nursing and materia medica. With another Sister Tutor, she also teaches us in the practical room. She seems to have been nursing for a very long time and we are convinced she served in the Boer War. In fact, she is one of those people of indeterminate age, but she is probably in her late forties.

She is short and round and her belt holds up her enormous breasts. When she laughs, which she does frequently, her bosom wobbles like ambulatory custard. Her laughter turns into rasping wheezes and coughs as she gasps for breath. At the same time, her face gradually turns blue and her eyes water. Fascinated by this display, I diagnose her as a case of emphysema and chronic bronchitis, forgetting that she would hardly be working if she had such serious conditions.

'Nursing is the art of making a sick person comfortable in bed,' she pronounces. Although she trained at a big London hospital she is always telling us that we are the best nurses in the world and how proud she is of all the LGI nurses who work in many different countries. She owns a pair of glasses that fold at the nosepiece. Her habit of standing in front of us folding and unfolding them has a mesmerising effect on us all, as instead of listening to her, we sit wondering which way the glasses will unfold next. She tries to instill in us a sense of dignity but as most of us are 19, it is an uphill task. 'You must always behave in a seemly manner and not let your profession down. Remember, it is a privilege to be a nurse.' This phrase becomes part of our vocabulary. When someone tells us about being puked on, for example, we say, 'Remember it is a privilege to be a nurse! Ha ha.'

It is during first block that we begin to worry about Blinks. The dilemma presented to us in PTS about a colleague who smells faces us in the form of Blinks. Whereas we routinely have a bath after coming off duty, Blinks goes straight to bed. She tells us she prefers to bathe when she gets up but we soon find out that she does not bathe at all. Judith, Sandy, Jess and I take it in turns to run a bath for her and then tell her it is ready. In her usual good-natured way, she thanks us and ambles off to the bathroom.

One day, I run a bath for her and she dutifully goes to the bathroom. In a couple of minutes she is back saying someone else is in there. It is Marie.

I knock on the door. 'Marie, this bath was for Blinks.'

'Well, no one was in it when I came so as far as I'm concerned, the bathroom was unoccupied.'

'That's not fair, Marie, Blinks was only going to be a minute.'

'What are you doing running a bath for her anyway? Why can't she run her own bath?'

I don't answer. Another bathroom becomes free and I run a bath for Blinks there.

The days speed by. In the practical room we learn how to apply leeches. Judith is astonished and says so. AJ accepts her comment philosophically. 'Application of leeches is still a requirement of the General Nursing Council and although it might, as you say, seem archaic, leeches are still used in the treatment of glaucoma – with good effect, I might add.'

AJ takes a small piece of flannel and cuts a tiny hole in the middle of it. 'You place the flannel on the patient with the hole over where you want the leech to suck, like this.' She rolls up her sleeve and places the flannel on her arm.

Three horrible, purple, worm-like creatures live in a stone jar partially filled with water. One of them has slimed its way to near the lid. AJ extracts it with a pair of forceps and places it on the flannel on her arm. There is a general 'Urrgh,' from us all as we stare in horror. The leech finds the small hole immediately and we watch it swell until it finally starts to move. At this moment, AJ picks it up again and replaces it in the jar.

She looks at our faces, all registering varying degrees of disgust. 'Really nurses, there is nothing to be so squeamish about! People in jungles all over the world get leeches on them all the time even though they aren't the same type as these. You don't feel anything.'

I walk into Blinks's room after supper one evening to find her looking like a Mad Woman in a gothic movie. She has not been brushing her hair, but as her cap usually hides the tangled thatch, we have not noticed it before.

'Blinks,' I say, 'let me brush your hair for you. It looks

awful.' Blinks grins at me and sits down to allow me to attack the tangle.

'Blinks, are you feeling alright?' I ask.

'Yes, of course I am. Why? Don't I look alright?'

'Yes, you look fine but you seem to be forgetting things lately.'

'Do you wonder? This place is enough to make anyone lose their mind!'

In addition to making sure she has a bath we take it in turns to do her hair and we check that she has her glasses and textbooks with her before we go to class.

We learn to set trays and trolleys for more advanced procedures such as catheterisations, tepid sponging and medical and surgical fomentations. Fomentations are the application of heat to reduce swelling; a surgical one is sterile, used when the skin is broken, and a medical one is not. We also learn how to pass a Ryle's tube. This long, thin, rubber tube is pushed up a patient's nostril and down into the stomach to obtain specimens of stomach contents, to give feeds, or as preparation for gastric surgery.

'This is an unpleasant procedure for the patient,' AJ says, 'so you must learn to do it gently. First you must ensure the tube is patent, that is, not blocked. You can see that there are three holes at the bottom of the tube and they can easily become blocked.' She passes a tube around for our inspection.

'These are the things you need.' AJ indicates a tray on

which sits a kidney dish, a bowl, lubricant, a syringe, litmus paper and various cotton wool balls. 'First you tell the patient what you are going to do, of course. It is better to do this before you arrive with the tray or else you might be chasing the patient down the corridor!' She starts to laugh. After the paroxysm of coughing ends, she carries on. 'You examine the nostrils and select the biggest. I don't suppose you know that one nostril is always bigger than the other do you? Well, turn to your neighbour and have a look.' We all look up each other's nostrils and sure enough, they are different sizes.

'You then clean that nostril with these swabs. You lubricate the catheter and insert it into the nostril. After about an inch you will meet some resistance. At that point, you ask the patient to swallow. Then the tube should slide down the throat into the stomach.'

I have watched this procedure on the wards and know it is not as simple as it sounds. AJ fails to mention how the tube makes the patient gag and how sometimes it comes out through the mouth making the patient look like a gargoyle.

'How will you know the tube is in the stomach?' AJ asks.

'Fluid should come back up the tube,' Wee Jess says.

'Yes. You attach the syringe, withdraw some of the fluid and test it with litmus paper. What colour should it turn?'

'It will turn red because the stomach contents are acid,' I answer, 'but how do you know that you are not in the lungs?'

'That is a very important question. You know the tube is not in the lungs because you would not be able to obtain any fluid. Also the patient would cough. If the tube is in the lungs and you give a feed, what would happen?'

'The patient would drown.'

'Exactly. Now I want you to be able to set the tray and it is up to you to find an opportunity to pass a Ryle's tube while a sister watches you.'

Not content with this directive, I go back to the practical room later to put a Ryle's tube down myself. I am always imagining what it feels like to be a patient and I believe that we should only do to patients what we have experienced ourselves. Someone has already told me which is my largest nostril so I carefully lubricate it and the tube. I poke the tube up my nostril but after about an inch it will not go any further. I poke and prod until the pain makes my eyes water. Good grief, I'll never be able to do this to someone. I take some deep breaths and push the tube so hard it finally goes down into my throat. I gag, but swallow hard until the tube slides down into my stomach.

At this moment AJ walks in to find me with a bloated face and a rubber tube protruding from my nose.

'What on earth are you doing, Nurse Ross?' she says. She isn't smiling.

'I wanted to know what it felt like,' I croak.

'Does this mean you are going to perform every procedure I teach on yourself? Are you going to catheterise yourself? Put stitches in yourself so you can take them out? I won't be able to leave you alone!'

YES SISTER, NO SISTER

I am in no position to make a dignified reply. Tears are streaming down my red and swollen face. A large globule of viscid fluid that increases in length by the second and threatens to drop onto my crisp, white apron, now accompanies the rubber tube dangling from my nose.

'No, Sister,' I manage to gasp.

AJ's voice is cold as she says, 'Take that tube out, Nurse, wash it and put it away.' She leaves the room. I can hear her wheezing.

I gingerly pull out the tube and thankfully sink my face into a basin of cold water. I feel mortified. I had not expected to be found by a sister but as I had, I think I should receive some commendation for wanting to experience what a patient goes through, not a rebuke.

Judith tells us an alarming story one day. She was talking to Blinks at breakfast and found out that Blinks thought it was Wednesday instead of Thursday.

'Nothing wrong with that,' I say, 'I often forget what day it is.'

'Yes, but Blinks couldn't remember anything that had happened the day before, that was what was so funny. Well you know I am on the ward above her, so I talked to her staff nurse and found out that Blinks had not shown up for duty on the Wednesday. No one seemed to worry too much; they didn't even go and check her room. Typical of the way they care about us.'

'Where was Blinks? Did she take a day off?'

'No. I think, and so does Blinks, that she slept the whole time. She went to bed on Tuesday, didn't get up on Wednesday, slept all day and all night, and got up on Thursday thinking it was Wednesday. Now, don't you think there is something wrong?'

I tell Judith about the time Blinks barged into my room without knocking and screamed at me. 'You have been poking around in my room, haven't you? Where is it?'

'Where's what Blinks? I haven't been near your room.' I was alarmed.

'My pocket watch. You came and took it.'

'No I didn't, Blinks,' I said gently, 'it's in your pocket.' I could see its chain behind the bib of her apron.

'Oh, yes. How silly of me. I'm sorry.'

When I talk to the others, they relate similar experiences. It doesn't occur to us, nor to the sisters, that there can be something wrong with Blinks. Now that we are in block and see Blinks every day, we notice how much she has changed. She is so forgetful that if we don't escort her to class she will go without the things she needs. She barely passes the weekly written tests and because she can't remember what goes on the various trays and trolleys, she fails the practical tests. AJ seems worried about her. She confides in me and tells me she is going to ask Blinks to set a tray for a medical fomentation in a test the next day.

'I think she just needs some encouragement and I would like her to get something right for a change. Will you go over the tray with her until she knows it inside-out?'

Blinks and I come back to the practical room after supper to practice setting trays and trolleys. I make sure Blinks sets the medical fomentation tray until she gets it right. She is delighted when she gets full marks next day and AJ gives me a conspiratorial smile. Blinks gets enough marks to scrape through.

We go home for a few days after block and when I return I notice that the door to Blinks's room is open. I see one of the Home Sisters packing up her things. A bare mattress stares at me with the same aura of death as a stripped bed on the wards.

'Where's Nurse Blinker?' I ask. I have a sick feeling of foreboding.

'I'm afraid she's left,' the Sister says. She continues to pack Blinks's trunk and doesn't look at me.

'Why? She had every intention of coming back four days ago.'

'She was ill when she got home and her parents took her to the doctor.' The Sister looks embarrassed.

'What's wrong with her? Is it something serious?'

'I'm afraid she has schizophrenia and is in her local mental hospital. She won't be coming back.'

Chapter 13

I AM ON A surgical ward at last but I cannot raise any enthusiasm for learning to change dressings, prepare patients for theatre, give injections or do any of the things I have longed to do. I am fairly senior too, as there are three student nurses who are junior to me. But somehow the ward routine seems humdrum and I wonder how I could ever have thought it exciting.

I receive a parcel and a letter from Blinks, which depresses me even more.

Dear Jen,
I am feeling a bit better. This place isn't too bad and the nurses are very kind. The psychiatrist doesn't think I will ever return to training so I want you to have my paediatric textbook, as I know you wanted one. Give my love to everyone.

Love Blinks

I cry in my anger over what has happened to such a sweet girl. Was there something we could have done? Why didn't

140

the sisters, who are supposed to know about disease, recognise that Blinks was ill? Instead, a monster like the Sod bullied her. We are simply robots, and as long as we do the tasks quickly and say, 'Yes Sister, no Sister, three bags full Sister,' we pass.

On my first day on this new ward I am down to do dressings with a perm. Sister Pearce gives us a list and on it she has marked the patients whose wounds she wants to inspect. We put white gowns over our uniforms and wear white cloth masks. I catch a glimpse of myself in the bathroom mirror but the sight does not fill me with joy. It is a reflection of just another nurse.

In the sterilising room, the perm sets up a dressing trolley for the first patient. She wipes it down with carbolic, then places on the top shelf two large stainless-steel bowls with lids that she takes out of the large steriliser with sterile tongs. She opens up a drum and removes two sterile green cloths, cotton wool swabs and gauze dressings with the tongs and puts them into one of the bowls. Into the second bowl she puts three pairs of forceps, a pair of scissors and a small container – all sterile. She pours alcohol into the small container and covers both the sterile bowls with their lids. Finally she places an unsterile bowl with a lid onto the bottom shelf of the trolley together with a chest blanket and a tray of rolls of tape, bandages and safety pins.

'Right, I think that's all,' she says, 'I will do the first

dressing and then you can do the rest. But first we need to put another set of bowls and instruments in to boil so they'll be sterile when we come back.'

Sterilisers are large, metal boxes on legs with knobs to regulate water entry and exit, and knobs to regulate heat. One steriliser is big enough to boil the stainless steel basins and lids while the smaller is for instruments and syringes.

The perm looks at the list. 'Let's start with young Jean. She had an appendicectomy five days ago and we might be able to take some of her stitches out.' She wheels the trolley to Jean's bed and says, 'Time to do your dressing, Jean. Can you lie flat please?'

I pull the curtains around the bed and we both go to wash our hands. I watch while the perm folds down the bedclothes to expose the dressing. Then she places the chest blanket over Jean's top half. She gently eases the plaster strips off the skin around the dressing and leaves it there while she takes the lids off the three bowls on the trolley. She lifts off the dressing with one pair of forceps and deposits it and the forceps into the unsterile bowl. Using two pairs of sterile forceps, one in each hand, she surrounds the wound with the green cloths, being careful not to touch them. A neatly stitched incision is exposed but the skin is red and swollen around each stitch entry and the edges are not quite healed.

The perm points to the edges with her forceps and says,

'The stitches are not quite ready to come out yet, Jean. I think we should give them another day or two.'

Jean squints down to see. 'It's really itchy,' she says, 'I'd love to give it a good scratch.'

'That's a good sign – means that it's healing,' the perm assures her as she moistens a swab with alcohol and with one motion, wipes the wound from top to bottom down the centre.

'You clean the wound from the top down and from within out, so that you're moving from the cleaner area to the less clean area,' she says to me. 'You use a swab only once. Don't wipe it up and down.'

After cleaning the wound, she puts clean gauze squares on it and fastens them on with white tape. Then we go to the sterilising room, empty the dirty dressing and swabs into a bin, and put all the bowls and instruments in the sink where I wash them in soapy water. The perm wipes the trolley with carbolic again and re-sets it as I turn on the steriliser for the washed bowls.

'Right,' she says, 'Your turn. I don't want to give you someone with stitches to come out until I've shown you how to do that, so let's go to – let me see,' she studies the list. 'Oh, yes. Mrs Ward. She had a pyelolithotomy two days ago.'

The morning flies by as I am absorbed in learning to do dressings. The hardest part is manipulating things, like the sterile cloths, with forceps in both hands. I feel very clumsy, as I am not used to using my left hand. When we come to a patient who needs stitches taking out, the perm takes over to show me how.

'Hold the knot with the forceps in your left hand and snip the stitch with the scissors, like this. Then press the flat part of the scissors on the wound as you pull out the stitch. It doesn't hurt as much if you press down with the scissors.' She snips the black stitch, presses down and pulls it out.

'Take every alternate stitch out first and then re-assess whether to take them all out or not. But before you take any stitches out, check with Sister or me, until we are sure you know how to judge properly.'

I am a two-five that day. After dinner, I go to my room, start to read and fall asleep. It's all I do in my off duty – sleep. I hear about young people joining clubs, going dancing, playing tennis, meeting in pubs, and wonder what it is like to have a social life. Or what it is like not to be continually tired. On my days off, I sleep until noon, some-times go shopping or visit Amma, and go to bed early. When I first arrived in Leeds, I joined the swimming club but I didn't last long as I was never off duty when they practised.

I go back to the ward at five o'clock to find I am to do treatments and 'preps'. Patients for surgery the next day have an enema, which a junior nurse gives, and then I shave the pubic area. If it is to be abdominal surgery, I

144

shave the abdomen also and paint the area with iodine. Treatments means giving injections, irrigating tubes, suctioning tubes and preparing inhalants to help patients cough. I also have to check the drainage systems used for various reasons. To apply suction to a tube, I rig up a bottle of water in the same fashion as an intravenous infusion, and allow it to drip into a bottle on the floor. The patient's tube is connected to a Y-connection. As the water flows down from one bottle to another, suction is created. I am kept very busy but it is nice not to be doing the menial jobs.

A few days later, Mrs Tubbs is admitted. She is a large, jovial woman who comes in to have her gall bladder out. I prep her for theatre and she bears it all with good humour. 'Serves me right for eating all them cream buns,' she says. 'Me doctor kept telling me to go on a diet but what's life without Yorkshire puds to go wi' tha' beef, and what's tea without a cream cake or two?'

That evening her entire family of husband and six children comes to visit, cheerfully ignoring the rule about only two visitors at a time. She tells me that all the children are adopted.

'I took one in coz he'd lost both parents in t'war, poor little mite, and then another came and another and they sort of grewed on me. Fred was exempt from service coz of his age but he was in t'ome Guard and kept finding lost little 'uns.'

In the morning, I give Mrs Tubbs her pre-op injection of omnopon and scopolamine and get her ready for theatre. I give her a white cap to wear, a 'mob' cap that covers all her hair, and make sure she has no hairpins or jewellery on and that her dentures are out.

'I look a right nana,' she says.

'Well, you're not going in for a beauty competition, Mrs Tubbs,' I say, 'and the surgeon is too young for you.'

'Call me Ma,' she says, 'Everyone does.'

'Right you are, Ma. Good luck. You'll be back here before you know it and ready to take us all on.'

That evening Ma Tubbs retches and vomits miserably. She is obviously one of the people who react badly to anaesthetic. The anaesthetist comes to see her and prescribes a drug but it does not help. I sponge her face and hold her as she heaves and strains, her empty stomach convulsing but unable to expel anything.

She remains cheerful. 'I felt like this when I went out on a boat trip round Filey Brig, but there's no smell o' sea air in 'ere.'

During one of the heaves, she yanks on her intravenous infusion and dislodges the needle, and the skin around the end of the needle balloons up. I inform Sister who calls the houseman to come and re-start the drip. I am late off duty as I stay to assist him.

'Goodnight Ma,' I say before I leave. 'I hope you'll feel better in the morning.'

As soon as I come on duty the next day, I go to see how Ma is doing. I am relieved to find her sleeping. When she wakes up, I help her sit up in the bed and encourage her to cough.

'I know it hurts to cough, Ma, but you must take deep breaths to expand your lungs. Here, press this pillow against your belly, like this, so it won't hurt as much.'

She gives me a wan smile and says, 'Bully!'

That evening she spikes a temperature and it is still up when I come on duty the next day. I sponge her down, change her bed and give her a fresh gown.

'Well, this is one way to get extra attention,' I say.

In the afternoon, she cannot urinate. I palpate her bladder. It is full. I try sitting her on a bedpan and dribbling warm water over her vulva with no result. The perm and I help her onto a commode beside the bed. No result. The perm tells me to catheterise her. I was shown this procedure by Sister Pearce a few days ago but I have only done one on my own, and then under supervision.

I remember Sister Pearce saying, 'There are few women who look like the anatomical drawings where the urethra is an obvious hole. You can't prod about with a catheter or you'll infect the bladder. So insert one catheter and if urine doesn't come out, leave it there and try with another. If you leave the first one in, you won't be trying for the same hole – which will be the vagina.'

I wheel the trolley up to Ma's bed and explain what I am

going to do. 'Seeing that your waterworks won't, Ma, I'm going to put a tube into your bladder to drain off the urine. It won't hurt but it's a bit uncomfortable, but it will make you feel better.'

'Right you are, luv. Anything you say.'

I swab Mrs Tubbs' vulva and then gently separate the labia to swab inside. I take a catheter, hold it a few inches from the insertion end, put the other end in a kidney basin and bend down to look for the urethra. Large though she is, Ma has not had children of her own and the urethra is plainly visible. I insert the catheter and urine pours out into the kidney basin.

'There you go, Ma, that's opened up the flood gates. Let's hope this does the trick and you can wee on your own now.'

'Didn't feel a thing, Nurse Ross. Thank you.'

Ma's temperature is still up the next day and she is told she has pneumonia. She is worn out with coughing and her indomitable spirit is beginning to flag. No more repartee or jokes from either of us.

I am wheeling a dressing trolley down the ward when she calls to me. 'Nurse Ross, I feel as if summat's given way. Will you 'ave a look?'

I close her curtains, lie her down and undo her many-tailed bandage. With the release of this pressure, her dressing is pushed off by a grey mass, which pokes out of her wound and steadily increases in bulk. I stare in horror.

A burst abdomen. A surgical emergency. It is when the stitches give way and the intestines fall out. If something is not done immediately the patient goes into severe shock and dies.

I quickly pull my dressing trolley into the cubicle, take out the sterile cloths to cover the wound, place a pillow on top of it and say, as calmly as I can, 'Hang tight onto this pillow, Ma. I need to get Sister to come and look.'

Sister is doing a round with a surgeon. Ignoring protocol, I tug at her sleeve and say, 'Sister, come quick. Mrs Tubbs has a burst abdomen.'

She and the surgeon come to look at the wound. He says to Ma, 'I am sorry, Mrs Tubbs, but you've come apart at the seams and we'll have to take you to theatre and stitch you up again.'

'Oh, no.' Ma starts to cry. 'I can't go through all that again.' I hold her hand.

Sister says, 'You're certainly having a rotten time, Ma, and I'm really sorry. But you will get a different anaesthetic this time so you won't be so sick.'

She and I wheel Ma to theatre in her bed. Moving her onto a trolley would be too risky as we might end up with yards of guts on our hands. I go off duty worrying about Ma and whether she will pull through. The anaesthetic does not make her as sick as before and over the next few days she slowly improves.

I am doing beds and backs for a change and when I get

to Ma, she says, 'It's time I put on me own nightie and feel human again.'

I find a flowered nightie in her locker and a pink crocheted bed jacket. 'This is a pretty bed jacket, Ma. Did you make it?'

'Aye, I did that. I knit and crochet a lot. In fact, I'll get hubby to bring in some wool so I'll have summat to do with my hands.'

Ma gets stronger as each day passes. She spends more time sitting up in a chair and gradually starts to walk. If she isn't busy crocheting something in sky-blue wool, she's going round the ward talking to patients, reading to them, giving them drinks or writing letters for them.

I am becoming more competent at changing dressings, removing stitches, shortening drains and am now a dab hand at catheterising women. Yet, although the work is more interesting, I cannot feel the former enthusiasm. I hardly see Judith or Sandy or any of my friends; they seem to have hibernated. If we meet in the dining room our conversation is about our wards. There isn't much laughter any more.

I receive a letter from my father.

Dear Jenny,

Just a quick note to let you know that Sophie is leaving in three months. They are going to live in Beirut. I bumped into Tom yesterday and he asked me to write and see if you would be interested in running the swimming school at Breach Candy. They need a reply as soon as possible as they will have to advertise if you don't want the job.

You can, of course, live with us. Our rates for lodgers are very reasonable.

Love Dad

I feel a huge relief. I can get away from here and go back to India. I lie on my bed and think about my life there. After the war years in Leeds, Bombay was another world. I sailed out on a P&O liner with my mother and baby brother. Shipboard life was a taste of what was to come: sunshine, good food, constant leisure. I bought three long evening dresses with matching evening gloves and I rotated through these as everyone dressed formally for dinner every night.

Port Said was my first encounter with a culture completely foreign to my own and I found it thrilling. The bustle of brown bodies, the noise of men calling out to entice us into their shops, constant honking of car horns, strange dried foods and herbs, pungent smells and gillie-gillie men who performed magic tricks.

As we sailed into Bombay harbour, I could see my father dressed in white slacks and a white short-sleeved shirt, waiting to meet us. He drove us to our new home, a huge ground-floor flat with three en-suite bedrooms, a living room that comfortably held a piano and two three-piece suites, a dining room and an inner sanctum ruled by Fergie the cook. The servants were lined up to greet us: Sammy the bearer, dignified in his turban and cummerbund, Ruth the ayah, or nanny, for my brother, Ali the houseboy and Fergie. They placed garlands of flowers around our necks as they greeted us with 'Namaste'.

I quickly settled into a life of days spent at Breach Candy, the outdoor European swimming pool that was a short walk away, where I took lessons from Sophie and learned to swim and dive. After a while I helped Sophie teach children how to swim. When I wasn't there, I was shopping with my mother, playing canasta or sitting around with three or four other teenaged European girls who lived in Bombay. We did not mix with Indian teenagers and I was too naive to wonder why. I resolve that when I go back, I will try to get to know Indian girls of my age.

Evenings were spent attending parties, dinners and dances. There were a few young men, who worked mainly in banks, and as young girls were scarce, I was in great demand. I get up to find my photo album. There I am in my navy broderie anglaise long dress dancing with Neville in a white sharkskin dinner jacket. We have been caught mid-step and are both laughing as we stare at the camera. I am brown and robust and my hair is bleached almost white by the sun.

I flick through the album. There's a picture of me with a large party dining at the Taj Mahal hotel. The host, fascinated by an insatiable appetite produced by a mile-long swim every day, encouraged me to order more and more courses until I could eat no more. There we are at Juhu beach. I swam in the sea there until I saw a four-foot water snake swim by, striped like a football jersey, and decided the pool was safer.

My time off flies by in a reverie as I recapture the mood of my former life and I return to work feeling buoyant and cheerful. After I come off duty, instead of having a bath and going to bed as usual, I go to Judith's room. She is in bed, reading.

'Guess what? I've had a letter from my father and I can go back to Bombay and teach swimming. Isn't that wonderful?'

'You mean, leave here?'

'Yes. Oh bliss! No more sick people, no more urine or bile or sputum. Goodbye shit, hello happiness,' I sing.

Judith lowers her book. 'I remember you telling me how useless your life in India was – how you could hardly wait to get away and do something worthwhile.'

'That was before I knew what it's like.'

'But Jen, you've always been so enthusiastic about nursing.'

I sit on her bed. 'Yes, I know. But I'm not now. The thought of leaving here is bliss. You've said many times that we're just slave labour and you're right.'

'But you've been doing a lot more than maid work, haven't you? You're pretty senior and I thought you were doing more interesting things.'

'Well, I am. But still…' I hesitate. I have forgotten all the things I don't like about India.

'Anyway,' Judith says, 'We can live out next month. I was talking to Sandy and Jess and they think the four of us should get a flat together. What do you think?'

'That would be nice but I don't think I'll be here.'

'Think about it. You don't have to write to your Dad just yet do you? Sleep on it.'

I go back to my room and fall asleep dreaming of Breach Candy and diving off springboards into clear blue water.

The next day, Mrs Tubbs goes home. I am doing a dressing when Sister Pearce comes in and says, 'When you've finished that dressing, Nurse Ross, will you come out into the foyer. Mrs Tubbs wants to say goodbye to you.'

Ma is sitting in a wheelchair waiting to be taken to an ambulance. 'I couldn't go without saying goodbye to you, and a big, big, thank you. Your cheery face and sweet ways right helped me along, they did. Every time summat went wrong, there you were, calm as a cucumber and making me feel everything would be OK.'

She takes hold of my hand and squeezes it. 'Here, I made this for you.' She thrusts a mound of blue wool into my hands. 'It's a bed-jacket like the one you liked. I chose this colour to match your eyes.'

Tears come into my eyes. 'Oh, thank you, Ma. It's lovely. I shall treasure it. I'm sad to see you go but – don't you dare come back!'

Sister Pearce is standing to one side and we open the main doors so the porter can push Mrs Tubbs through.

'Is it alright to accept this present?' I ask.

'She made it just for you so it would be ungracious to refuse. It's money or expensive presents we can't accept. Mrs Tubbs thought the world of you, as do many of the patients, I might add. You seem to cheer them up.'

That night, I meet with Judith, Sandy and Jess to discuss taking a flat together. The thought of living out is exciting and we stay up late talking about it.

'What about Marie?' I ask.

'Her calling might suffer if she lives out so she wants to live in,' Judith says as she raises her eyes to the ceiling. 'Besides, even though she's not quite the clot she used to be, I still couldn't live with her.'

'Will your father let you live out?' I ask Sandy.

'I put my foot down. I told him I am nearly 21 and old enough to make up my own mind. I also told him to get a house-keeper as I am not spending my days off doing housework any more.'

'Good for you! How did he take it?'

'Well, he was surprised at first and then came around. I said I would still visit frequently but he'd have to find someone else to run the house.'

Judith says, 'I've got a copy of the *Yorkshire Evening News* and marked some of the furnished flats for rent that are on a tram route to here. When can we all go and look at some?'

It turns out that we are all a two-five on Thursday so we plan to go flat hunting. I write to my father.

Dear Dad,
Thank you for your letter. Please thank Tom for his offer and while the prospect of coming back to a job in Bombay is appealing, I still want to be a nurse.

Love Jenny

P.S. Four of us are going to live out. Can you lend me some money to buy a scooter?

Chapter 14

15 Waterford Gardens
Bramwood, Leeds

15 March 1954

Dear Mum and Dad,

I am writing to tell you my new address, though if you still send letters to the Infirmary, I will get them. Yes, we've moved out – Judith, Sandy, Jess and me. Marie decided to live in, which is a good thing as she and Judith don't get on and, anyway, it's difficult to find a flat for more than four.

We looked at several flats and chose this one coz a) it has nice furniture, b) it is on a tram route, c) it is big, d) we can afford it. It is £4 a week and so that is only £1 each a week. We get more money living out so I think I will be getting something like £20 a month.

We have the main floor of a big detached house with a nice garden full of shrubs. There are three more flats upstairs but they have another entrance at the back. Our entrance is what used to be the original front door. It has stained glass windows and is very grand. It opens into a big hall and off this is a living room that we could entertain the queen in. It has a high ceiling with ornate plasterwork and a picture rail that gathers dust. There's a fireplace with a gas poker so it's easy to light a fire. We can draw the long velvet curtains across the bay windows, light a fire and be really cosy. And the armchairs are so comfy!

There's two big bedrooms and a bathroom with one of those deep baths with feet. Judith and I share one room and Sandy and Jess the other. We had to bring linens but everything else is provided. So I'm glad I brought that sheet and towel set from Bombay and Amma has lent me a couple of blankets. I splurged and bought myself a quilt so I'm nice and warm in bed.

The kitchen is at the back and has a door into the back garden where there's a coal bin. It's enormous (the kitchen I mean, not the coal bin) and has a table in it so we can eat there as well as in the main room. There's a fairly new gas stove with an eye-level grill and bags of cupboards.

We all put money into the kitty for coal and food but we don't need much food as we can still eat at the Infirmary. Jess and I are both a five-to tonight and we made a sort of risotto but it didn't taste very good. Sandy is the only one who can cook something other than scrambled eggs and junkets.

We've made a work list and we're taking it in turns to clean and shop etc. Sandy is organising us!!

There's a tram every ten minutes to the Infirmary and it only takes ten minutes to get there so if we get the 7am tram we can be on duty at 7.30 all right. We change at the hospital and we each have a locker there. There are bathrooms too, so we can have a bath and save the hot water here. We have to put a shilling in the meter to get hot water and the bath uses a lot.

We take prelims next month. If we pass we get a purple stripe on one sleeve. I'm glad to hear that Anthony can do the crawl. I wish I were there to see him.

Love Jenny

15 Waterford Gardens
Bramwood, Leeds

20 April 1954

Dear Mum and Dad,
I've bought it!! Went out last week, did a test ride and I collected it the next day. I looked at Vespas too but decided on a Lambretta because I like the look of it better. It is very safe and, yes, I have a crash helmet. In fact, I have two but I can't carry a passenger until I've passed my test, which is next week. I have to have L-plates on until then.

It is so wonderful and many, many thank yous. I went for a ride in the Dales on my day off. It is so nice to get out of Leeds and see green fields. I stopped to watch a sheep cleaning her lamb that had just been born. It was so sweet!

It was a bit cold on the scooter but of course the windshield helps and I have a pair of motorbike gloves to keep my hands warm. I keep it in the garage here and the bike shed at the Infirmary so it's never standing out in the rain for long. I've learned how to take the spark plug out and clean it. That's the main thing that goes wrong.

30 April. I didn't get this finished but will write more now and post it tomorrow. I passed my test so now the others fight over who is going to ride on the pillion. I don't have to leave until nearly 7.15 to be on duty for 7.30 so that's an extra 15 minutes in bed.

You wanted to know more about Sandy, Jess and Judith. Well, Sandy is the eldest and keeps us in order! She has run a house for her father so she knows how to cook and clean. She makes sure we do. She's a bit of a chatterbox. Jess is a small lass and we call her 'Wee Jess' but she doesn't like that as she's self-conscious about being four foot eight inches. She says the patients don't think she is capable of lifting them or doing things for them. She was born with a cleft palate and a hair lip, which she had repaired of course, but she

YES SISTER, NO SISTER

speaks with a sort of whistley lisp. Judith is the clever one – always has her nose in a book. I don't know why she's in nursing as she should be in university. She doesn't get very good reports as she questions every-thing and the sisters don't like that. She thinks the way they run the hospital is inane.

Sorry to hear Fergie has been sick and I hope he is better soon. Give my love to everyone.

Love Jenny

15 Waterford Gardens
Bramwood, Leeds

10 June 1954

Dear Mum and Dad,
I'm writing this on duty as I am doing nights at the Ida and Robert Arthington Hospital, known as the Ida. It is the convalescent hospital for the Infirmary and it's in Cookridge – way out in the country. It used to be a TB sanatorium so the wards have verandas – big enough to put all the beds out on them if we want to. There are only four wards and I'm on a male ward with some kids in the sideward. Most of the patients are getting better and sleep all night so for once, I have the chance to sit down.

I am really grateful for the scooter as I can ride

straight here instead of going to the Infirmary and then being taken here by bus. It saves me an hour. Boo hoo. I scratched it. On the garage door.

There's a bunch of university students in the other flats and we all go out together. If we're off on Saturday we go to the university Union dance. We've been to the pictures several times and sometimes we get fish and chips and eat them in our flat, as it's the biggest. We are having a party next Friday and some medical students are coming as well as the usual gang.

Yes, I am careful on the scooter and, no, I don't go too fast and, yes, I always wear my crash helmet. Don't worry!! I offered to take Amma for a ride on it but she declined for some reason!!

A patient has just had an asthma attack so that's all the time I have.

Love Jenny

15 Waterford Gardens
Bramwood, Leeds

5 September 1954

Dear Mum and Dad,
Wow, we've nearly finished second year! I never thought I'd make it but time is flying by. We're in second block so we have every evening off and Sundays.

Which is nice because I have a boyfriend! His name is Nick and he's an architectural student in his third year. In fact, we all have boyfriends but none of them serious, so don't worry.

Block is quite interesting as we are learning more about the diseases that afflict us. We had a doctor give a lecture on tropical diseases, which are quite nasty so watch out! We're also learning about specialities, like eyes, and we each get to spend time in various clinics. All except Rose Cottage, the VD clinic, we don't go there.

We also visited the special units at LGI, though students don't work there. There are only two dialysis units in the whole of England and we have one of them. Boast, boast! We are the north of England centre for the treatment of tetanus too. The patients are on curare and a respirator until they recover so there is always an anaesthetist on the ward.

Nick and I went to Buckden on the scooter on Sunday and had lunch in the pub there. Then we walked along the Wharfe. It was a beautiful day and the colour of the trees was spectacular.

The ward allocation lists have gone up and Judith and I are both in theatre when we have finished block.

Love Jenny

Chapter 15

JUDITH AND I enter the theatre doors at 7.30am to find two other student nurses, Burton and Mackie, junior to us, also starting today. I have worked with Burton before; she is one of the clumsiest girls I have ever met and she is always in trouble for dropping things, spilling things or falling over things. We stand around at a T-junction of corridors with doors off each side, wondering what to do. I have been as far as the short arm of the T when I have accompanied patients into the anaesthetic rooms here, but the long corridor holding the actual operating theatres is an unknown. The place is bustling with people in white, wearing masks, but no one takes any notice of us.

'What do you think we should do?' I ask Judith.

'Wait here, I suppose, until someone comes to find us. We can't go wandering around dressed like this.'

In a few minutes, a figure in a white dress and a butterfly-type cap appears. 'I'm Sister Jackson,' she says, 'Theatre Superintendent. Come with me and I'll show you where to change.'

We are ushered into a room full of lockers, with toilets and showers at one end. Jackson points to a rack of white, short-sleeved, V-necked dresses. 'Put one of these on. No slips, stockings or suspender belts. There are only four sizes so find the nearest fit. Put your uniforms into an empty locker. I'll be back in a few minutes.'

I find a dress that fits but is too long. Then I notice the tie-belts and when one of these is on, my dress is not too bad. It is comfortable anyway, and I'm glad to be rid of the stiff collar. I don't know what we wear on our feet but when Jackson comes back, she points to a row of white plimsolls and says, 'Find a pair of those that fits and then keep them in your locker. They can go in the laundry once in a while.'

We all find a pair of plimsolls and put them on. They feel cold and uncomfortable.

'Now make sure your hair is all concealed under one of these,' Sister Jackson says as she hands us each a square of soft white cloth. 'You can either make it into a turban or wear it like mine. You don't need to wear a mask unless you're actually in a theatre. Now, I will show you round briefly but as the lists are about to start I don't want to take you into a theatre.'

We follow Jackson as she walks briskly down the main corridor and points out theatres that are numbered one through six. Each pair has a sponge room in between and a door with a glass window in it. We peer into one. I see autoclaves run down one side and sinks for scrubbing instruments down the other.

We turn to retrace our steps and walk down to the other end of the corridor. Suddenly, a tall man in white trousers and top and white Wellington boots comes out of a theatre. He says to Sister Jackson, 'Sister, I must have a theatre this afternoon.'

'Mr Townsend, you know very well the theatres are all booked until six o'clock. You can have one then.'

He falls on his knees in supplication. 'But Sister, if I don't get a theatre this afternoon, the patient will die!'

'Mr Townsend,' Jackson says firmly, 'get up and don't

brandish a shroud at me. If the case is so desperate then rearrange your morning list.'

The surgeon gives a sort of snort and goes back into the theatre. Jackson walks on saying, 'Sometimes they behave like spoiled little boys!'

We enter the instrument room. It is lined with glass-shelved cupboards holding equipment that would look at home in a blacksmith's forge if it weren't so shiny. On to the table in the middle, Jackson places a metal crate filled with neatly arranged instruments.

'This is a general set. Before you can do anything useful, you must know the name of each of these instruments and the order in which they go in the set. I will give you an hour or two. When I come back I will dump the set out and you each must be able to name the instruments and put them back in the right order.'

She leaves us with a list. Judith says, 'Right. We must be careful not to disturb them until we know what each one is. This is a Rampley sponge forcep. Look, it has a circular end and a ratchet on the bottom. Next is a Mohnihan clamp – it has serrated edges and is quite big.' She takes each instrument out, names it, describes it and then we rehearse by someone randomly picking one for us to iden-tify. Judith remembers the set after one rehearsal but she patiently helps us all so that when Sister Jackson returns we feel more or less ready for the test.

'Before we play with the set, come and have coffee,'

Jackson says. 'We have it all together in the sitting room. The surgeons have their own room but they usually join us as it's more lively.'

The sitting room is full of white-clad figures and without identifying uniforms, I cannot tell who is a sister, who is a surgeon or who is a technician. We four are huddled over our coffee when someone joins us.

'Hello. I'm Sylvia Cotswold, in second year. Is this your first day?'

'Yes. How long have you been here?'

'A month. I love it! I'm sure you will too when you get used to it. Has Daisy given you the set test yet?'

'After coffee. Why do you call her Daisy? Isn't her name Pamela Jackson?' I ask.

'Oh, some story about her riding on the back of a tandem down the main corridor when she was first a theatre sister. She's been known as Daisy ever since. They're all crazy, you know. It gets very tense in here. The surgeons have temper tantrums and throw instruments at the walls and the sisters hold trolley races and fool around.'

'Have you taken anyone yet?' Judith asks.

'Yes, a few times. We don't take the consultants of course but when the registrars operate, the sisters usually give them a student.'

'What's it like?' Mackie says.

'They're very patient – ask for what they want and don't

get their knickers in a knot if you can't find the right instrument stat. [at once].'

'What's it like looking inside an abdomen?' Barton asks. 'I'm afraid I might faint.'

'Most of the time you can't see a thing. You're too busy scurrying around picking up swabs, changing washbowls or autoclaving. The first case I took was on a knee so it wasn't sick-making at all.'

We finish our coffee and Daisy, as we now call her, leads us back to the instrument room. As promised, she up-ends the crate and shuffles the instruments around. 'Right,' she says, 'Who's first?'

We all look at Judith who promptly selects two Rampley sponge forceps, two Mohnihan clamps, two Parkers clamps and so on, as she puts the set together.

'Well done,' Daisy says. 'You're very quick.' She up-ends the set again and I have a go. I name the instruments correctly but mix up the order a bit. 'Well done,' says Daisy again. After Mackie and Burton manage the task, she says, 'I've never had a group as quick as you. Usually it takes a whole day for students to learn the general set. Now I'll show you how to use the autoclaves.'

We put on masks, which are made of two layers of cotton with a piece of cellophane between them, to enter a sponge room. Daisy explains how the knobs and dials of the giant autoclaves work. They make me think of submarines with their tightly closed doors, hissing steam and wheel-like handles. We are shown how to remove sterile instrument sets with tongs and place them on round trolleys with removable sterile tops.

We go for dinner after we have changed back into our regular uniforms and as we have to change again when we return, our dinnertime is reduced to 20 minutes. When we return we are each sent into a theatre where the runner is to show us what to do.

Over the next few days we learn how to be a runner, our primary role. We hear stories about Mr Stephen Penfield, a plastic surgeon. I have seen his tall, elegantly dressed figure many times, striding down the main corridor, hands behind his back, muttering to himself. On the wards he has a reputation for being charming and courteous to patients but in theatre he is so impossible, no theatre sister will take him permanently. Each theatre sister has her own surgeons that she always takes unless she is away or sick. There is a roster for Mr Penfield who complains to Daisy weekly that he hasn't a permanent sister.

'If you would behave yourself, Mr Penfield, I might persuade a sister to take you on. As it is, no one will. I can't say I blame them. Why only last week you threw a Babcock at Sister Hale.'

Judith is the first one to run in Mr Penfield's theatre with Daisy scrubbed up. 'What was he like?' I ask Judith over supper at home.

'He's a right sod!' she says. 'He stands on a swab so you can't pick it up or else he hides one by leaning against it.'

Swabs are gauze oblongs about 18 x 4in, which hold a small metal insert so they can be detected by X-ray. They, as well as the instruments and needles, are counted before being used and again before the wound is sewn up, to be sure that nothing is left in the patient. A mobile rack with rows of ten pegs is part of the equipment and on it we hang used swabs. At the end of a case, the rows of dangling, bloody swabs look like a bizarre form of Christmas tree.

'But I got the better of him,' Judith went on. 'He complained his wash-hand basin water was too cold. When I added hot water, it was too hot. So I went for a sterile thermometer, took it and two jugs of water into theatre and asked him exactly what temperature he would like his water. He glared at me over his mask and I glared back. I don't think he knows the temperature of water so he just said it was OK.'

The next morning, Daisy says to Judith, 'Well, Nurse Horsfall, you certainly made an impression on Mr Penfield! He thinks you're very intelligent and wants you as a permanent runner.' She laughs when she sees Judith's face. 'Don't worry, I told him students have to rotate to gain experience. Then he wanted to know if you would like to perm in theatre. He's still hoping someone will take him on. Would you like to perm here?'

'Not if it means working with him, thank you.' Judith says. 'I suppose that's flattering but I can imagine no worse fate.'

The four of us who started on the same day, and Sylvia Cotswold, try to have coffee together, but as we can only go when the sister and surgeon decide to break, it is not often that we can. We have a greater chance of meeting at teatime in the afternoon when the majority of operations have been done and we spend our time cleaning. At this time we exchange stories about the peculiarities of surgeons.

Mackie sits down one day and says, 'Have any of you run for Mr Pearson?' We shake our heads. 'He's urology isn't he?'

'Yes. He looks just like Oliver Hardy of Laurel and Hardy. He's nuts! I know they are all nuts but he's nuttier than the rest.'

'Why?' Sylvia asks.

'After he scrubs up, he holds his arms straight out in front of him like Lady Macbeth.' Mackie walks round the room with her arms extended and a gormless, ghostly look on her face. 'Then he says to his theatre sister, "The surgeon will have the instruments in the usual order," like a Shakespearean actor. But you know what? He says it every time – for every single case. He would drive me crazy!'

'Me too,' Sylvia says. 'I've run for the other urology surgeon, Mr Cokes. He's nuts too but not that bad. He's quite polite usually but when anything upsets him, he yells, "A thousand bloody hells, ten thousand bloodier hells," at the top of his voice.'

One of the perms sits with us one day and tells us to be very careful about what we say in theatre. 'One student is still famous, two years later, because she walked up behind a registrar whose gown was undone. She pulled at his belt and said, 'Everything that dangles should be pulled.' She was never allowed to forget it!'

We all laugh though I am not quite sure why it is funny.

'Yes,' the perm went on. 'A sister put her foot in it too. Her patient, a man, was in lithotomy position and draped so that only his genitals were showing. Well, she was over at the desk reading the chart, saw his name and said, "Oh, I know this man." The anaesthetist heard her and the story was all over theatre in a flash.'

'I still think Mr Penfield gets the prize for sheer lunacy,' Judith says.

'Well, at least he's polite,' Burton says. 'I ran for Mr Cartwright yesterday and he tells dirty stories the whole time. I couldn't hear all that he was saying but he was talking about his son's girlfriend. I did hear him say, "If she fell out of a ship she'd come up on Neptune's prong."'

The day comes when I am down to run in Mr Penfield's theatre. Sister Goodrich is taking him. I have run for her before and I get a great charge out of the way she soon has her set all mixed up, then has to rummage like a cat in a litter box for an instrument. Last time I was with her, the surgeon, impatient for a clip, made the mistake of reaching for it.

'Get off my instrument trolley,' she shouted at him. 'Leave the buggers alone.'

We start the list and my mouth is ready to smile under my mask. I don't have to wait for long. Mr Penfield says something to her that I can't hear, but her reply is clear and concise. 'I do have an opinion but I don't have a medical degree so you'll have to make your own mind up.'

After that, nothing untoward happens. I am disappointed, as I want to go to the dining room with a Penfield story. The last case is a baby for repair of harelip. One of the sterile requirements is an 8 x 4in tin of Vaseline gauze. At the end of the procedure, Sister Goodrich cuts a one-inch square from the beginning of the 10 yards folded in the tin and Penfield places it carefully on the sutures.

He is about to stride out when he turns and says to Goodrich, 'Will that tin of Vaseline gauze be used again?'

'Yes, after it has been sterilised again.'

'I'll make sure it isn't,' Penfield says, picking up the tin. He hands it to me. 'Here, hold this.' He grabs a pair of forceps, takes hold of the end of the gauze with them and runs round and round the theatre until there is 10 yards of sticky Vaseline gauze draped over everything.

Goodrich is furious. 'I'll report you to Sister Jackson for this,' she shouts, but the tall figure has already marched out of the swing doors. 'When he dies, I'll see they plant the bugger, or burn him.' We start to clean up. 'And I'll tell Daisy that if I have to take that sod again, I'm leaving!'

It is early Monday morning and it is Burton's turn to run in Penfield's theatre. She is nervous at the best of times but she is especially shaky today, as we have told her what he is like. She brings the three-legged trolley into the sponge room and places it ready to receive the sterile upper tray and the set of instruments out of the autoclave. I am doing the same thing for the theatre next door. As the wheels of the trolleys are always stiff, Burton exerts some pressure to push hers into her theatre, but instead of its usual arthritic movement, the trolley develops the limbs of an athlete, flies across the theatre, bumps into Mr Penfield as he scrubs up and spews the instruments, container and tray all over the floor. There is a noise like a thousand metal dustbins falling from a height that seems, like an echo, to take an eternity to diminish.

Daisy is scrubbed and waiting for the instruments. Mr Penfield stops scrubbing to stare and Burton and I stand in the entrance of their theatre in a state of shock.

'Oh dear,' says Daisy quietly, 'We had the wheels of the trolleys oiled this weekend and perhaps they are a bit too smooth. Never mind, Nurse Burton, just bring me another set before you pick up this one.'

'I'm not having that woman in my theatre,' Mr Penfield growls. 'She's dangerous.'

'You will have whichever nurse I see fit to put in my operating theatre, Mr Penfield. Now perhaps we can proceed with this case.'

Good for you, Daisy, I think as I push my trolley into my theatre – very carefully. Poor Burton. It really wasn't her fault, but she is so unnerved that Daisy tells her and me to change places. Nothing happens though. Mr Penfield seems a little subdued and doesn't even stand on swabs.

I am the first of the four of us to go on nights. Theatre works out its own off duty and we each do a week of nights while we are there. My main job is to wash, dry and powder mounds of rubber gloves, and pack them ready to be sterilised. First I have to blow each one out and inspect it for holes. If I find a hole, I repair it like the inner tube of a bicycle wheel. Then I powder each one, make sure I have a pair the same size, and lie them side-by-side on a cloth which I fold into a packet and place in a drum.

It is pretty boring work and I long for an emergency. Just as I am giving up hope we get word that there is an acute appendicitis coming in and Jack Moulton, a surgical registrar, is to operate. The sister-on-call is brought in from the Nurses' Home, where they sleep when on call. Sister Brodie, a nice woman, is on call and when she arrives she tells me to scrub up. I am to take the case and she will run. I am thrilled.

I scrub my hands and forearms with a sterilised nailbrush following the pattern I have been shown. Then I rinse, dry my hands on a sterile towel Brodie hands me, pick up my sterile gown, insert my arms into the long sleeves and hold the ties out so Brodie can tie them behind me. I put on rubber gloves and walk to my table of instruments holding my hands up. There should be a chord from a full orchestra at least, or a camera crew ready to record my triumphant moment.

Jack Moulton finishes scrubbing and Brodie ties his gown. 'This is Nurse Ross, Jack,' she says as he walks over to the table. 'This is the first case she's taken, so be kind to her.' He winks at me over his mask and then asks the anaesthetist if he can begin.

The patient is a young woman with many stretch marks on her abdomen. 'How many children has she had?' Jack asks Brodie.

She goes to the desk to look at the notes. 'Five, and she's only 28.'

'No wonder her abdomen is so flabby,' Jack says as I hand him a sponge holder and a swab soaked in iodine. He swabs the abdomen, then sheets up as I give him towels and towel clips. Then I hand him a knife handle into which I have slid a blade. He makes an incision.

I seem to float in time as I pass him instruments and peer into an abdomen. Jack points out the various organs as he explores their condition. Then he locates the appendix and brings it to the surface. I can see that it is enlarged and inflamed. I do not feel at all sickened; the opening into the abdomen surrounded by sterile cloths does not seem to be connected to a human body.

He crunches off the appendix and asks for a ligature. I

find the glass phial of catgut, wrap it in a towel, snap the phial and cut a length to hand to him. I am warm under the huge round light. The atmosphere is tranquil, not like days, and the only sound is the whoosh, whoosh of the anaesthetic machine. I hardly notice the anaesthetist, as he is screened from me, so I am startled when a deep voice suddenly says, 'Can we get some bacon and eggs when we're done?'

Brodie says, 'Yes, I've already ordered four plates and they'll be up in twenty minutes. And I'll make tea.'

Jack sews up and I put a dressing on the incision. Then we all transfer the patient on to a trolley and wheel her into the corridor.

'I've phoned for a porter and the ward nurse,' Brodie says. 'They'll be here in a minute.'

'I'll go with her until she is round,' the anaesthetist says, 'but make sure my bacon and eggs are still hot for when I come back.'

He isn't long and we sit in the sitting room enjoying toast, bacon and eggs and tea. I am glad of the meal as I missed tea but my main enjoyment is the sense of camaraderie. I feel like an accepted member of a team. No matter that I am the one who goes back into the theatre to scrub the instruments and mop the floor, the feeling stays with me until morning. When Judith comes on, I crow about being the first to take a case and go home feeling important.

Chapter 16

BACK ON DAYS again and I find that I am not down for any theatre. I look for Daisy. Has she forgotten that I am on? I find her in the instrument room and ask her what she would like me to do.

'Ah yes, Nurse Ross. I want you to help Bob today as several anaesthetic machines need a good clean. He's in the store room.'

Bob is a theatre technician who sees to the lights, adjusts the operating tables for each surgery and services the anaesthetic machines. The storeroom is a large room lined with shelves that house everything that no one knows where else to put. Bob is muttering over three Boyle anaesthetic machines that are heaped with instruments and cloths.

'Bugger PA,' he says. 'It's all very well trying out heart operations on weekends but does he have to make such a bloody mess?'

'Never mind, Bob,' I say. 'I've been sent to help you.'

'I told Daisy I'd never have these machines ready for use

today if I didn't get any help. Now one of the autoclaves is playing silly devils and I have to go to the basement for some more tanks.'

'Well, I'll clean these machines for a start. How on earth did they get like this?' I look closer at the blood and dog hair clinging to most parts of the machine.

'It's Philip Allison – he's trying to work out how to stop the heart long enough to operate on it and keep the blood flowing. So he experiments on dogs. Though how he makes this mess, I don't know.'

Philip Allison is a thoracic surgeon with a reputation for improvisation. A few years ago a woman inhaled an open safety pin and PA designed an instrument to remove it prior to operating on her. Nowadays, he uses two eggbeaters he bought at Woolworth's for 1s 6d each, as chest retractors. I have not run in PA's theatre as heart surgery is so specialised. He has his own team of nurses, both in theatre and on the wards. They are able to do mitral valvotomys, which take all day, and which involve freezing the patient, but PA is anxious to do more.

I wheel the first Boyle machine closer to the sink, which I fill with soapy water. The machine is a two-tiered trolley with shelves about two feet square. Beneath the lower shelf is a drawer for different sized rubber masks and attachments. A rack on the side holds small tanks of oxygen, air and nitrous oxide, and these are controlled by glass flow meters, which rise from the top shelf.

As I scrub, I am wondering if this is history in the making and if PA succeeds in operating on hearts, whether I, who scrubbed an anaesthetic machine free of dog blood and hair, will be remembered. I imagine a movie's list of credits rolling by: Philip Allison is the star, there is a supporting cast, and there, in tiny print, Manual Labourer – Jennifer Ross.

After I finish cleaning the machines, I seek out Daisy to find out what I am to do next. 'Put on a mask and go round the anaesthetists to see if there is anything they need. Take the DDA (Dangerous Drug Act) book with you and record the pethidine, or anything else they've used,' she directs.

I always forget the anaesthetists and how important their work is. They sit quietly beside their patient's head and as they don't act like the prima donnas at the operating table, they fade into the background. They are all very pleasant as I replenish their supplies. One of them asks me to watch his patient while he goes for coffee.

'Nothing will happen,' he says when he sees my eyes widen. 'Just sit here and make sure this bag goes in and out.'

'What if it doesn't?' I ask.

'It will. But if anything goes wrong, go out of the door and yell "Andrew" at the top of your voice. Watch this drip as well. I've just changed the bottle so it won't run dry. Thanks.'

I sit at the patient's head not daring to take my eyes off

the black rubber bag that expands and contracts as the patient breathes. Andrew returns after ten minutes, just as I am beginning to relax.

'There, now you know that there's nothing to being an anaesthetist. We just sit here playing with our knobs!'

Bob prepares a fresh anaesthetic machine for each case and today I help. We wipe each with carbolic, check the tanks, replace them if necessary and put out clean, sterilised syringes. Just before dinner, I go into a theatre where the list has finished, to claim the used anaesthetic machine. The anaesthetist is still there. He is sitting giving himself an injection into his arm.

'I'm a diabetic,' he says, 'and this is my a.c. [before meals] insulin.' He smiles at me.

I think nothing of the incident but a couple of days later I am running for Daisy and the same anaesthetist is working. As we clean up afterwards, I ask Daisy, 'How difficult is it for a doctor to work if he has diabetes? Will it affect him much?'

'Why? Who has diabetes?'

'The anaesthetist who's just done this case.'

'He hasn't got diabetes. What makes you think he has?' She stops what she's doing to stare at me.

'I found him on Monday giving himself his insulin,' I say, feeling confused.

'What!' Daisy startles me with the explosive way she says the word. 'Come into my office.'

Thoroughly alarmed and wondering what I've done, I follow Daisy to her office.

'Sit down,' she says as she reaches for paper and a pen. 'Tell me exactly what happened.'

Daisy writes as I relate what I saw. When I have finished she says, 'Don't say anything about this to anyone, Nurse Ross, but you may be required to tell this story again.'

'I don't understand, Sister. If he isn't a diabetic, what was he injecting?'

'Pethidine probably.'

'But all his DDAs were accounted for.'

'He could say he'd given a patient some and hadn't or, more likely, he gave only part of each ampoule to several patients and used the rest. However he did it, this is very serious.'

'What will happen to him?' I really like the anaesthetist. He had helped me fill out the DDA book with the patient's names and seemed particularly conscientious about his records.

'I shall have to tell the chief anaesthetist and he'll deal with it. Don't look so alarmed – he'll be helped to get off drugs and when he does, he'll be able to work again under supervision. It's an occupational hazard.'

I am dying to discuss this incident with Judith but Daisy has asked me to keep quiet. When we are at home one evening a few days later, I decide to broach the subject in a general way.

'Do you know much about drug addiction in nurses and doctors?' I ask Judith as we sit down to a supper of mushrooms on toast.

'There's an article about it in the last *Nursing Times*,' Judith says. 'It seems to be more prevalent than we think.'

'I can't understand how anyone would begin to take drugs, especially the DDAs, when they know they're addictive.'

'Oh, it's easy. You have a pain, a toothache for example and you're on duty, so you give yourself something so you can keep working. Then you have another shot, then another, and Bob's your uncle, you're hooked. Look at you, you've taken the odd Seconal when you can't sleep, haven't you?'

'Yes, but they're not addictive,' I say feeling guilty.

'They are habit-forming. Don't start in on the heavy stuff though – you'll lose your license before you've even got it!' Judith gets up from the table. 'Come on, you promised me a ride into the country and it's a lovely evening.'

As we ride out into the glorious Yorkshire countryside and I feel the wind on my face and see the bright green of the fields, I am glad I am healthy. I see so many ill people that I forget that most of the world is not sick.

We park the scooter and walk along a public footpath through fields to a small village. Unlike Sandy, Judith does not need to talk the whole time, so in companionable silence we enjoy only the occasional baa of sheep and the call of wood pigeons.

'Want a cider?' Judith asks when we reach the village with its centuries-old inn.

We order a pint of draught cider and packages of Smith's crisps each before finding a seat in one corner of the beamed room.

'We should do this more often,' Judith says. 'When I think about our lives and see that all we do is work and sleep, I wonder why I'm doing this. I had an old school friend ask me what I do for fun and I couldn't answer.'

'We go to the theatre and the cinema frequently,' I say, 'but it's difficult to have a boyfriend unless he's a medical student because they simply don't understand how hard we work. If they're medical students they're exhausted all the time as well.' I take a long drink of cool, refreshing cider. 'Nick and I only went out together for a few months. I think he got tired of listening to my excuses about why I couldn't go out when I come off duty at nine.'

'This is very pleasant,' Judith says as she licks salt from the crisps off her fingers. 'We must make ourselves go out more and see how the rest of the world lives.'

'It's a bargain,' I say. We down our ciders and walk back to the scooter in the evening mist.

Chapter 17

WHEN WE ARE all home one evening, Judith calls for everyone to sit down as she wants to discuss something.

'But I want to do thome washing,' Wee Jess says.

'You can do it later. I want to discuss the dullness of our lives.'

'Speak for yourself,' Sandy says. 'My life is hectic.'

'Yes, but it's hectic in the wrong ways. Look at us – worn out all the time. All we do in our off duty is sleep. If we do go out, we want to be in bed by 11. Anyone would think we're in our seventies, not our twenties.'

'What do you suggest?'

'Jen and I were out on her scooter on Tuesday evening and we had a lovely walk and ended up in a pub. We should get out more.'

Sandy brings in the ironing board and plugs in the iron. 'If we're just talking, I can iron as well, can't I?' she says when she sees Judith's exasperated look. 'Anyway, there isn't room for four on the scooter.'

'I'm not suggesting we always go on the scooter. I'm thinking we should make an effort to just go out more.'

Sandy starts to iron one of her numerous starched petticoats that she wears under full skirts. 'We all go to the theatre regularly even if we don't all go together, and we're not often off together.'

'And I usually go home on my day off and so do you,' Wee Jess says.

'Oh, what's the use!' Judith swings her legs over the arm of her easy chair. 'I just think we are wasting our youth – giving it to dear old Leeds General Infirmary.'

'What would you like to do?' I ask.

'I would like to take some evening classes, join a club, go riding, play tennis – lots of things. But meet people who aren't old, sick, or treating the sick.'

'But we do get four weeks holiday a year to make up for it,' Sandy says. 'You and Jenny went skiing in February and pony-trekking last autumn. We could all do something together next holiday.'

'I'm not wanting your company, I want to meet different people who are more interesting than you lot.'

'She's saying we're not interesting, that we're not fun, that we add no colour to her life,' I say. I hold both arms out horizontally and sing, 'I can-can like you can-can, we all can-can...' Sandy and Jess join me and we prance round the room. Judith holds a cushion over her head and groans.

When we're in bed, Judith and I talk more about adding variety to our lives. 'I agree with you,' I say, 'My life is dull. It is too easy to sit down and collapse when we come home but I felt so much better after we'd been out on Tuesday. I would like to learn to ride and there's no reason we can't do that in a two-five. There's a stable in Bramhope. I'll find out more about it, shall I?'

'Yes, and I'll get the Aston Adult Education programme. We can see what they offer in the afternoon. It's easier to get a two-five than a five-to, but then we'll be going on nights and that will ruin it.'

'We don't go on nights for another three months. There's time to take one course.'

'I'll find out anyway. I feel better just thinking about it,' Judith says. She turns on her side. 'Good night.'

'We could learn to play a musical instrument. A trumpet perhaps?' But Judith is asleep.

The ward allocation lists go up and our days in theatre are numbered. I am to go to Casualty, Judith to the hospital for women and Sandy into theatre. I feel sorry for Jess – she is down for the Dragon's ward.

A back door of the hospital leads from a parking area for ambulances straight into the Casualty department. The sister is a male nurse, Joe Barnes, so of course we call him Brother Barnes, or BB for short. He is middle-aged with a shiny, bald pate. Dark-brown eyes sparkle behind his glasses and his mouth and expression are of one ready to smile. He wears a white coat with a name-pin stating simply, 'Joe Barnes, SRN.'

BB was a nurse in Singapore during the war. When it fell to the Japanese, he spent three years in Changi. During the 'check-up' we do prior to every change of ward, I find out that he was once punished by the Japanese by being shut in a metal box and left out in the sun all day.

My informant also tells me that BB is constantly at war with Matron's office and that he is usually the victor. He can't stand red tape or formalities, such as sisters putting on cuffs when Assistant Matrons enter the ward. When they visit Casualty, he goes out of his way to be sitting so that he can remain seated. He addresses student nurses by their first names and refers to them as such to the Assistant Matrons.

When I first meet him, he asks if I am called Jennifer or Jenny. 'Jenny,' I say. 'Jennifer reminds me of school, especially when the emphasis is on the first syllable.'

'Right Jenny, if you think Casualty is one long saga of saving lives and performing extraordinary feats with tubes, you're in for a big disappointment. Most of the time we see kids who've stuck pencils up their noses or stones up their bums, and adults who've done something daft and cut themselves. Then we have our share of drama queens who overdose on aspirin to 'show' their lovers, Saturday night drunks and people with warts who think they need attention at two o'clock in the morning. Sordid – yes, exciting – no, but we keep cheerful anyhow.'

He shows me round. There's a room with several curtained cubicles, two walled rooms with examining tables, two small theatres and a plaster room.

'I want you to take this cubicle,' BB says, pointing to one. 'The triage nurse will send you dressings to change or stitches to come out.'

'What's a triage nurse?'

'The nurse who assesses each person in the big queue that's forming and sends each to the appropriate nurse or doc. Patients who are waiting to see you will sit here,' he says, indicating a row of chairs. 'The sterilising room and dressing trolleys are over there. I will help you at first as you have to be able to judge whether a patient should come back or not, or if further treatment, such as physio, is needed. Some of them need to see a Lady Almoner as well.'

I am busy all morning dressing burns and other wounds, putting drops in eyes and removing stitches. BB keeps a careful watch on what I am doing. I soon learn which patients need to return and to whom I can say, 'No need to come back.' I am so occupied in my little space that I don't know what is happening in the rest of Casualty.

At coffee break, which, like theatre, is taken in the staff sitting room, I am introduced to the physician-in-charge, Alexander John. As BB is known as Brother, Dr John is privately called Father John. He is a quiet man with an enormous black moustache and large baby-blue eyes. He is renowned for being able to suture wounds that leave no scar so all facial injuries are referred to him. There is the same lack of formality here as in theatre. The difference is that here everyone seems relatively sane.

I am a two-five and on in the evening with BB. A woman who has overdosed herself on some unknown substance is brought in unconscious. BB shows me how to pass a thick rubber tube into her stomach and how to wash it out. I sit with her, administering oxygen, as the doctor starts an intravenous drip. Her sister, who found her, is in the waiting room. When the drip is up, I fetch her to come and visit.

'This is typical of our Ivy,' she says. 'She's lucky I happened to drop in or she'd have been a goner this time.'

'Has she done this before?' I ask.

'Oh yes. I think this must be the sixth, or is it the seventh time? Row with her boyfriend, I expect. What she doesn't realise is that instead of making them feel sorry for her, she makes them run a mile.'

After about an hour, Ivy starts to regain consciousness and is admitted to a ward. No sooner has she gone than four people who have been in a car accident are wheeled in. One of them has a serious head injury and is attended to by BB and the doctor while the other nurse and I see to the rest. They have minor cuts and bruises but are in shock so need warmth and oxygen before we dress the wounds. As they lie recovering, a policeman brings in an unconscious man who reeks of alcohol.

'Not sure about this one, nurse,' the bobby says. The police take upright drunks to the cells but they bring unconscious people to us, as alcohol can mask serious conditions. I take the man's temperature, pulse and respirations, check his blood pressure and neurological signs and lie him on his side so that if he vomits, he won't choke on it. When the doctor and BB have finished attending to the car accident patient, they come to examine the alcohol man.

Another policeman is here to take details of the car accident and as there is a lull, everyone, including the police, sits down for a cup of tea. Not for long. There is the sound of a child crying and I go out to find an eight-year-old boy with his wrist looking like a dinner fork, accompanied by yet another bobby.

'He won't say who he is,' the policeman says, 'so I've brought him here. Then I'll go and track his parents.'

BB appears. 'What's your name, son?' he whispers to the boy. 'Tell me. I won't give you up to the police!' He bends his head down to the boy can whisper in his ear. 'OK, son. It looks as if you've lost your stuffing and you're going to need a cast on that arm. Come with me.

BB leads the boy into the plaster room. In a couple of minutes he reappears to say to the policeman, 'He's Tom Bates of 9 Springfield Crescent.'

'Thanks,' says the bobby. 'I'll go and get his parents.'

'Now's your chance to put on a cast, Jenny,' BB says to me. 'It's a simple Colles. I'll show you how.'

In the plaster room I learn how to wet a roll of plaster of Paris bandage and wind it over the stockinette sleeve I first put on Tom's arm. Then I smooth out the plaster and bring over the edges of the stockinette to make a soft cuff. I check the cast is not too tight and that Tom can move his fingers before I take him to a cubicle where he can wait for his parents.

'Would you like an ice-cream?' I ask him.

'Ooh, yes please.' Tom's eyes light up and he stops whimpering. I tell BB where I'm going and then walk to the main kitchen where there is always Walls ice cream in the freezer. It is time to go off duty when I return as the night staff has come on.

'That was a pretty normal evening,' BB says when I ask him if I may go. 'See you in the morning.'

Several days pass before I have a chance to ask Sandy how she likes theatre. 'They're all nuttier than fruit cakes, aren't they?' Sandy is ironing her petticoats again. 'The funniest thing happened on Sunday. Two housemen put Sister Hale in one of those big laundry bags on wheels and took her for a ride down the main corridor. Then they saw Matron coming and they shot into the nearest ward, leaving Hale sitting in the bag. She didn't know why they had stopped so she stood up to see what was happening and found Matron looking at her. And you know what Matron said?'

'What? Go on.'

'She said, "Really, Sister, if you must behave like this, at least the housemen could be gentlemen enough to help you out," and walked on.'

'She's quite a lass, isn't she?' I say. I like our present Matron. She had recently been on a trip to the United States. When she found out that a Matron there is a lavatory attendant, we heard that she introduced herself as someone who is in charge of toilets but that these are included in a thousand-bed hospital.

I am the triage nurse one day when a woman, typically dressed in a headscarf and shapeless coat, patiently waits her turn.

'What's wrong?' I ask. She hands me a folded handkerchief. I open it to find a finger. It is all I can do not to shriek and hurl it from me but instead I ask to see her hand. She has it wrapped in a bloodstained towel concealed beneath a blanket. I take her to an empty cubicle and have her lie down.

'You needn't have waited in the queue, luv,' I say, 'something like this needs immediate attention.'

'Nay, lass,' she says, 'there's folk much worse than me.'

I get BB to come and take care of her and go back to the queue. Later I ask him what happened to her and he tells me she has been admitted, as she needs surgery to clean up the stump. I say, 'can you imagine someone who has just chopped off their finger, standing in a queue? I think I would have sent for an ambulance.'

'You're not a stoical Yorkshire woman,' BB says.

'Oh yes I am!' I am indignant. 'But I still think losing a finger is more than a trifle.'

'Why, is it a baked custard?'

I throw a towel at him and carry on.

BB is forthright and down-to-earth with the patients and I learn a lot from his approach. A young boy of about ten comes in one day with a thin layer of skin hanging from his calf. He is screaming like a banshee and refusing to be touched when BB comes to see what all the fuss is about.

'What's your name?' he quietly asks the child.

'Mike,' comes the answer.

'Well Mike, it's like this. You have cut your leg badly. All this needs to be sewn back into place.' He points to the flap of skin. 'Now you can either have that done and go home with a mended leg or you can refuse and go home with it like this. It's entirely up to you; you have to decide. Which is it to be?'

'Sew me up then,' mutters Mike.

'Well now Mike, I will sew you up as you request but I will not do it if you scream and yell. It will hurt a bit but no more than you're used to. I expect you to act like you usually do when you're hurt. You don't usually yell do you?'

I am amazed how Mike suddenly becomes mature. He and BB chat about cricket, discuss who is going to win the

Test match, and argue over who is the best bowler, as BB sews up the flap. They shake hands and Mike promises to return the next day for his leg to be checked.

We all learn to suture wounds. The first one I get is a deep gash in a thigh from an accident with a saw. I take the man into one of the operating rooms and expect BB or the doctor to come and sew him up, but after ten minutes neither has appeared so I go to find out what they are doing.

'I thought you would do it,' BB says.

'I've never done it before and I don't think I can,' I say.

'Can you sew?' BB asks.

'Well yes, but material, not skin.'

'No difference. Here, I'll come and show you. First you inject some local anaesthetic and when that's had a chance to work, you just sew the edges together like you would a skirt.'

I am quite proud of my neat stitching as I dress the wound. I say as I help the man off the table, 'Come back in five days to have it checked. Or sooner if it bothers you or if you get a temperature or anything like that, but it is a nice clean wound and should heal easily.'

That night we are all home for a change. Sandy tells us about a nurse in theatre who sat on a shelf and got a circular needle stuck in her bum.

'Both ends of the needle went in and one of the surgeons had to extract it. Boy, was she embarrassed. Can you imagine? And she's only been in theatre a week. Now she has to live that down!'

'How are you getting on with the Dragon?' I ask Jess.

'She took one look at me and thaw how thweet and charming I am so I've had no trouble.' Wee Jess says as she lays her bent head on her folded hands and flutters her eyelashes at me. 'She's horrible to Cartwright though – behind her all the time.'

'That was me,' I say, 'and Milbury was the blue-eyed girl.'

'How's Casualty?'

'Great fun! BB is such a treat after some of the sisters I've worked with. No nonsense. He expects us to make decisions. I love it.'

My upbringing and education were vague about male reproductive organs and so far nurse training hasn't helped me overcome my shyness.

When we bathe male patients and get to the 'private parts', we hand the patient a flannel for him to wash himself 'down there'. It is only when laying out dead men that I have actually handled these parts and I am embarrassed to even refer to them. So when we get the vicar of the church next to the hospital into Casualty, clutching himself where he has been hit by a cricket ball, and BB tells me to put heparin compresses on his genitals every five minutes, I become immobilised.

BB sees my hesitation and says, 'What's the matter with

you, woman? Don't you know how to make a heparin compress?'

'It's not that,' I say, 'It's...'

'Don't tell me you're being maidenish about a man's groin! Oh, for heaven's sake Jenny, he's more embarrassed than you are. Pretend it's his foot you're putting compresses on and have some sympathy for the pain he's in.'

I make up the compresses and go into the cubicle where the vicar is lying. His dog collar and shirt on the top half look incongruous with the sheet covering his legs and his exposed swollen genitals. I wring out the first compress. Without looking at his face, I place it gently over the affected area as I pretend it's his foot.

'This should help the pain,' I say, and it seems to as he relaxes with a sigh. 'I'll be putting fresh compresses on every five minutes so I'll be back in a jiff.'

The next time I go in, I look at his face. He is quite young and has a sandy-coloured moustache. He looks at the ceiling as I replace the compress and doesn't speak. After the third compress, I ask how he's feeling.

'A bit better, thank you nurse. At least the pain is better but this will go down as my most embarrassing moment!'

'Just pretend it's your foot that's sticking out,' I say. 'That should help.'

Our eyes meet, we laugh, and he reaches for my hand to give it a squeeze.

One morning I come on duty and poke my head into a

cubicle to see BB and the houseman attending a man with a hugely swollen penis. It has a ring on it so that it looks like a long inflated balloon that has been twisted in the middle. I stare in wonder until BB tells me to go away. Later, I ask him how the man got a ring on his penis. He is strangely reticent despite the incident with the vicar. 'You're too young to understand.'

'Don't be silly, tell me,' I insist. After much nagging he tells me a prostitute has put it on because he wouldn't pay. I don't believe him and it is not until I consult Sheila that I learn the truth.

'Sheila, you seem to know all about penises! We got a man into Casualty who had a ring on his. How do you think it got there?'

'I expect he was masturbating with it,' Sheila says. I am not quite sure what the word means but don't like to admit it. I will look it up later.

'While we're on the subject, a man can't die with an erection, can he? You were kidding us.'

'Of course I was kidding! An erection is a sign of life if there ever is one.'

Chapter 18

'WHAT HO, GIRLS.' A voice, an octave above the average and with an amplitude that could be heard across a gymkhana ground, greets us as Judith and I enter the Chestnut Stable. 'Jolly good that you want some fresh air and exercise to blow away the cobwebs, what? Nurses, eh? Can't say that job would suit me – I'd keel over at the first sight of blood. Good job someone can do it, what? But you must be really hard.'

I grit my teeth. It infuriates me when people say we must be 'hard' to do the job they couldn't do. We do it because we care enough, not because we are so indifferent that we are hardened to suffering.

Chestnut Stable is run by Olivia Alcock-Brown, an aristocratic young woman who, I was informed by a mutual acquaintance, is too dense to go to college or train for a career, so was set up by her wealthy parents with a riding stable. It was a fortunate choice as both she and the stable flourish.

'Now which of you is Judith and which Jennifer? You've

ridden before, Judith? Good show. I'll put you on Thunder and you, Jennifer, on Sable. Call me Livvy, by the way. But not Olive – that name goes right up me nose as the Australians say.'

She helps us onto our horses and then mounts her own, a frisky white mare. 'Steady on, Snowy, steady there.' She reaches over to pat her mount's neck, which, as she is nearly six feet tall, is not difficult.

'I'll take you into Harefield House estate today. I have permission from the Earl, you know. Went to school with his daughter. Dear old Flip just got herself harnessed – to a banker, don't you know. Nice fella but a bit wet. Jennifer, hold your reins like this. He can't tell a mare from a stallion. No seat whatsoever. Only interested in figures. The arithmetical kind I mean. Don't think he'd know what to do with the others. Got his libido stomped out of him at Harrow. All those cold showers and running up and down hills. Glad we didn't do that at Cheltenham.'

Livvy keeps up a running commentary on her life and the people in it and occasionally throws out directions about how to sit, steer and stop.

'Jolly good show,' she says when we return after an hour and a half. 'Hope you're not too stiff. Try some Sloan's liniment on the old rear if you are. Works wonders.'

We pay her ten shillings each and leave. Unfortunately we can't talk on the scooter so I don't hear Judith's impressions until we're going to bed.

'Fraightfully jolly, what?' Judith says and this expression becomes part of our vocabulary. 'She's a good rider though and her horses are in perfect condition. I think she's a hoot. I'm going to enjoy this.'

'It's nice to ride in Harefield House grounds isn't it?' I say. 'I've always imagined myself cantering over those acres of green that all stately homes seem to have.'

It is Wednesday and I am looking forward to our ride this afternoon. The queue of patients has been quite short and we are clearing up after it when BB calls us.

'Action stations! There's been a bomb explosion in the centre of Leeds. We are to expect dozens of casualties. I've alerted Matron's office and they're sending more staff and Dr John has mobilised the medical staff.'

'What happened?' I ask.

'The police think it's an IRA attack. Here they come.' We hear ambulance sirens sounding like approaching cats in distress. 'Dr John and I will triage. Jenny, you take cubicle one, Jean, two, Heather, in three. As soon as more staff come, I will assign them to you and you supervise them.'

The swing doors to outside are flung open. Trolleys are rushed in. Father John and BB quickly examine each patient and send him or her in different directions.

'Jenny,' BB calls, 'before you do anything else, phone Jim and ask for every trolley in the hospital to he brought here. Then here's your first patient.'

I phone Jim and wheel my trolley into my cubicle. On it is a girl, about nine years old. Her face is black, her head is bleeding and she is unconscious. Her school uniform is in tatters. Blood is seeping through a wound in one arm. I panic. What am I to do?

'Keep calm,' I say to myself. 'First, see to her airway, then examine her.' I wipe some of the black soot off the girl's face so I can see her colour. Her lips are blue and mottled. Her respirations are shallow and irregular. Her pulse is extremely rapid. The head wound, after I have cleaned it a little, seems to be superficial but it is bleeding profusely. Help me, someone, I don't know what to do. Should I intubate? An anaesthetist showed me how not long ago. She is certainly not breathing well nor getting enough oxygen. Do it lass. Can't do her any harm and may save her life. I grab the laryngoscope, tilt her head back and insert an airway that I then attach to breathing apparatus with oxygen. I start to squeeze the oxygen bag rhythmically and watch her chest rise and fall. Her lips change from blue to pink. So far so good.

Still squeezing the bag, I try to expose the arm that is bleeding. At that moment the curtains are pulled aside and a student nurse comes in.

'Mr Barnes told me to come and help you. What can I do?'

'Could you squeeze this oxygen bag while I have a look at her arm?' I cut off the sleeve of the blood-soaked blazer and blouse. It is as if I have released a tap. Blood squirts everywhere. I grab a piece of rubber tubing and tie it around the upper arm. The blood flow stops a little allowing me to see torn flesh and exposed muscle. I can't do this. I don't how to stop this. I want to cry.

'Father John,' I yell forgetting to use his correct title. He comes in. 'She's bleeding badly from this arm and I don't know how to stop it.'

'You've put on a tourniquet and you've got her intubated. That's good,' Dr. John says calmly. 'Now let's see if we can clamp the artery that's bleeding. Got a clamp?'

I hand him one and he pokes around in the wound.

'No good,' he says. 'She'll have to go to theatre. Who is she?'

I look at the child's satchel that I have taken off her shoulder. Inside the flap is written 'Christine Stacey, 153 Bellevue Road, Leeds, Yorkshire, England, Great Britain, World, Universe'.

'Her name's Christine Stacey.'

'Well, we haven't time for consent. We need to stop her bleeding straight away. She'll have to go to theatre as quickly as possible.'

As we wheel the trolley out into the corridor, Daisy appears from nowhere. 'This patient has a severed artery in one arm and needs urgent surgery,' I tell her.

'Right, I'll help this nurse take her. Will you tell BB that the lists are stopped and we're freeing all theatres as soon as

the current patients are done. The surgeons and anaesthetists are standing by so just wheel them in.'

Daisy and the nurse, whose name I still haven't found out,
run down the corridor with the trolley. I look for BB.
Casualty is bedlam. Trolleys holding battered, bleeding forms
are everywhere and more are coming in through the door.
There is the sound of children crying and ambulance sirens
in the distance. I see a man with half his face blown away,
one eye dangling from its socket. Another man has bleeding
stumps sticking out of his trousers and I am reminded of Bill
Stokes. Everyone is black. Clothing is in rags. I am nauseated
by a terrible smell of burned flesh and clothing.

I give BB Daisy's message. 'Try and find out their names
and write them here,' he says indicating a clipboard. 'The
relatives will be here soon and will want to know. Also put
where they are. If you've got someone that can go home,
wheel them into physio.'

I write, 'Christine Stacey – theatre,' on the list and wheel
the next trolley from the line into my cubicle. It's another
little girl. She is also unconscious. I check her pulse and
respirations. There are none. She is dead.

I go to find BB. 'That child I just got is dead. Did she die
here?' I say waving my arm around. I can hear the hysteria
in my voice. 'Or have I just killed her, or what?'

'Sorry, Jenny. She was dead on arrival. She was put in the
wrong place. I am sorry, but it's chaotic out here. Wheel her
into the store room, will you?'

I cover the child with a sheet and wheel the trolley to the storeroom. It is so full of other trolleys with sheets covering small humps that I can't get mine in. Where else can she go? There's a visitor's waiting room. I wheel her in there and hurry back. Life is unreal. Am I in a film? A dream? Can this horror be really happening?

'BB, the store room is full so I've put her in the visitor's waiting room.'

'I'll get someone to move them all and clean them up for identification. We're going to need the visitor's room, as the relatives will be showing up soon. The worst cases are in so they won't be as bad from now on, I hope. We're trying to give nurses ones they can handle alone as all the docs are tied up. So you'll have to make the best decisions you can.' He gives my arm a squeeze. 'If you think they need surgery, take them to theatre. If you think they need admitting, admit them. If they need stitching, stitch them. We'll sort it all out eventually.' BB's usually placid face is strained but his voice is even. 'Go to it, kid. You're one of the best I've got. And if you make the wrong decision, which you won't, I'll back you all the way.'

I suddenly feel I am up to this, I can cope after all. I find my next patient.

The nurse who is helping me comes back from theatre and I find out that her name is Markham. 'I think I'm going to be sick,' she says.

'Oh no you're not! If anyone's going to be sick, it's me,' I say. 'Besides, we haven't got time.'

We wheel our trolley into our cubicle. Another little girl. Huge eyes stare at me from a blackened face.

'What's your name?' I ask her.

'Margaret Jones.'

'Do you hurt anywhere, Margaret?' I ask as I begin to wash her face. Her skin is pink. I examine her head. No signs of bruises or cuts.

'My back hurts here,' the child says as she tries to turn over.

'Don't move just yet.' I examine her legs and test her reflexes. After Markham and I undress her, I press her abdomen in different places to see if she reacts.

'I have to stand up,' Margaret says suddenly. 'My back hurts lying on it.'

I raise the head of the trolley and help her bend forward. The right side of her back from her shoulder to her waist looks as if someone has scraped it with sandpaper. I touch it. 'Ouch,' she says.

'It's all scraped. We'll clean it, which will sting a lot, but then you'll be OK. Can you remember what happened?'

'We were all waiting at a bus stop. Our class was going back to school from a trip to the art gallery. I heard this great big bang and then I was lying on the pavement. There was lots of shouting and a man came to see if I was all right. He told me to lie still and an ambulance would come, and it did.' She starts to cry. 'I want my mummy.'

'She'll be here very soon and then you can go home. But

first I have to put a dressing on your back.' I gently clean the wound but it still hurts her. She cries silently until I have finished. Then she stops and smiles at me.

'That feels better, thank you,' she says. I want to hug her. She is so remarkably composed for her age that her stoicism helps me control my own anxiety. We help her up and walk her to the physiotherapy department. As we approach, I can hear singing and when we enter the main hall of the department we find all those waiting to go home are sitting wrapped in blankets singing 'Pack up your troubles in your old kit bag'. Kitchen has produced a trolley with an urn of tea and trays of sandwiches covered with damp cloths. I give Margaret a cup of milky sweet tea and a sandwich and tell her that I want to speak to her mother before she goes home. Then I hand her over to one of the nurses who are looking after these patients.

After Margaret there are no more children but I am busy stitching gashes made by flying glass, dressing grazes and dealing with people who are shivering and dazed with shock. I take one woman with a glass shard sticking out of her eye to theatre, and I admit two people with fractures. BB tells us to grab tea and sandwiches when we can and Kitchen keeps everything replenished. At one point I am told that a Mrs Jones wants to see me.

'Your little Trojan can go home,' I say to her. 'She's been a right champion. She may have been knocked out by the blast so you need to keep a good eye on her. I am sure she'll be alright but it will be wise to wake her up every hour during the night to make sure she is conscious and to check her pupils with a torch, like this.' I show her how to test the pupils. 'If they become very tiny or very large or different sizes, call an ambulance and bring her in. We would keep her in normally but, as you can see, we are overwhelmed.'

'I quite understand. Do you know how the others are?' Mrs Jones asks.

'I'm afraid I don't, Mrs Jones. We were just swamped with casualties and I've been too busy to get the general picture.' I don't want to tell her about the small humps I'd seen under sheets. There must have been at least six.

I am seeing one case after another and lose all track of time. It is nice to have Markham to help as she does all the sterilising, which makes it quicker for me. She also takes the patients who can go home to physio and gives them tea. The little bus-type ambulances, used to transport patients to and from hospital, are beginning to clear the room so patients do not have to wait for long now.

BB comes in. 'That's the first wave of patients. They were on the street. Now we can expect those that have been buried under rubble. A store collapsed on top of them. So far the only ones they've got out are dead.'

I look at my watch. It is nearly eight o'clock. I can hardly believe it. I have been attending to casualties for over eight hours without a break. Then I think, 'Oh no – we were supposed to go riding and I didn't let Livvy know.' I don't suppose Judith did either as all off duty was cancelled throughout the hospital. Those who should have been off were sent to help here or in theatre. There is a lull so I go to the phone in the tiny room that serves as BB's office to call Livvy.

'Livvy here,' a voice booms after two rings. I hold the phone away from my ear.

'Livvy, it's Jennifer. I'm terribly sorry that we didn't let you know we weren't coming but there's been a disaster.'

'Don't worry old bean. Heard about the bomb. Guessed you'd be busy, as I know you're in Casualty. Good thing you can handle it – hardened to it I expect.'

Something gives way. 'Hardened to it,' I shriek down the phone. 'Hardened to seeing little kiddies blown to bits, people with their faces half blown off, a man with no feet and...' I start to cry. There's a pause.

'Look, I'm terribly sorry old thing. Didn't mean it. It's just that...' Livvy's voice hesitates, 'I'm no good at anything, you know. I couldn't do what you and Judith do. I do admire you. See you next week, I hope.'

'Yes you will,' I manage to say before I hang up. Then I put my head on my arms and sob. All the horror and exhaustion drain out of me as I let it out through tears.

BB comes in. 'What's this? I thought you were a stoical Yorkshire woman?'

'Well, I'm not,' I snivel.

He puts an arm over my shoulders. 'You did OK, kid. Now go over to the Nurses' Home and powder your nose or whatever you women do, and put on a clean pinny. You look like a butcher. Then come back in ten minutes and there will be bacon, eggs and chips for everyone. That'll cheer you up.'

When I return, Casualty is quiet and we are able to sit and eat our bacon and eggs undisturbed. I do feel more cheerful. I didn't realise I was so hungry. Everyone in the room looks exhausted, especially Father John. He and BB have had the awful job of getting people to identify the dead. Most of them were children. I had seen the stricken parents waiting for news as I flew in and out of my cubicle. I was lucky – the only parents I saw were the ones who could take their child home. As I munch I feel the same sense of camaraderie I felt in theatre and I am proud to be one of this group – proud to be a nurse. If I can cope with today, I can handle anything.

Sister Busby comes in. It must be nine o'clock and the night staff is on. Not much chance of us going off yet as we are expecting victims who have been buried. The police have let us know that the diggers have nearly broken through the rubble and that several people are trapped but alive.

'I hear you've had a somewhat busy day, BB,' Busby says. 'Just like old times, eh?'

'With this team, we can only win.' BB looks round at us.

Today must be like the war was and those two have been through it. But it wasn't just one day for them but day after day after day. How on earth did they survive? I look at them with new respect.

'Sister Busby,' I say. 'I'd like to know what happened to a little girl called Christine Stacey. She had a head injury and went to theatre with a severed artery in her arm.'

Busby looks through her reports. 'She's on Ward 10. She had her arm amputated. But she's conscious now. You can go and see her if you like.'

There is the sound of ambulances again but this time many of the casualties walk in. They are in shock but not badly injured. They had been in the back of the store that collapsed and were trapped. Some of them have broken limbs and need to be admitted, but after we have examined them and attended to any small wounds, the rest can go home.

It is midnight when I get home. Judith and Jess are there but not Sandy. We catch up on each other's news.

'I've been in theatre all day. Sandy is still there but on the last case, I think,' Judith says.

'We had to thend as many patients home as possible and we had loadth of admissions,' Wee Jess says. 'It was awful. Most of them were thurgical cases even though we're a medical ward and don't have the right equipment.'

'What was it like for you, Jen?' Judith asks as she puts down a mug of cocoa for each of us.

'It was terrible. The first lot was all little girls. They had been in a bus queue right next to where the bomb went off. There were some horrible injures and several deaths. After today, nothing worse can happen to me.' I sip my cocoa. 'You know, I don't care what cause the IRA stands for, to set off a bomb among ordinary people, including children, is simply barbaric. I hate them and all they stand for and will do for the rest of my life.'

Chapter 19

I AM TO SPEND my third night duty on Princess Mary, the ward for sick infants. Before I can be in charge on nights I have to present myself, in a completely clean uniform, for two days orientation. I am excited though nervous about the prospect of looking after babies. My only contact with wee bairns has been my brother, who was born when I was 14, but that was not enough experience to give me confidence.

Sister Howes greets me. For some reason, I expected a large motherly type but she is small, cheerful and energetic. She asks me what my off duty is.

'I don't know, Sister. It's up to you.'

'Well, the evening routine is much like the afternoon so you may as well have a five-to today, and tomorrow as well.' She smiles at me. I immediately like her; she does not seem to be officious or rule-bound, two qualities I can't stand. To ask about my off duty straight away indicates that she has sympathy for students.

'I'll show you how to change and feed a baby first as that is what we mostly do.'

Sister Howes puts on the white gown hanging beside a cot, opens the locker and slides out a tray with a small bowl, cotton-wool balls and baby talcum powder. She fills the bowl with warm water. Then she lowers the cot side and picks up a tiny, wizened baby.

'This is Matthew. Failure to thrive. We get quite a few of these in as we're the centre for the whole of Yorkshire. It's heart-breaking, as we can't find the reason. They just don't grow.' She lays Matthew on her lap, takes off his nappy and puts it in a bowl on the floor. Then she carefully washes and dries his groin with cotton wool. She folds a muslin square into a triangle, folds it again and places it under the baby.

'You bring this flap up like this and fold the other two ends across. Then, holding your fingers under where the safety pin goes, you pin it. Keeping your fingers here means you prick yourself, not the baby, if you push too hard.' She puts Matthew back in his cot while she washes her hands. Then she picks him up again, settles into a chair with her feet on a stool, takes up a glass feeding bottle from a jug of hot water, tests a drop of milk on her forearm and puts the teat in his mouth.

Matthew sucks weakly. 'This one isn't interested but some of them are proper little guts-aches. Come on, Matthew, there's a good boy.' Sister Howes jiggles the bottle. After a while she puts it back in the hot water and sits Matthew up.

'This is how you burp them. Don't be afraid to bang on their backs – they're not made of porcelain.' Matthew's expression is one of profound concentration. Then he gives a giant burp for one so small and his expression relaxes. 'Now, perhaps you could change and feed Shirley in the next cot. She's eight months old and came in with gastro-enteritis but she's better now and ready to go home.'

I feel extraordinarily happy holding a baby on my lap and cradled in my arm. I spontaneously start to sing a lullaby. Shirley has round blue eyes, pink cheeks and sucks her bottle with gusto. I hold her tiny hand and admire the miniature nails. I nuzzle my chin on her head and feel the softness of her hair. She smells of baby powder. Then I look up guiltily. Perhaps I shouldn't be cuddling a baby. Perhaps I will infect her.

Sister Howes comes over and puts her hand on my shoulder. 'I am glad to see you cuddling Shirley. They need that as much as food and clean nappies.'

The ward reminds me of Peter Pan and Wendy as it looks like an old-fashioned nursery. At the far end there is a large fireplace with a brass fender around the hearth and a coal fire burning. A clothes horse is bent around one side of the fire and a medley of tiny woollen garments hangs out to dry. Six white-painted metal cots flank each side of the room. One of them holds several stuffed animals and a chubby-cheeked baby who is standing up mouthing the cot rail.

After I finish feeding Shirley, Sister Howes says, 'It's time for David to have his penicillin. I want you to give it.'

'I can't inject a baby,' I say in horror.

'Yes, you can. You have to. It's the same as an adult only you use a smaller needle.'

I take David's nappy off and stare at the tiny bottom. 'I'm going to hurt him,' I say to Sister.

'Yes, you are. But he has to have his medicine. Go on – brace yourself and give it.'

I quickly insert the needle into the tiny bottom and press down the plunger. There is a moment's silence and then a furious howl. David's little face is screwed up and his mouth is wide open. His whole body is letting the world know of his affront. I pick him up and hold him against my shoulder.

'Oh, David, I'm sorry. There, there.' I cuddle him until he stops crying and put him back in his cot.

Sister Howes is laughing at me. 'You'll soon get used to it.'

We have admitted a baby with pyloric stenosis and we are getting him ready for theatre. I learn how to give subcutaneous saline (sub-cut). Instead of an intravenous infusion, saline is injected under the skin in an attempt to keep the baby hydrated. I also learn how to pass a tube through the baby's mouth into his stomach to wash it out.

'Pyloric stenosis is quite common,' Sister Howes says. The diagnosis is made when a baby vomits and it shoots across the room – projectile vomiting. Luckily, it's a simple matter to cut the pylorus, which is all that needs to happen. Then it's OK after it heals.'

She holds up the shrivelled little baby. 'You watch,' she says, 'he'll be so plump next week you won't recognise him.'

We all start night duty the next day and although I hate nights I am looking forward to working on Princess Mary. It is so peaceful. I am busy all the time but it is not the frantic rush of the adult wards. As the ward is small, and as I sit down a lot to feed babies, I don't get as tired as usual.

A few nights later I admit a three-month old with gastro-enteritis. Her mother, who wears a headscarf over her curlers, a man's overcoat fastened with safety pins and down-at-heel shoes, carries Nancy in. She smells and I am thinking how I wish she would take a bath when I remember my day with the district nurse in PTS. This woman probably lives in a one-up, one-down with one cold water tap. Nevertheless, the baby is clean. I start to undress her and peel off layer upon layer of hand-knitted clothes. Finally she is dressed only in a nappy and I can almost hear her say 'Whew.'

I take off the nappy, which is dirty with liquid green stool, and wrap it and the clothes for the mother to take home. 'There you are Mrs Naylor, you take these and bring in a clean nappy and clothes when you come to take her home again.'

'Do you think she'll be alright, nurse?' Mrs Naylor looks tired and anxious. 'She's been fretful all day like and hasn't kept nowt down. And look at her bum! It's all red and sore but I've been changing her often, honest I have.' She starts to cry.

'I'm sure you have,' I say. 'It's difficult to keep them clean when they have constant diarrhoea. But there's every good chance Nancy will recover quickly and she'll soon be home with you. The doctor is coming to examine her and he will explain what is wrong and what we are going to do. Perhaps you could wait in the waiting room until he arrives.'

I weigh Nancy, take her temperature and dress her in clean clothes. I have just finished when the paediatric houseman and the night sister come in.

'Is the mother still here?' the houseman asks. 'I'll get a history from her before I examine the baby.'

'Yes, she's in the waiting room,' I say.

The night sister tells me to put Nancy in traction. When babies have severe diarrhoea we put splints on their legs, then hang them up onto pulleys suspended from two poles which traverse the cot ends. In this way their bottoms are exposed to the air and they are not sitting in stool.

The houseman comes back from the waiting room with Mrs Naylor, who leans over the cot to give her baby a goodbye kiss.

'Phone in the morning Mrs Naylor, to find out how she is,' I say as I see her out of the ward. 'Visiting hours are from two to four and from seven to eight or you can make arrangements with Sister to visit when it suits you.' I touch her arm. 'You brought Nancy in before she's really bad so I don't think it will be long before she's home and keeping you on your toes.'

I give Nancy her first sub-cut and then go to make up her feeds. I scrub up to enter the milk kitchen. It is bright and gleaming with a long stainless steel counter above which is a shelf holding large round tins of National Dried Milk powder. Those with blue labels hold full-cream, those with red labels, half-cream. There are also jars of Benger's food and other special milk powders. A big Brown Betty teapot looks strange among the tins and jars but I need it now as babies with diarrhoea have their feeds made up with tea. There is little else we can do for the numerous babies we get with gastro-enteritis: try to keep them hydrated, stop the skin of their buttocks from becoming excoriated, and wait. If we get them before they are severely dehydrated, the prognosis is good.

Nancy soon recovers. Sister Howes gives Mrs Naylor lessons on the importance of sterilisation of bottles and teats and the use of boiled water to make up feeds, before she takes her baby home.

In my own home, we are all excited as Judith announces, looking uncharacteristically embarrassed, that she is engaged to be married. She waves her fourth finger at us to show off a ring. It does not hold a diamond but an amethyst. She says she prefers that stone and thinks diamonds are over-rated.

'Well, you're a dark horse. I had no idea,' I say. 'Who is the lucky chap?' I feel hurt that she hasn't told me before the general announcement. I am her best friend after all.

'His name is Alan King and he was a dresser at the women's hospital. I've been out with him a few times but I didn't tell you lot because you would have ribbed me too much. He's coming for supper on Saturday so if any of you are around, you can meet him.'

'What's he like?' Sandy asks.

'He's dark, not particularly tall, brown eyes, nice smile. Rather gorgeous really.' I am amused by Judith's dreamy look as she says this. What a transformation!

'I'm going to be in on Saturday if it means refusing an invitation from the Queen,' I say. 'When's the wedding? How about a double event with Marie?'

Judith gives me a withering look. 'We don't have a date planned as I want to finish and do Midder. Alan wants to specialise in something, he's not sure what.'

When we're in bed Judith says, 'Will you be my brides-maid, Jen?'

'Yes, I'd love to,' I say. 'As long as I don't have to wear frills and lace.'

Judith laughs. 'No, it will be a very quiet affair in a registry office. No one there but our parents and you.'

My hurt disappears. Judith has always been reserved and

I appreciate the fact that I am the one she chooses to debate with. When the four of us are together she doesn't say much but when she and I are alone, we discuss books, philosophy and how much better we could run the hospital.

Judith spends the entire Saturday shopping and preparing food. I am not allowed to help or even lay the table. Her normal eating habits are absent-minded so I am amused by her industry. She prepares spaghetti bolognaise, salad, crusty bread, a creamy pudding and arranges Camembert cheese and grapes on the table. She has also bought an expensive wine rather than our usual plonk.

Alan arrives as Sandy and Jess get up and we all sit down to eat. He is handsome but I don't like the way his dark eyebrows nearly meet or the blue-dark shadow where he has recently shaved. He reminds me of Heathcliffe.

'This is very good, dear,' he says to Judith after a few mouthfuls. 'I can see I'm going to be well fed.'

The adoring look Judith gives him makes me want to shake her.

'Judith has often said that cooking should be shared by married couples,' I say to Alan. 'How are you in the kitchen?'

'Oh, I didn't mean all the time,' Judith says hastily. 'Just once in a while.'

'The kitchen is the woman's domain,' Alan says. 'My mother wouldn't let me in hers – said I made too much mess.' He takes a sip of wine. 'Ah, Cabernet Sauvignon. An excellent choice, dear.'

'You patronising ass,' I think. I cannot understand why Judith has fallen for such an idiot. I want to shout 'Wake up, where are you?' to her but I know I would simply lose her as a friend. I hope she comes to her senses before the wedding.

I am silent for the rest of the meal. Thankfully Sandy is able to chatter away. She, Jess and I wash up. We leave Judith and Alan alone in the living room Then Sandy and Jess go to work and I tactfully take myself out to the pictures.

I come on duty after nights off to find a baby with TB meningitis. He is nine months old and has ginger hair. His back is arched so badly that his head touches his heels and he has a dreadful scream-like cry.

Sister Howes gives the report. 'He has had a lumbar puncture and the cerebro-spinal pressure was 480mm of water instead of the normal 100mm. Streptomycin was injected into the subarachnoid space and he is on it intramuscularly also. But I'm afraid there's no hope. He is going to die – probably tonight. I have talked to his parents. They have gone out for something to eat and will be back later.'

We walk over to the baby's cot and I feel a heavy sense of uselessness, as I look at the pathetic little human. Why does this have to happen to babies? I can accept the death of old people philosophically. Indeed, many of the patients I have nursed are ready for death and resent any intrusion other than pain control.

'Deaths of babies are always hard,' Sister Howes says. 'It just doesn't seem right.' She goes off duty. The night sister visits shortly after as she has heard about the dying baby. I carry on feeding and changing babies with a heavy heart. I can see Nicholas, for that is his name, from wherever I sit and his piercing cry reverberates through my head like the penetrating screech of a train whistle. His parents return and the night sister comes back to talk to them.

'Can I hold 'im, Sister?' the mother says. 'I want to 'old 'im while he passes on so 'e knows 'e's loved.'

'Of course you can,' the Sister says. 'Put on this gown and sit here.' She gently lifts the arched form and places him in his mother's arms. The father stands with his arm around his wife's shoulder. Nicholas starts to convulse. The mother can barely hold him but she clings on to her baby. I am ready to cry but both parents are showing enormous restraint so I do too.

After an hour Nicholas gives one last jerk and is still. His mother cuddles him and kisses him. 'Goodbye darling,' she says as she puts him in his cot. 'Remember we loved you.' I can't help it. Tears run down my cheeks and I find the parents are comforting me, not vice versa as it should be.

'These things 'appen, nurse,' the father says. 'Can't be 'elped.'

'The doctor said he'd be retarded like if 'e lived and that would be no life would it? It's for the best.'

I can't believe their fortitude but I'm looking at a generation that has just lived through a major war where death was a daily occurrence and mourning a luxury.

I phone the night sister to inform her of the death and ask her to come and certify it. Sister Busby arrives. She is now Night Superintendent. 'Hello, Nurse Ross. I'd forgotten you're on here. Which baby is it?' I show her the dead baby. She listens to the heart with a stethoscope and then asks me if I have laid out a baby before.

'No Sister,' I say. I feel unprofessional and foolish with my red eyes.

'Come outside,' she says. We leave the ward to sit in the tiny visitor's room. Sister Busby just looks at me and she seems so sympathetic, I start to cry with a vengeance.

'Don't feel ashamed of crying,' she says gently. 'It's when we stop crying we're in trouble. Some sisters may tell you you're unprofessional but I am delighted that you care so much.' I dry my eyes. 'Do you think you can lay him out now? Do it with love and compassion as your last nursing act for him.'

Sister Busby really is a grand lass and when I'm a sister I want to be like her. I wash the little baby and put on a clean white nightie. Then I fold his hands around a white flower I get from the ward next door. I wrap him in a sheet.

'Goodbye Nicholas,' I say as a porter comes to take him away.

1955 is nearly half over when Sandy suggests that we give a party to celebrate our 21st birthdays, all of which fall in that year. 'I have a patient who owns the Daleswood Arms and he will let us use the rooms for free,' she says.

In a matter of days we have a party organised. Other patients donate the crockery, cutlery and drinks, someone's brother plays in a dance band and promises to bring them and Marie surprises us by producing an uncle who volunteers to act as Master of Ceremonies. We provide the food. One hundred student nurses and medical students have a super time eating, drinking and dancing. The whole affair costs six of us, we four with Marie and another girl, two pounds and ten shillings each.

I never fail to be amazed at, and grateful for, the generosity and affection Leeds people show nurses. Our distinguishing purple, black and white scarves earn us smiles and all number of price reductions when we are out, that I know other students do not receive.

My time on Princess Mary quickly passes. The only other death I have is of a newborn with such awful deformities, the death was a blessing.

I give report to Sister Howes at the end of my last night. I tell her I have finished the rotation and who is coming on tonight.

'Would you like to perm for me?' she says. I am surprised, then flattered. Sisters sometimes ask student nurses to come back as staff nurses when they get on well with them, as it is important that the trained staff on a ward work well together.

I haven't really thought about where I want to staff but the prospect of working with Sister Howes, whom I admire, and nursing babies, who I love, fills me with pleasure.

'Yes,' I say, 'I would like that very much.'

Chapter 20

Dear Madam,

I have much pleasure in informing you that your application for registration has been approved and your name has now been entered on the General part of the Register of Nurses maintained by the General Nursing Council for England and Wales. Your registration number is 235802 and you are now entitled to call yourself a Registered Nurse; your date of registration is 4 April, 1956.

Your State Registered Badge will be sent to you direct from the manufacturers; owing to restrictions in supplies of metal there is a delay of approximately six months. When you receive the badge great care should be taken of it in order that it may not fall into the hands of any unauthorised person; it is the property of the Council and arrangements should be made for its return to these offices on the death of a nurse.

Yours faithfully,
Registrar

15 Waterford Gardens
Bramwood, Leeds

10 April 1956

Dear Mum and Dad,

Many thanks for the roses. They are simply beautiful and add a touch of elegance to our humdrum living room. It is nice to have *something* to acknowledge I've finished. We all went over to the Nurses' Home at nine o'clock last Wednesday to get our letters saying whether we've passed or not. We all have. All 13 of us that is, out of 33 that started. Then we went to the sewing room for a length of purple grosgrain to go round our waists as a belt to show that we are staff nurses. And that was it! Back to the wards and business as usual.

American nurses have a big ceremony when they graduate. They wear white uniforms, carry a bunch of red roses each, have photographs taken, parents come – a general celebration. Us? We just went to Matron's office. She congratulated us and said sorry that our badges aren't ready but there's a metal shortage coz of the war. And we're to go on nights next month just to add insult to injury.

Judith is in love! I told you she's engaged didn't I? His name is Alan King and he finishes medical school at the end of this month and then has a year as a houseman before they can even think of getting married. Marie's wedding is on 23 June.

Love Jenny

15 Waterford Gardens
Bramwood, Leeds

30 June 1956

Dear Mum and Dad,
We all got nights off together so we could go to Marie's wedding last week. It was a lovely wedding. Marie looked stunning. She's pretty anyway but as a bride, she was simply gorgeous.

I enclose two snaps. Number one is Marie and Charles. Don't they make a nice couple? Number two is us in our hats. Aren't we a scream? That's me under that mass of pink fur stuff and that's the coat Sandy helped me buy. That's Judith on my right looking like Vita Sackville-West. Wee Jess looks like a mushroom and Sandy is under that bonnet of flowers.

We got up early and took the train to York and had a look round before going to the church. The reception was at a guildhall – I can't remember which one – and was very lively. All Marie's Italian relatives were there – men in hats with coloured ribbons hanging from them and the women in lots of frills. They certainly know how to enjoy themselves. And because we are Marie's friends, we were all hugged and kissed by everyone when we arrived and again when we left. Judith said she felt like a teddy bear.

Marie is not going to stay until the end of the year so she won't get her hospital badge and certificate, but she doesn't care – she's still an SRN. They sail off to Africa after their honeymoon. Judith thinks they have no business meddling in other cultures and imposing their beliefs even if they do provide medical care. I agree with her.

Nothing much else to say. I'm on nights on Princess Mary but it's been moved temporarily to the private patients wing so it can be refurbished. Judith and I still go riding when we can and Sandy and I have started walking more in the Dales. The scooter is going well.

Love Jenny

15 Waterford Gardens
Bramwood, Leeds

3 December 1956

Dear Mum and Dad,
Four years ago today I started training here! I can hardly believe it. Today I became a permanent staff nurse and wear a purple uniform with long sleeves

and a little cape. The sleeves end in solid cuffs which the hospital provide but we have to buy the little muslin cuffs to wear when we roll up our sleeves, which is most of the time.

I am on days now and won't have to do any more nights unless I choose to become a night sister. Yippee!! I am still on Princess Mary and last month we moved to our new ward. They've ruined it. All glass and hygiene – each baby in a separate cubicle. They put a built-in bath in each cubicle and they've put them too high for us, as we sit down to bath babies. We told them, but who listens to nurses? I really miss the old nursery-type ward with the fireplace.

I was really touched last week. A very much wanted baby of an older couple died. We couldn't find out why – he just didn't grow. I laid him out and we usually place a white flower in their hands. The parents came to visit him and held him for ages and as usual, I had to cry with them. I can't help it! Well, the next day they came back with a huge bunch of flowers for me because I had put a flower in their baby's hands. It is so unbearably sad when a baby dies. I still haven't got used to it.

This year we're in the pantomime. It happens every year and is put on by the sisters and perms to poke fun at the consultants and the housemen and the Ass. Mats. of course. We have started rehearsals and it is great fun. I will tell you all about it later.

We had a letter from Marie last month. It took two months to get here. They both got severe diarrhoea and vomiting when they first arrived and I suspect that Marie doesn't find it quite as glamorous as she expected. We have all written back as she is very homesick, she says.

Love Jenny

15 Waterford Gardens
Bramwood, Leeds

15 April 1957

Dear Mum and Dad,
Sorry I haven't written for so long but there's not much to say. We are all perms and because of that, we get every other weekend off. We have managed to get the same ones so finally we have some social life. We meet the housemen all the time at work and we've had a few parties with them. Last month we hired a bus and went to Blackpool but by the time we had stopped at every pub on the way, it was time to come back again!

Wee Jess is organising a cricket match between us and them to be held one Saturday next month. Lots of fun with a nice group but only Judith has someone special – her Alan, who is now in the house. I didn't like him at first but now I know him better, he's not so bad. Being a houseman has knocked some of the arrogance out of him!

The big news is that we're all going to do Midder (midwifery), starting 1 August. We've all applied for Queen Charlotte's Hospital in London. As it doesn't have medical students, there is no competition for deliveries and it has a very good reputation. It should be fun living in London, though I'll be sorry to give up this flat.

A Chinese restaurant has opened in Harrogate. Jess and I went there on the scooter last week. It is quite good but not as good as the Chinese food in Bombay.

People are really funny about it. They don't know what Chinese food is and are very suspicious – as if it contains fish eyes or something!

Love Jenny

Queen Charlotte's Hospital
London

15 January 1958

Dear Mum and Dad,
Only two more weeks in this awful place – I can hardly wait to get out of here. I shall never eat peas again! We have peas with every meal. They are bright

green. I don't know how anyone can start with a healthy pea and end up with a fluorescent one but they manage somehow.

You ask why I hate it here. Well, it's not the mothers and babes; I love them and I love delivering babies. It's the way we are treated. For example, we don't change rooms when we're on nights like at LGI. Fair enough but there is no attempt to be quiet while we are sleeping. The cleaners even come in and clean our rooms while we are in bed! One day when I was asleep, my door was flung open and my clean laundry was dumped on top of me.

The sisters are unbelievable. If I thought the ones at LGI were autocratic they are as lambs compared with this lot. One even expected me to get off the public phone because she was waiting for it. Because I wouldn't, she spent the time banging on the glass door. On duty they treat us like skivvies instead of State Registered Nurses.

We have lectures every weekday from 8.30 to 10am and you have to be there. So if you're a day off, you have to get up and if you're on nights you have to stay up and try and keep awake.

We should have known there was trouble ahead when we arrived as there isn't a single London-trained nurse in our set. They know better! Anyway, not for much longer. We have to stay in London in February to take two days of exams but of course, they've arranged them so that there isn't two weeks between them for a holiday. Sandy and Jess are staying here for the month but I am going to live with Judith in the flat she's taken in Wimbledon. I will try and get a job.

Sandy and I are going to Austria on 2 March, skiing. We are going to a little village called Westendorf. It's £50 for 2 weeks and that includes room, food, travel, ski rental and 4 hours of lessons every day.

Alan is joining Judith some time in February and they're getting married quietly after he arrives. She doesn't want a big do. Jess is going to do Part II Midder straight away. She wants to be a district midwife. Sandy and I will go back to Leeds after our holiday. She's going back to LGI and I'm doing Part II in Leeds.

Love Jenny

Pontings
Kensington High Street

23 February 1958

Dear Mum and Dad,

I am writing this at work, if you can call sitting around from 9 to 5 with an hour for lunch, work. I've never had it so easy! Mind you, getting a job was not easy and I feel sorry for those who have to try. I started off at Pontings and the personnel manager was very nice and said that if I couldn't get a job anywhere else, to come back. I tried every store in the High Street and every store in Oxford Street with no luck. They didn't want anyone for such a short time or they thought I was over-qualified.

So I came back to Pontings at the end of the day and she gave me a job as a 'floating biller'. When people respond to newspaper ads and want, say, a pair of pyjamas and some shelves, I have to make sure that these items, from different departments, meet up to go in the same parcel. It's dead easy. It is such a change to go home and not feel tired.

Because I got holiday pay from the hospital, which I used to pay for Austria, I didn't get paid here for two weeks so I have been absolutely broke. So was Judith. We lived on herb omelettes for two weeks.

Alan arrives tomorrow so I am going to sleep on the sofa. They are getting married on Tuesday and only want me and their parents there.

Love Jenny

Chapter 21

I PARK MY SCOOTER and walk into LGI with a feeling of relief. I feel hugged by the warm familiar smell and cheered by the well-known sounds and sights. When I reach the main corridor I hear a voice say, 'Hello Ross. Where've you been? Haven't seen you for ages.'

It's Jordan, a perm I know quite well. 'Hello Jordan. I've been doing Midder at Queen Charlotte's. I was supposed to start Part II today but there's been a mix-up in the dates and I can't start until June. So now I'm looking for a job. What's been happening in dear old LGI?'

'Well, we've a new Matron for one thing. I can't stop now but why don't you come to first dinner and I'll fill you in. Save me a place if you get there first.'

She hurries off and I enter Matron's office. The first person I see is Miss Darcy, the Deputy Matron. 'Well Nurse Ross, good to see you. My word, you do look brown! Where have you been?'

'Austria. Skiing. And before that doing Midder.'

'It's disgusting to look like that in the middle of winter!

Is this just a visit or are you back with us? I don't remember seeing your name anywhere.'

'I was supposed to start Part II Midder today but when I got there yesterday I was told I should have arrived on 2 March. I had phoned a few months ago to see if I could be two weeks late so I could get in a holiday and they said yes. But now I have to wait until June, so I'm out of a job.'

Miss Darcy leans back in her chair and gives me a radiant smile. 'The Lord works in wondrous ways! Sister Jenner on Ward 5 has just been diagnosed with glandular fever and is expected to be off for three months. Her perm leaves on Friday. I was at my wit's end wondering what to do, when you show up. Sister Jenner's replacement! When can you start? Now?'

'I haven't anywhere to live yet. And I've no uniform.' Events are moving too fast for me. 'Besides, I'm not sure I'm capable of taking charge of an adult ward – remember I was on Princess Mary before I left.'

'Well that's one thing I am sure of. You can live in until you find a place and I expect your uniform is still in the sewing room. Why don't you go over and see while I do the paper work?' She gets up from her desk and almost gives me a hug. 'You're the answer to my major problem.'

I leave, in a daze, to go to the sewing room where Betty finds my uniform in two bags in a storeroom. I go up to sick bay to find a Home Sister to see about a room and find an unfamiliar figure wearing the head Home Sister's uniform.

'Hello, I'm Nurse Ross. I left here seven months ago to do Midder and now I'm starting again as a perm. I haven't anywhere to live yet so Miss Darcy said I should live in for a while.'

'I'm Sister Appleby. I just started here.' She's an older woman with prematurely silver hair and an open face. 'Now let me see. We have a Nurse Sandstone just moved in. She's a perm. Do you know her?'

'Oh yes. We shared a flat for years and did Midder together. She doesn't know I'm here – she thinks I'm doing Part II but it's been postponed.'

'Well this will be a nice surprise for her. She's in East 221. I'll put you in East 225 which is close by.' She hands me keys, which I sign for, and then I collect my uniform and find my room.

When I go back to Matron's office, Miss Darcy says, 'I thought you'd be in uniform ready to go on duty.'

'Oh come off it!' I say. 'I can't start yet. I haven't got my clothes or anything.' 'You've got your uniform haven't you?'

'Yes, but I can't wear it barefoot.'

'When can you start?'

'How about one o'clock tomorrow?'

'All right. I'll let the ward know. You will have three days with Nurse Mason before you take over, so I'll tell her to give you the same off duty as herself.'

I sign various forms and leave for the dining room, as it

is time for first dinner. I look for Sandy but she must be coming to second dinner. I can't wait to see her face when she sees me back at LGI.

Jordan arrives. I tell her about starting on Ward 5 and then say, 'Tell me about the new Matron. What's she like?'

'Her name is Ann Wilks and she trained at Barts.' She says 'Barts' with a long 'a' and at the same time, holds an extended forefinger under her nose. 'We're not allowed to say "poorly" anymore.'

'That's ridiculous! All the patients say they're nicely or poorly.'

'Yes, but *we* mustn't use those words.'

'She sounds as if she's a nut case if she chooses such trivial things to worry about. Does she have any redeeming qualities?'

'Hmmm. Well, she owns an orange mini.'

'Really? What fun.'

'Doesn't go with the rest of her. She's tall and thin and pale. When she first came, she wore a severe black dress that made her look as if she was death at the door. One day she did a round on Ward 1 and a patient said, 'Ee luv, black does nowt for thee!' We both laugh. 'Now she wears navy blue. I don't know whether that remark influenced her or not but she does look less funereal.'

I am served a bowl of tapioca pudding and as I put a dollop of jam into it I say, 'Where's the Sod? There was a different head Home Sister when I went over there.'

'Yes. Appleby. The Sod was so drunk one night she walked into AJ's room by mistake and got into her bed while AJ was in the bathroom. AJ came back to find the Sod in her bed and vomiting all over her room.'

I laugh with glee. 'Was she fired at last?'

'Yes. She's gone to be dried out but we don't think she'll come back.'

'What's Appleby like?'

'Really sweet. Well anyone would be after the Sod, but the Apple is lovely. She's a widow. Her husband died not long ago so she came back into nursing until she retires. She's got two grown-up children. Her daughter's a nurse in Canada.'

Jordan looks at her watch. 'Must go. See you later.'

I get a bus to Amma's and after supper, take a taxi to carry my luggage and me to the Nurses' Home. I could wait until morning but I want to unpack and settle in. I also want to surprise Sandy. I have almost finished unpacking when I hear her key in her lock.

'Hi there, Sandy.' She has just taken off her cap and is tousling her hair.

'What are you doing here? Have they thrown you out already?'

'Guess who is in charge of Ward 5?' I bow.

'What? Here, sit down and tell me what's happened.'

We talk well into the night even though it's only two days since we parted. I hear about Sandy settling into the skin diseases ward that she requested. She gets a peculiar satisfaction from smoothing ointments over bodies and having her hands permanently stained with gentian violet. I tell her about going to the Nurses' Home of the midwifery course only to find I couldn't start training after all and that I had come to LGI expecting to beg for a job and been greeted with open arms.

'Darcy wanted me to start stat. but I told her I didn't have any clothes or anywhere to live so I'm starting tomorrow at one. My room is next door but one.'

'We'll have to find a flat as soon as we can,' Sandy says. 'After six months living at Charlotte's, and now this...' She waves her arm to indicate the room.

'I'm supposed to start Part II on 1 June so it's not worth it,' I say. 'This isn't too bad. At least we don't need late passes. We're Big Girls now!'

Ward 5 is a male medical ward where the consultants specialise in chest complaints. I go on duty after dinner and by the time the night staff comes on, I feel as though I have never been away. Mason leaves at the end of the week and after three intensive days with her, I think I can cope with running the ward. After all, it is temporary. If it was really my ward, I would make the changes I have been contemplating all through training but I'm sure Sister Jenner would not appreciate coming back to different routines.

The day after Mason leaves I enter the ward at eight, alone. There are two staff nurses. Miss Darcy has promised a third, but I am the only perm. I walk to the centre table and all the nurses hurry over to it. We kneel and I read a prayer, randomly chosen from the cards that have been put out by the night staff. I feel a fraud. I am not a Christian and mouthing these words makes me feel insincere. But, I tell myself, it is part of the job.

I take the report from the senior night nurse. The staff nurses, Isobel Dawson and Carol Klein, make no move to join me so I call them over. Although they are not perms, they will function as such until Sister Jenner returns.

After report I say to them, 'You two will be acting as perms until Sister comes back so that is how I shall treat you. You still have to come on at 7.30 but otherwise we'll have coffee in the sideward and share weekends off – that sort of thing.' Their faces light up and I wonder what Jenner has been like.

I go over the report with them and ask Carol to make out the work list. As she is the senior of the two, she is my replacement. I start a round which means dragging the mobile file carrier with me, finding out how each man feels, examining him if necessary and checking each chart to see whether lab or other results are back. There are 34 patients on this ward and most of them have that wan, strained look of people with breathing difficulties.

Two patients have tracheotomies. A hole is made into the trachea and a small, metal, hollow tube is inserted and held in place by tapes that tie round the neck. An inner tube can be removed for cleaning. A spare is kept in hydrogen peroxide on a tray beside the bed. In most cases the inner tube is frequently blocked by mucous so it must be suctioned regularly. These patient's beds are surrounded by equipment: the tray for cleaning the tube, a portable suction, a tray of tubes to suction with and oxygen, which is delivered through a mask over the tracheotomy opening.

Before I have finished the round both ward doors are flung open and a large, florid man, in a blue pinstriped suit, strides in followed by an entourage of white-coated young men. It is Dr Harper, senior consultant on the ward. I go to meet him, trailing the file cabinet behind me.

'Who are you?' he asks without formality.

'Nurse Ross. I am Sister Jenner's replacement while she is off sick with glandular fever.'

'Oh.' Gimlet eyes stare at me and I stare back. I sense that here is a man who likes to intimidate. I refuse to be cowed. He gives way first and at his first bed his registrar takes the patient's chart that I hand him. He explains to the chief the diagnostic test results, treatment and progress since his last visit. As he talks, Dr Harper stares at me with a thoughtful gaze and I feel like a mouse in front of a snake.

He moves to the head of the bed and takes the patient's wrist to feel his pulse. 'How are you, my man?'

'Nicely, thank you sir,' the thin, breathless patient replies.

'I'd like to listen to your chest if I may.'

I pull the curtains and the group of medical students huddles closer to the bed. I help the patient off with his pyjama top so that Dr Harper can palpate and auscultate his chest.

'Did you examine his chest this morning, Nurse?'

I am taken aback by the question. Is he testing me? 'Yes, I did.' I do not add 'Sir'; in Yorkshire we do not use the title.

'And what did you hear?' The eyes are boring into me again.

'I heard rales at both bases and an irregular heart rhythm.'

'What is his sputum like?'

I take the sputum mug from the locker, open it and hold it out for Dr Harper to see.

'Is he having physio?' he asks.

'Yes, the physiotherapist comes every day and we do postural drainage as well.'

'What's his appetite like?'

I haven't been on the ward long enough to remember every patient's food intake but I say to the patient, 'You're not very hungry are you Mr Sykes?' and bless him, he says, 'Nay Doctor, I don't feel like eating nowt even though t'nurses try to make me tackle summat. Just not up to it, tha knows.'

'Good, good. Now you students, I want you each to listen to this man's chest. Nurse Ross has told you what you'll hear so I am going to watch your technique rather than hear your opinion.'

I seem to have passed his test of me, as he doesn't question me again. However, at the fourth patient, the round is held up because the patient's X-rays are not back from the radiography department.

'I will send someone to get them,' I say. 'They will be here before you finish so perhaps we can move on and come back to this patient.' I get the gimlet stare again but he doesn't say anything.

This is the first time I have attended a formal round. The two Princess Mary's consultants tend to breeze in and out and rarely do formal rounds. No one has instructed me on my role so I work it out for myself. First, I ensure that the patient's privacy is respected and that he is left comfortable after the physicians and students have examined him. Then I must be familiar with each patient's progress – how he sleeps, eats, moves and evacuates, and what the latest lab results show, or indeed, any other test. Finally, I must note all requests for further tests, such as stool or sputum examinations, blood work or X-rays, and make sure that requisitions and samples are sent. I must also arrange for discharge to home or to the Ida, and make appointments for other consultations such as with psychiatry.

A major round is conducted every day by one or other of the five consultants who have beds on Ward 5. In addition, I do rounds with their registrars, and sometimes housemen, although they are in and out all day. I am beginning to find out that being in charge is not quite the picnic I thought it was going to be.

Nurses decide how much a patient should be up, what he should eat or drink, whether he needs a laxative, how often his dressings are changed and when his stitches, if any, should come out. If a patient is ready to go home, it is the nurse's responsibility to ensure that there will be adequate care and arrange for the district nurse or home help, organise an ambulance to take him home and call the Lady Almoner if there is financial need.

I am gasping for a cup of coffee and as soon as Dr Harper and his firm have left, I head for the sideward. Sidewards used to he just that, places with one or two beds for patients on isolation, but now they are offices for sisters and perms and much of the ward business is conducted there over coffee or tea. I have just sat down when there is a knock at the door. I open it.

A student nurse says, 'Matron is on the ward.'

Damn! I start to unroll my sleeves as I enter the ward to see a tall, thin woman in a navy blue dress and a plain white cap standing by my desk. She is completely shapeless; straight up and down with no curves where one would expect to see them. I immediately think of an African carving of a Zulu. Her face is round and flat like a plate, housing two pale blue, watery eyes. It is a kind face though, and I think I could like her.

'Good morning, Matron.' I grab my cuffs from the desk and put them on.

'Good morning, Nurse Ross. I would like to do a full round.'

I escort her to the first bed and tell her about the patient there. I feel annoyed; mornings are our busiest times and Matron and her staff usually visit in the afternoon or evening. She says, 'Good morning, how are you?' to each patient but makes no comment to me. On the last lap, we come to a large, heavy man who is slumped down in the bed.

'I think he needs to sit up more, don't you Nurse? I will help you lift him.'

I take off my cuffs and we face each other on either side of the patient. I ask him to bend his knees and lean forward, and then we place our arms across his back and under his legs and grasp each other's forearms. A nod and we lift. The patient nearly shoots out of the top of the bed! Some nurses never manage to synchronise their lifts and find the load heavy and a strain on the back. When two experts lift together, it is effortless and effective. I appreciate that this Matron is clinically able and I look at her with respect. Is it my imagination or is she looking at me in the same way?

As she is about to leave, she stands at the door and says, 'I think your ward could be a little tidier, don't you nurse? And I noticed that one student's hair was not completely within her cap.'

She leaves. I feel like sticking my tongue out at her retreating figure. I want to say, 'For heaven's sake woman, how about an encouraging word for me? I've never been in complete charge before and all you can say is that the ward is untidy and someone's hair is loose.' I stomp into the sideward for my cold coffee wondering why I like her.

Chapter 22

28 April 1958

Dear Judith,

Thank you for your postcard from Portugal. That was a sensible place to choose for a honeymoon – the weather here's been terrible.

You will have got my long letter telling you about my hol in Austria and then coming back here. When I'd been back about a month, I decided to hell with Part II. Don't need it. And the thought of being up all night then having to work all day was too much. You know how I love my kip!

So, having made this big decision, Sandy and I found this flat. It's really nice; two bedrooms and more modern furniture than the last place. We even have a tiny fridge and a Hoovermatic washing machine. Mind you, we pay more, but as we're perms, we can afford it. We're going halvers on a television – howzat for luxury?

You know I told you this new Matron says we can't say 'poorly'? Well now she wants us to say 'in' a ward, not 'on' a ward! I try and find a reason to write 'on the ward' every time I send in a report.

I am working with two staff nurses, Isobel Dawson and Carol Klein. Do you know them? We are having a lot of fun together and our sideward is where the men come for coffee now. I gather that Jenner is a bit rigid. I'm not looking forward to her coming back as I'm enjoying being in charge.

What ho – I went riding last week for the first time since I got back. Livvy sends her love. She's just the same. 'Met this fella, Charles, at the Hunt Ball. I think he's tightening his girth to pop the question. Don't know what I'll say. Pop likes him. Good seat. But there's something odd about his tack. Wears strange cravats.'

I miss you. Love Jenny

3B Rosemount Crescent
Leeds

15 May 1958

Dear Judith,
Many thanks for your letter. I am so glad you're applying for Cambridge. I do hope you'll get in. The clinic job sounds lousy so I hope things look up soon.

If you get into Cambridge, will Alan set up practice there?

Sandy and I came off the scooter last week – I don't know why. She was OK but I've fractured my scaphoid so my arm is in a cast. Thank goodness it's my left arm so I can still write. The best thing about it all is I am under the care of Geoff Mitchell, the orthopaedic registrar. He is absolutely gorgeous! He is tall and wears cavalry twill trousers and check shirts. I get breathless when I see him!! I have to have this cast on for six weeks so it will still be on when Jenner comes back. He says to see him if I'm worried about the cast. Can you think of a good reason why I should be? I thought of 'accidentally' getting into the bath with it on, but then I thought he'd think I'm stupid. Do you know of a drug that makes your arms swell?

The funniest thing happened. Remember I told you Matron has an orange mini? You know her garage has two doors – one to the outside and one you can reach from the hospital. Well, the housemen broke in one night and carried the car out into the main corridor. It blocked the traffic for hours before someone told her. She's had a padlock put on the door.

Love Jen

3B Rosemount Crescent
Leeds

15 June 1958

Dear Judith,

Thank you for your letter. I think it is wonderful that
you are moving to Cambridge and Alan has a shared
practice. When will you hear from the university?

Jenner is back. The first thing she did was check the
supplies and complain that there weren't enough new
thermometers. I had ordered them but she didn't want
to hear. Isobel and Carol aren't allowed to have coffee
in the sideward any more and the men have stopped
coming. Some poor nurse forgot to plug in the food
trolley so the plates weren't hot enough for her, so she
made them wash them in hot water. While they were
doing this, the supper got cold! I'm going to the office
soon to see where I can move to.

I get my cast off this week. Sandy sends her love.
Oh, I nearly forgot. We had a letter from Marie. She's
pregnant but wants to come home to have the baby.

Love Jenny

Ward 9

Leeds General Infirmary

17 July 1958

Dear Judith,

Many thanks for the Get Well card. Sandy told me she'd written to tell you I was in. NO, I did not do this just to see Geoff Mitchell! Though, I must say he is the only bright spark on an otherwise dull horizon. He comes to see me every day. Mmmm!

Well, I got my cast off, had two weeks of physio and then I went to see Gorgeous for my final check. The very next day, I went riding. I was on a new horse and we were just standing after a gallop when it suddenly took off. Before I could get my balance, it ran under a tree and a branch knocked me off. I have cracked my pelvis and two ribs. Bloody painful I can tell you. Nothing displaced though, so I don't have to be in a cast. I can probably go home next week on crutches.

It's quite interesting being on the other side of the bed so to speak. You certainly find out which nurses you want and which you don't. Some leave you feeling comfy for hours and some leave you feeling as if you are sitting on sandpaper.

I got a huge bunch of flowers from Livvy. She feels terrible but it wasn't her fault.

Matron came round yesterday. She didn't seem

terribly sympathetic. Said she hoped I'd be back on my feet soon and to be more careful in future. Miss Darcy was really kind. When I told her I was going to sell my jodhpurs and give up riding for knitting, she said, 'Oh no, you mustn't do that. Get back on a horse as soon as you can.' She sat down and we talked for ages. She used to ride and came off several times.

Must end. It's difficult to write in this position.

Love Jen

Amma's House
Leeds

6 August 1958

Dear Judith,

CONGRATULATIONS! How wonderful! When does term start? When you're a famous barrister, will you still talk to me? I'm going to brag about my friend who is reading law at Cambridge!

I'm at Amma's being spoilt by her and my aunts. I have to be on crutches for another two weeks and then I can start to walk. I hope to be back at work by the end of the month. I'm bored stiff!

Sandy has applied for a night sister's job. I expect she'll get it so she'll be on nights on 1 September.

Love Jenny

3B Rosemount Crescent

Leeds

12 September 1958

Dear Judith,

Thank you for your letter. I'm glad Alan is enjoying his practice and that you both love Cambridge. Your new flat sounds very posh.

Not much to tell you. Sandy is in blue, on nights, so I hardly see her. I'm back on Jenner's ward because both Sylvia and Carol left and they need me until the new staff nurse has settled in. Then I might be able to transfer.

Saw Wee Jess briefly as she passed through Leeds. She's a fully-fledged midwife now and is going on the district near Settle.

Love Jenny

3B Rosemount Crescent

Leeds

3 October 1958

Dear Judith,

What's it like being an undergraduate student? Do you wear a gown and ride a bicycle? Write a long letter and tell me all about it.

I have applied for a night sister's job starting 1 November. When I took my application in to Matron, she said she had grave misgivings about putting my name forward. 'You're not exactly harum-scarum but...' Honestly – just because I fell off a scooter and a horse does not make me an unsuitable sister. No one else has applied so I expect I'll get it. I shall be glad to leave Ward 5. Jenner manages to make the ward a dull place to work. She's so routine-bound, she drives me crazy. When I'm a ward sister my ward is going to be fun to work on.

When are you coming north again?

Love Jenny

Chapter 23

Dear Miss Ross,

It gives me great pleasure to inform you that your appointment as a night sister was confirmed at the meeting of the House Committee yesterday. Your appointment will commence on 1 November 1958.

Yours sincerely,
Ann Wilks, Matron

A SISTER AT LAST! I change into my long-sleeved blue dress with its stiff collar and fasten on the familiar apron. I handle my LGI badge affectionately as I pin it on the bib. I went through a lot to earn it. Then comes the bonnet. Sandy showed me how to make the semi-circle of starched muslin with its fluted edge into a mass of frill that I am about to place on my head. It required sewing a running stitch with strong thread and then pulling the thread to gather the stiff material into the size of a small pudding basin. Two starched ribbons are pinned to the inside and the loose ends tie in a bow under my chin.

Sandy also showed me how to wet the starch out of the parts that run next to my neck so that they don't chafe. I already have a permanent red mark around my neck from my collar and I don't need more disfigurements.

I had my hair set this afternoon and I have to admit that I am pleased with the image in the mirror. Perhaps I am not so old-looking after all. Perhaps those wrinkles under my eyes will disappear with sleep. I am 24.

It is nearly 9pm. I dread leaving the locker room. I wish Sandy was here but as junior night sister, she is up at the Ida. I know that as I meet nurses coming off duty they will say to each other, 'Hey, look! Ross is in blue,' the sort of comment I have made many times before.

I brace myself and head down the covered passage from the Nurses' Home to Matron's office. I am excited. It will be fun to be on nights with Sandy, and Sister Busby is the Night Superintendent. She is with Matron when I arrive and I greet the other two night sisters whom I know slightly. They are busy with pieces of paper but I have no idea what to do.

'I don't know what section Buzz will give you, so I can't be much help I'm afraid,' Todd says. 'The first thing we do is find out who the sickest patients are and who has been to theatre. You need to know quickly because their relatives phone about 11.' She hands me a small black box that I clip into my pocket. 'As soon as you know which wards you're covering, phone the front-hall porter and give him the number of your beeper and your wards. When you get phone calls from outside or from your wards, he'll beep you.'

Sister Busby emerges from the inner sanctum. 'Well, Jen Ross, I thought you'd show up sooner or later. Nice to see you. How does it feel to be in blue?'

'I feel damn silly as a matter of fact. I have no idea what I'm doing.'

'Oh, you'll soon get the hang of it. I'm letting you off lightly tonight as I will take two of your wards.' She hands me a list of wards and a sheaf of reports. 'I'll take these wards,' she says as she ticks off two numbers, 'and you do the others. I do theatre and casualty every night. Let's go.'

We walk down the main corridor that is empty except for a hurrying houseman in the distance. Even though Busby has taken two of my wards I am still responsible for 170 patients.

'Just go into your wards and see the sickest. It's a lot easier now that staff nurses are on some wards at night as they can give out the sleeping pills. We had to do that at one time, remember? Let me see – you better go to Ward 18 first and then 17, as there are student nurses in charge and you will have to do the o.n.'s [sleeping pills]. Visit them more often as well, especially 18 as Sage is on.' Buzz rolls her eyes. 'Sage is a misnomer if ever there was one – she's as thick as two planks! See you later. Beep me if you need help.' She swings through the outer door of a ward as I walk on towards Ward 18.

I want to be a good sister. I think I am competent but mostly I want to be a good teacher. I remember how much I learned from Busby when she was my night sister. She taught me how and what to observe, what was important, what wasn't, and she inspired me to study my textbooks. I do not want to be a stickler for trivial detail like the Dragon nor a bully like the Sod. I do not want to instill fear in the students but nor do I want to let poor nursing care pass me by.

Ward 18 is a male ear, nose and throat (ENT) ward. There have been nine surgeries today but all minor, such as removal of nasal polyps. It should he fairly quiet but there is a general air of disturbance, as if two emergencies have just been admitted. There is certainly no sense that here is a ward settling down for the night.

A big, heavy-set student nurse lumbers down the ward to meet me. From the stripe on her sleeve I see that she is in third year, so this must he Nurse Sage.

'Good evening, Sister,' she says. I almost want to look over my shoulder to see whom she is talking to. It is the first time I have been addressed as 'Sister' and I wonder how long it will take me to get used to it.

'Good evening, Nurse Sage. Shall we do the o.n's? Where is your runner?'

'I'll go and get her.' Sage trudges down to the bottom of the ward. I stand fuming. She seems surprised that we are to give out sleeping pills at this time of night. I look at my notes and start to check on the post-op patients. At the third patient, Sage and the runner come to tell me they are ready.

We all move to the first bed. 'Where are the drugs?' I ask.

'Oh, I'm sorry. I left them on the desk. I'll just get them.' Sage goes to the desk and finds the tray of bottles of sleeping pills.

'Nurse Sage, you know perfectly well that you don't leave o.n. drugs lying around. They are to be kept locked up at all times.'

'Well, I knew you would be here soon, so I left them ready.'

'That is no reason to leave them unlocked. You do not get them out until the night sister is actually on the ward.' I have only been in blue an hour and here I am telling someone off. Only moments before I was dreaming of being a super teacher who doesn't carp, but leaving narcotics where patients could get them is serious and Sage should know better.

We make our way round the ward. I check the bottles from which Sage takes the pills against the patient's charts. All her movements are so slow that I want to shake her but at least she can read and hands me the right bottles. I do manage to examine the post-ops on the way round but I am way behind time.

My beeper buzzes as we near the end and the runner heads for the phone to find out where I am needed. She reaches the door, then turns, comes to me and says 'I'm sorry Sister, but I don't know your name.'

'Ross,' I say. 'I should have introduced myself.' The call is from a relative. Fortunately, about one of the patients I have just seen.

The next ward is in darkness when I enter and the two students quickly come to me, the senior with the tray of sleeping pills she has just removed from the cupboard. We make rapid progress around the ward. I finish the round with them, go to see the sickest patients, then set off for my next four wards. These have staff nurses on so I only need to visit the patients on my list.

Promptly at 11pm my beeper starts buzzing as relatives phone to inquire about their loved ones. I try to remember something about the patients so that I don't sound like an automaton. I refer to the patient by name and say, for example, that she is having a bit of pain but that we have given her something, or that she will feel better in the morning. Or else, 'Well, he's still very poorly luv, but we're doing all we can to make him comfortable.' I am over-whelmed by the gratitude that is expressed.

When I finish my last round, I head for the office where I can sit and deal with the phone calls over a cup of tea. The others are doing the same and several housemen are lounging around drinking tea. I know most of them but not the one for ENT. Before I have time to ask, a pale, sandy haired young man says, 'Are you doing Wards 17 and 18?'

'Yes, I'm Jenny Ross. It's my first night.'

'I'm Mike Cardiff – ENT houseman. How are things?'

'Pretty quiet. There is one man, Phillips I think.' I shuffle through my notes. 'Yes, Phillips. He's got half his packing out already. Says it's making him itch. What would you like me to do if he pulls it all out?'

'Just leave it. If he starts to bleed you can re-pack but I don't think he will.' Mike yawns. 'There's a woman on 17 I'm a bit worried about. Mrs Tufts. She sprang a temperature today and I'm not sure what's going on. Keep an eye on her, will you?'

I write down 'Tufts' on Ward 17's page. The other night sisters are also comparing notes with housemen. When they have finished, the housemen go to bed and we all head for the dining room for dinner. I walk alongside Busby.

'It's our job to see they get a good night's sleep,' she says. 'They're on call 24 hours a day with a half day off a week. It's ridiculous! How can they be expected to function if they're up half the night?' We swing off down the stairs to the dining room. 'So you'll have to make decisions for them. Don't get them up to certify a death if it's expected – only if it's not. And make judgements about treatment. They'll back you up.'

We collect our dinners from the kitchen, as there is no maid service at night.

'We had one houseman, Geoff Spratley. Do you remember him?' Busby continues. I nod. 'He comes bouncing in as Houseman of the Year, cocky as hell, didn't want us to make decisions for him, oh no. How could we, mere nurses, know anything? Well, it only took about two weeks of waking him up every hour about something and he was begging for mercy.' She chuckles. 'We stop them from getting too big for their boots.'

'Nurse Sage.' I say to Busby. She grins. 'How on earth has she got this far?'

'Yes she is difficult to handle but she is better than she used to be.'

'She drove me crazy within five minutes. She'd left the o.n's on the desk all ready for a patient to come and help himself.'

'I hope you reprimanded her.'

'Yes, I did. My first encounter with a nurse as a sister and I'm telling her off. Good start, eh?'

'As long as you're telling them with the intent of teaching them.' Busby pauses. 'Jen, you have to remember, these are students. We expect far too much of them as it is and we must allow them to grow up and make mistakes.'

'I do want to be a good teacher,' I say. 'I find it hard to correct them because I remember, only too well, certain sisters making my life a misery by continually picking on me. I am not going to be like that.'

Busby's beeper goes off and she gets up to use the phone. 'Got to go to Casualty,' she says as she stuffs sponge pudding into her mouth. 'See you later.'

There are three other night sisters, two I met in the office and one who is on the Brotherton Wing for private patients. 'What happens now?' I ask.

'We do full rounds. You can make it a teaching round with the junior if you like, but it's better to know the patients before you do. We're usually back in the office at three, if we're lucky.'

I love the hospital at night. It's dimmed lights, hushed quiet and empty corridors are such a contrast to the bustle of the day. I stop to gaze at the huge stained-glass windows which flank the main staircase, showing angels succouring the sick and wounded. I have never really looked at them before. They are so very Victorian; like the rest of the hospital.

A full round on my first ward is interrupted by a call to give morphia, which student nurses must have checked by a State Registered Nurse. Morphia now comes in glass ampoules, not as tablets to be melted in a teaspoon over a spirit lamp. I have to flick the ampoule with my forefinger to make the fluid in the stem sink down, saw off the stem with a small file, and then withdraw the fluid with a syringe.

I enter Ward 18 telling myself that I must not get exasperated with Nurse Sage but my resolution is short-lived. There is not a nurse in sight. I walk down the length of the ward and find Sage and her runner in the sterilising room.

'Surely the rule that there must be a nurse on the ward at all times was drummed into you when you were peaks?

Supposing a patient called out or fell out of bed while you were both in here?'

The runner looks as if she's just been sentenced to life imprisonment but Sage's expression is vacant and she says nothing.

'I would like to do a full round, Nurse Sage,' I say and march back on to the ward to the first bed. I am fuming, not only because of her error but because she has so quickly shattered my image of myself as a tolerant, benevolent sister. Is this why sisters become over-bearing? People like Buzz do not respond to students with exasperation but I do remember that she tore a strip off Marie for praying beside a patient's bed. I must consult with her on how to deal with stupid nurses like Sage.

I calm down as we go round. Sage knows her patients well and I hear her address a sleepless patient in a warm, kind way. Just as our round is over I get an urgent call to see a woman with a plugged tracheotomy. The nurse had removed the inner tube to clean it but before she could insert a clean one, the patient coughed violently and plugged the outer tube.

'We'll have to change the outer tube,' I say to the staff nurse. 'Have you done it before?'

'No, Sister,' she says. 'I'm too scared to.'

Out of the hearing of the patient I say, 'Stand by with a pair of forceps, just in case the hole starts to close before I can get the new one in.'

A slit trachea will close immediately if the object holding it open is removed. I select a new outer tube and prepare the tapes for it. I explain what I am going to do to the patient and ask her to try not to cough. I cut the tapes of the blocked tube, twist it, pull it out and quickly insert the clean one. I hold it in place while the staff nurse ties the tapes and then we insert a fresh inner tube.

At the door, I ask the nurse if she thinks she could do that again. 'Remember to check that all the parts fit before you do it,' I say. 'I put one in once and none of the inner tubes were the right size. Big flap to find the right ones.'

More calls: a post-op patient's wound is bleeding, a diabetic is sweating, a man can't urinate, a drip is plugged, a suction won't suck. 'Much like days,' I think, 'except I have to walk further.' So far nothing has happened that I can't cope with and I am enjoying the alacrity with which the nurses move to meet me. Their respectful attitude reminds me of the power of the uniform I am wearing. I vow not to abuse it.

I manage to be in the office for tea at three. I get a call from the Ida hospital. 'How's it going?' Sandy asks.

'Not so bad. Busy all the time even though Buzz is covering a couple of wards for me. How's it up there?'

'Quiet as a grave as usual. Boring. Anyway, not much longer. In a few weeks, you'll be up here until a new night sister comes on.'

'Todd's leaving, so it won't be for long.'

'Is she? Where's she going?'

'Into the RAF. More chance of meeting a man she says.'

'Have you met Philip Brown yet?' Sandy asks. 'I've got quite a crush on him. He's so much fun! Livens everyone up.'

'No, he wasn't in the office tonight. He's houseman for Pearson and Cokes isn't he?' I yawn loudly. I always feel terrible between three and four in the morning.

'Yes, but they all change over at the end of the month so he'll be on one of the medical firms.'

'Whoops, there goes my beeper. Got to go.' I hang up and dial the hall porter to see where I'm needed. Urgent call for Ward 11. There's a staff nurse in charge so it must be something serious. I hurry down the main corridor.

In Ward 11, there are curtains drawn around a bed and a dim light silhouettes the figures of two nurses. I enter the cubicle to see a staff nurse placing an oxygen mask over a man's face. He is deathly pale, breathing in deep sighs, and is unconscious.

'It's Mr Peterson, Sister. Cancer of the liver. He was open and shut about a week ago. Metastases everywhere. He was alright until a few minutes ago, then he collapsed.'

'Can you get me his chart, please.' I note that he has a wife, does not have a telephone, like the majority of people in Leeds, and that he is Roman Catholic.

I go to the phone outside the inner ward doors, call the

hall porter and ask Busby to call me on Ward 11. A couple of minutes later the phone rings. I answer it.

'Sister Ross.'

'Buzz here. What's up?'

I tell her about the patient and then ask if I should get the houseman up.

'What do you think?' Trust Busby to throw the ball back to me.

'Well, as he's riddled with cancer, there's nothing the houseman can do, so I wouldn't get him up. I'd leave a note for him to come here first thing in the morning.'

'Right. I agree with you. What else are you going to do?'

'Send for his wife. He lives in Armley. How do I find the number of the local police station?'

'The front desk will have it.'

'Also, he's R.C. Is it the same number for a priest as on days?'

'Yes,' says Busby. 'You seem to be coping OK. Bye.'

I phone the hall porter, get the number of the Armley police station and dial it.

'Armley police.'

'This is Sister Ross at the Infirmary. I wonder if you could go and knock up a Mrs Peterson at 5 Pooley Grove and ask her to phone me.'

'Right you are, Sister. Her husband is it? I'll stay with her.'

The police are wonderful. They are so kind to the people we ask them to deliver bad news to; they stay with them at the telephone kiosk, ring for a taxi, see to pets in the house, and inform the neighbours the next day. We couldn't do without them.

A priest says he'll be there in 15 minutes and I go into the ward to ask the staff nurse to get ready for last rites. My buzzer goes. Mrs Peterson is on the phone.

'Hello, Mrs Peterson. This is Sister Ross. I'm afraid I have bad news for you.'

'Been taken badly, has he Sister?'

'Yes luv. I think it's best if you come here right away.'

'Ay, I'll do that. We're Catholics tha' knows. Shall I send for t'priest?'

'I've already done that, Mrs Peterson. Ask the bobby to get you a taxi and I'll see you when you get here.'

I ask the staff nurse to let me know when Mrs Peterson arrives and go back to the office. The others are putting on clean aprons for morning rounds and I do the same. We wear the same one to start the next night but we like to look fresh in the morning when the patients are awake.

The last phone call of the night is at about 7am. A staff nurse tells me that one of her patients put a denture cup, with her false teeth in it, on the bathroom windowsill and a seagull has flown off with them.

'You're kidding me,' I say.

'No, I'm not Sister,' she says laughing. 'It's true. The patient saw the gull swoop down and before she could do anything, it picked up her teeth and flew off.'

I phone the nearest police station. 'Sister Ross from the Infirmary. If you see a seagull with false teeth, would you arrest it for theft?'

Chapter 24

'SANDY, TELL ME something funny or interesting before I drop dead from boredom,' I say on the phone.

Now I am night sister at the Ida, I can understand why Sandy was anxious to return to the Infirmary. The four wards of convalescing patients, staffed by eight student nurses, do not provide enough work or stimulation to keep me interested. Even though I do at least one teaching round every night, I still have hours of empty time and as these occur between three and six, it is hard to keep awake. Phoning the Infirmary, when I know the night sisters will be having tea in the office, is the highlight of my night.

'Well, you know this group of housemen, with Philip Brown as ringleader, is completely crazy? Tonight one of them jumped out of a first-floor window into a blanket the others were holding but the blanket gave way. Now he's in Casualty with a query fractured pelvis.'

'Who was it?'

'Hamid Imam. Do you know him?'

'Yes, he was on Ward 5. What else has been happening?'

'I wish I could talk but my beeper has just gone. Bye.'

I wish my beeper would go but I don't even have one as my office is within easy reach of the four wards. I make myself a tray of tea in the main kitchen and return, yawning, to my office.

The Ida hospital is in the countryside outside Leeds. Instead of sounds of traffic, we hear cocks crowing, owls hooting and the rustling of grass made by nocturnal creatures. Wards are smaller than the main hospital and beds are arranged in rooms that lead off each other. This more casual arrangement and the reduction in bustle makes for a peaceful, tranquil atmosphere.

Most of the patients are convalescing. Instead of tables being used for treatment equipment, they are covered with jigsaw puzzles and crib boards. Six children, all bedridden at present, are kept entertained by adult patients and during the day their cots are wheeled out on to the veranda.

Some patients, those without family, come here to die, though we do not admit this. We try to pretend that patients are getting well, but in my experience so far, they know very well that they are dying. We keep up the pretence anyway. Families are told the prognosis and it is up to them to inform the patient. In most cases, they do not.

'Sister, come quick! I think Mr Ravinsky has died.' The junior nurse sounds alarmed.

'You seem surprised,' I say. 'Didn't you know he was dying?'

'No Sister,' she says and starts to cry.

'Sit down a minute. Have a cup of tea. There's no need to rush back.' I remember how Buzz had comforted me when baby Nicholas died. 'Some sisters might think you're unprofessional when you cry, but I'm pleased that you care so much. It's when we stop crying that we're in trouble.'

'He was such a nice man,' the young nurse sobs. 'I feel so sorry for him. He lost all his family in the concentration camps. He was only 62. I'm sure he died of a broken heart.'

'You're probably right, even though he had cancer.' When she calms down a bit, I say, 'Let's both lay him out as our last act of respect for him.'

There is no morgue at the Ida so we wheel the body into a garage to await transport in the morning. Mr Ravinsky has only a distant cousin living in London so I decide to wait until morning to notify her.

I am sitting addressing Christmas cards and writing annual letters one night when the phone rings. It is Sandy. 'Good news, Jen. There's a new night sister coming on next week. Guess who it is?'

'No idea. Tell me.'

'Milbury.'

I suddenly feel awake. 'Oh no! Don't tell me I have to work with her again. I can't stand her.' My thoughts go back to the Dragon's ward when Milbury lied about her seniority and told the staff nurse that I had not changed a patient. I have seen her in the corridor sometimes. She always gives me a big smile. I smile back through gritted teeth.

'It will be a long time before you actually do work with her because she'll be going to the Ida. As no one has plans to leave, she might be there a long time. I don't think you'll make it down here for Christmas though, as she starts December first and should have a month here.'

'I'll have to start praying.' I don't want to be here, alone, for Christmas and miss all the fun at the Infirmary.

A couple of weeks later I am heating up my dinner in the kitchen when I hear a car draw up. The outside door bursts open and six housemen, rather the worse for beer, tumble in singing 'The First Noel'. Philip Brown, an enormous young man who should be a champion rugby player, picks me up and whirls me round the kitchen.

'Thought we'd come and cheer you up,' he says. 'What have you got in the way of cheer?' He opens the fridge. 'A dry house, I see. We'll have to do something about that!' He leaves the kitchen to go to the car and returns with several bottles of beer.

We sit round the table drinking except for Paul who is peering at the clocking-in machine. 'What's this?'

'It's for the domestic staff to clock in and out,' I say.

'How does it work?'

'They take their card from that rack, put it in that slot

and pull the handle. The time they do it is … NO, don't fool with their cards – they'll get into trouble.'

Unfortunately, there's a pile of letters, mostly Christmas cards, for Miss Hawkins, the Assistant Matron in charge of the Ida. Before I can stop him, Paul takes each letter and runs it through the machine so that it ends up with a hole in it and a time stamped on it. I sigh as I wonder what excuses to make up.

I am feeling so cheerful after they all leave that I stop worrying about the letters and take the empty beer bottles out to my scooter bag. Then I leave the door to the kitchen open to get rid of the smell of a pub.

Mid-December and I am still at the Ida. I am resigned to spending Christmas there. Then the phone rings.

'Buzz here. I want you back at the Infirmary after your nights off. Milbury will replace you. You will have to cover her nights off sometimes, like the others, but otherwise you'll be down here.'

I am overjoyed. A few minutes later Sandy phones. 'You got the good news?' Her voice lowers. 'To be perfectly honest, I don't think Buzz can stand Milbury. She's always sucking up to her and that does not go down with Buzz at all. She's always saying, "Yes Sister Busby, No Sister Busby." It's enough to make you puke.'

'So she hasn't changed much – still the blue-eyed girl. What does Buzz do?'

'Nothing really. It's just the expression on her face that gives her away. Anyway, I'm so pleased you'll he here. No one is nights off on the 24th or 25th so we'll have a really good time.'

I have my nights off and go back to work on Christmas Eve. As we are all on, we have fewer wards to cover and as these are half-empty, we are not at all busy. Sandy and I meet after our first round to visit the wards to look at the decorations.

Decorating the wards at Christmas is a major activity at the Infirmary. It is so important that a silver cup is awarded to the best-decorated ward. Each ward has an enormous tree in the middle covered in baubles and hangings that patients have made or donated over the years. After that, it is up to the ingenuity of the ward staff and patients. The one we like best has cardboard cutouts of stockings with toys hanging out of them, attached to each vertical bed rail. On the centre table is a cardboard sleigh and a Father Christmas made of stuffed clothes and a papier mache head. The sleigh is filled with gaily-covered parcels.

'That's really clever,' Sandy says. 'I hope they win the cup.'

We go back to the office, which is packed with housemen, some drinking from the teapot and others from various bottles. They pair each other off and take it in turns to be on call and therefore sober. Philip is wearing a Santa hat to go with his false beard and red robes that are draped over a chair. He has been elected to visit the children's wards and fill their stockings. All the patients hang up stockings that the night staff fill with nuts, tangerines and toiletries, but only the children receive a visit from Father Christmas.

Philip comes up to me. 'Have you been a good little girl?'

'Oh yes, Santa,' I say in a falsetto voice.

He gives me a big kiss as a reward. At midnight he sets off with his sack as we go for dinner and the other housemen go to bed. They have left a coal fire burning in their sitting room so we go there after dinner rather than to the office. We are in and out attending to our wards but otherwise we sit in the glow of the fire enjoying our leisure and each other's company.

'Buzz,' I say sleepily, 'I want to know what you got the MBE for.'

'Do you now?'

'Yes, come on Buzz, tell us,' the others say.

'I got it for doing my duty, which is more than I can say for you lot right now.' She won't tell us even though we go on nagging.

We sleep through Christmas Day and so miss the consultants' visits with their families, the carving of the turkey in the middle of the ward by one of them and the tea for patients and their visitors. We also miss the staff dinner when the sisters wait on the nurses and the housemen wait on the sisters. The cup for the best-decorated ward is given out at the sisters' dinner. We hear later that the ward with the Santa in the sleigh won it.

By the time we come on duty the hospital is quiet, though some parties are still going on in side wards. I arrive early so I can visit Casualty before BB goes off but they are busy with a car accident, a child who swallowed a sixpence in the Christmas pudding, several drunks and a man with his finger lodged in a 'build-yourself-a-clock' part. So I go up to Princess Mary to say hello to Howes and admire the theme of spinning tops they have used as decorations.

'I hear you're leaving,' I say to Howes.

'Yes, at the end of February. I'm joining the RAF. Four of us are.'

'How are you at saluting?' I ask.

'We have a month of drills and things but then we're posted to a hospital and it will be much as usual. It's time I left. When the housemen start looking like boys, it's time to go. Why don't you apply for the ward?'

I hesitate. 'Much as I love it, I want more experience with adults. And it's too soon for me; I'll only have been on nights for three months.'

I wonder if I should apply. With my experience as a perm there, I stand a good chance. But such a special ward is out of the mainstream and my experience would then be limited to sick infants. I would like to be well rounded so I can travel in the future. I give up the idea.

A few days later the sister's pantomime is performed. Because we're on duty at nine we have to go to the first house at seven when the audience is mostly night staff and patients. The second house at 9.30 is much more interesting as Matron and the consultants are there.

BB organises the pantomime. All who are interested meet in November and join one of three teams: actors who revise a script and play parts in the actual pantomime, the dance chorus and the singing chorus. One or other of the choruses separates scenes of the plot. This year it is *Aladdin in LGI*. Part of the repertoire of the dance chorus is 'She wore an itsy-bitsy, teeny-weeny, yellow polka dot bikini,' with the nurses dressed accordingly.

The singing chorus composes verses to well-known tunes and there are songs for housemen, registrars, surgeons, physicians, and nurses. The housemen's song is to the tune of 'John Peel'. One of the verses is:

> *Philip Brown is too big by far*
> *To try and drive a midget car,*
> *For we'd rather have you as you are,*
> *So don't drive so fast, is our warning.*

'My Old Man's a Dustman' is the tune for the surgeons' song. One verse is:

Oh, way down in the cellar
You'll find the ENT
Syringing in the darkness
We have Consultants three.

Tom, Oliver and Peter are such a jolly crew
It gives us all great pleasure
To clean out ears for you.

Of all the songs, I enjoy the verse about Matron the best.
To the tune of 'Quartermaster's Store', we hear:

In navy blue, blue, the new girl takes her pew
Sitting there, in Matron's chair.
In a while, while, we may even see her smile
And she'll lose that icy stare.

I wish I could have seen her face.

Two nights later, the housemen retaliate and their show
has a printed programme.

LOOK BACK IN ANGER
Or
THE ATOMIC PILE

Part the first:
1. Good Fairy Mason
2. When in Casualty do as the Romans do

3. Dr Benghatti impersonated by Dr H. Imam
4. FLASH for inner cleanliness
5. From here to Maternity
6. I'll be sewing you

INTERMISSION

Part the second:
1. Dance: Staphs and Streps Forever by the Corpses des Ballet
2. The RMO's Lament: It had to be flu
3. Myxoedema Madness
4. It's spleen a long, long time
5. Old Man's Liver
6. Thanks for the Mammaries
7. Dance Macabre

Produced and written by Alan and Dick
BROWN appears by kind permission of the night sisters.
IMAM appears by kind permission of President Nasser.
WICKHAM appears without permission.

The housemen traditionally perform one of the dances from the sister's pantomime wearing the same costumes. Of course they dance to 'She Wore An Itsy-Bitsy, Teeny-Weeny, Yellow Polka Dot Bikini'. The itsy-bitsy bikinis are stretched to breaking point but they just manage to prevent the show from becoming pornographic.

Christmas celebrations at LGI end with a grass hockey match between the housemen and sisters and perms. As many as possible play and the rules are ill-defined and flexible. Not everyone has a hockey stick but we rob physiotherapy of its walking sticks and use them. There is often more than one ball.

Running up and down a field in the fresh air is just what we all need after the intense activity of the last few days. We know the hospital will fill up so we make the most of our leisure. I go home glowing from the exercise and thinking that although our social activities are restricted to the hospital, we have much more fun than those outside it.

Chapter 25

3B Rosemount Crescent

Leeds

15 January 1959

Dear Mum and Dad,

Very many thanks for the cheque. I'm saving it for my holiday in Norway next month. A group of housemen and trained staff are going to a youth hostel there. It is in the middle of nowhere I believe, so all there is to do is ski.

I had a wonderful Christmas and it sounds like you did too. How did you enjoy being Father Christmas, Dad? I was on duty but we have such a good time no one wants to be off duty except the very new nurses. I hope I am not on nights this coming Christmas, as I want to be in the pantomime.

The scooter is running well though it has let me down a few times and it's looking a bit battered now. Can't think of anything else to say.

Love Jenny

3B Rosemount Crescent

Leeds

4 March 1959

Dear Judith,

I'm writing this at the Ida where I'm relieving
Milbury's nights off. She's stuck with being up here
because she's the junior and as no one plans on
leaving, she'll be here for a while. Ha ha!

I had a super time in Norway. Our party of 16 took
over the youth hostel though there were one or two
others. Eight housemen, five sisters and three perms
went. We skied from the door but there was no lift so
we had to walk up the hill to ski down. You should see
my muscles!

As everyone was so exhausted when we arrived, we
slept for several days and they thought we were the
dullest lot that had ever been there. When we recov-
ered, they changed their minds! We had to make our
own entertainment but with people like Philip Brown
and Hamid Imam, that wasn't difficult. They've all
finished in the house now and are off in all directions.
Philip is going into general practice in York, Hamid is
going home and Paul Wickham wants to be a surgeon.
I shall miss them. I am sure the next lot will be dull by
comparison.

The youth hostel had amazing bedding – great big

down-filled bags in white covers that kept you so warm. Why we can't get them in England, I don't know. And they had central heating. Why are we so backward?

Are you getting on any better with your tutor? He sounds *trés formidable*. Write soon.

Love Jenny

3B Rosemount Crescent
Leeds

1 June 1959

Dear Judith,
Good luck in your exams. I am sure you will do well, as usual.

Yes, I'm still on nights. I'm getting tired – never do sleep well during the day. Sandy and I have had nights off together for a while now and we have been hiking in the Dales a lot. Busby is still around and Milbury has finally come down from the Ida. She has improved, has stopped sucking up to Buzz and although I don't like her, I can tolerate her.

Did I say the next group of housemen would be dull? I was wrong. Their favourite antic was trolley races down the main corridor with one of them on the trolley, until the RMO [Resident Medical Officer] put a stop to it when someone fell off and was admitted with a head injury. Then Sam Spooner got drunk one night, passed out and the others put stitches in his abdomen. They told him he'd had his appendix out. He believed them until he realised there was no incision.

You remember that bust of a famous surgeon halfway up the main staircase? Well, the housemen kept chalking eye patches and noses on it so Management protected it with a round glass cover like a porthole. How they did it, I don't know, but the housemen managed to fill it with water and put gold-fish in it. Funniest sight I've seen for a long time – fish swimming around Lord M's physog.

I did a round with a junior the other night and she was so nervous, her notes shook. I don't know what to do so they aren't scared of me. Not everyone is mind you. I had done my 3am round on a ward but forgot something. When I went back, a nurse was carrying a tray of tea and a fry-up into the ward. She looked at me, said, 'Whoops' and whirled back into the kitchen. I suppose I should have said something but I didn't. It's neglect of patients that I scream about, not things like eating on the ward. I did my nut when I found the GU (genito-urinary) ward with all the lights on at midnight. The nurse had put them on to change the drainage bottles. Can you believe it? Instead of using a torch, she woke everyone up.

The one thing I hate about nights is having to give

the report to Matron every morning. We take it in turns because the last one in doesn't get off duty until 9am. She is such a cold fish but somehow I sense that she would like to reach out only she doesn't know how. I think she believes that if she lets down her guard she will lose our respect. The only time she was human was when Bates rubbed her eyes and her contact lens fell on the floor. They were both on their knees looking for it!

I am so looking forward to seeing you when you come home in the hols.

Love Jen

3B Rosemount Crescent
Leeds

19 August 1959

Dear Mum and Dad,
Guess what? I have bought a new Lambretta. I was able to trade in the old one and with the money you sent for my birthday and some savings, a gleaming, beautiful scooter sits in the driveway. It has much better brakes, starts easier and has a better windscreen.

Judith was home for a few days. I went over to see her on the new scooter and we had several runs out as the weather was wonderful. She did really well in her exams as I thought she would. She really is very bright and deserves to be at Cambridge. She and Alan seem to be happy enough though they don't see much of each other as he has a busy practice and she is studying all the time.

Sandy started on days as ward sister on the skin ward on 1 August. It is just the ward she wanted. I shall apply for the next ward that comes up as I'm tired of nights.

Love Jenny

3B Rosemount Crescent
Leeds

24 September 1959

Dear Judith,

I have now spent three years of my life on night duty and I'm only 25. But not for much longer. Meet the next ward sister of Ward 1 – a female medical ward you may recall. It will be much easier at home with us both on days. Sandy misses the scooter rides.

The housemen are still up to their tricks. The flower ladies had an edifice built in the front hall to hold large bunches of flowers. It's ghastly. Made of bricks and looks like a fountain. It starts with a sort of moat and then a pillar rises from it to hold a large, metal bowl. One night the housemen all peed in it. I must say I agree with their opinion.

Another one did a round on a bicycle in the middle of the night. Apparently one of the patients said to him the next day, 'I don't rightly knows what's in them pills tha's giving me doctor, but they're making me see things. I thought I saw you on a bicycle in t'night.'

Had a letter from Marie not long ago. She had a baby boy you know but she had to have it in Africa. She's pregnant again and this time wants to come home for the birth. They've never been back since they went and that's over three years ago.

Love Jenny

Chapter 26

Dear Sister Ross,

It gives me great pleasure to write and inform you that your appointment as sister-in-charge of Ward 1 was confirmed at the meeting of the House Committee yesterday. Your appointment will commence on 1 October 1959.

I hope you will be very happy working in Ward 1.

Yours sincerely,
Ann Wilks, Matron

A WARD SISTER AT last! As I walk to my ward on the first morning, I think of all the sisters who have influenced me. I want to emulate Busby, BB and Howes. I do not want to be like the Dragon, the Sod or Jenner. My ward will be interesting for the student nurses, a place where they can learn and grow. I see my job as fostering them and in turn, they will nurture the patients. Lockers will be wiped once a day only. Teaching will be as routine as bedmaking and teaching sessions will be held daily. Each student will be allocated a patient and she will be expected to study the condition, medical treatment and nursing care of that patient. In fact, she will give the nursing care. Because we go round the ward doing all treatments, all medicines, all TPRs and so on, it is difficult for students to see the entirety of the nursing care provided.

I am aware that a ward reflects the character of the sister. Rigid, rule-bound sisters create wards where the bed-tables are lined up, the counterpanes are even and the patients almost breathe in and out in unison. Student nurses are fearful, and as a consequence, lack confidence. Liberal wards, on the other hand, are not regimentally tidy, nor are they disorderly. Students are free to use judgement and so take more interest in their patients.

I plan on making several changes and when I heard I'd got the ward, I told Buzz some of the things I want to do. 'It's ridiculous that the work list is made out according to seniority. That means the junior nurses never learn to give out medicines or do treatments. Nor do the seniors learn to be in charge. When they finish, one day they are a student and the next a staff nurse, who, without any preparation, is expected to take charge. I intend to make out the work list so I am doing kitchen and bedpans sometimes – that should shake them!'

'I am sure your ward will be exciting, but Jen, a word of advice. Don't go waving a broom to make a clean sweep. Take your time. Wait two or three months and then introduce changes very slowly.' Buzz had poured herself a cup of tea and settled back in her chair before continuing. 'People don't like change and if you start off by making major reforms, they will resist and wear you down. So take it slowly. Get your staff nurses particularly on your side before doing anything.'

I am thinking of her words as I enter the foyer of Ward 1 to find Joan Sutcliffe, the perm, waiting for me. I dropped by one morning last week to introduce myself and tell her I would be starting on 3 October as it is a Saturday and the weekend gives me time to know the patients before the consultant's rounds.

'Good morning, Sister,' she says.

'Good morning, Joan. Please call me Jenny or Jen. Shall we go in?'

The nurses are already gathered around the centre table waiting for me to say prayers. My experience on Ward 5 allows me to proceed with confidence. After prayers we move to the desk to receive the report from the night nurse. I notice that Brenda McFarlane, the staff nurse, does not join us. Well, that's one change I'm not waiting for. 'Brenda, please come and take report.' How can a nurse be expected to take charge of the ward if she's not up-to-date with what is happening? 'Also, you are to have coffee in the sideward with us, in case that's not what you usually do.'

When we've had the report I ask Joan to take charge so I can spend the morning getting to know the ward and doing a thorough round of the patients. It is a 34-bed, female medical ward specialising in rheumatology and neurology but with the usual medical complaints such as chronic bronchitis. I have five consultants, the two prominent ones being Jack Hartman, a rheumatologist, and Hugh Dingwall, a neurologist.

Before I start my round I go out to the kitchen to pay attention to the domestic staff. Ignoring them can spell trouble as they have many ways to make my life a misery. Although each of the three has her own supervisor, I am responsible for the day-to-day operation of the ward and for the part they play in it. I find Eva, the non-nursing orderly, Mavis, the cleaner, and Francesca, the maid, beginning to wash up the patient's breakfast dishes. I ask if they can stop for a minute.

'I'm Sister Ross,' I say. 'I wanted to introduce myself and find out if there's anything you need or anything I can do to help you.'

'I'm Eva,' the orderly says. She is a thin, haggard, middle-aged woman with wispy bleached hair springing out from her blue cap. 'And this is Mavis and that's Francesca. Francesca doesn't speak much English but she's a right hard worker.'

I say hello to Mavis, a short, solid woman with thick legs who could, without trying, play the role of a typical Yorkshire working-class woman, and to Francesca, a young dark-haired, dark-eyed, pretty Spanish girl. They all smile at me.

'There's one thing tha' can do,' says Mavis. 'Tha' can see to it that there's more staff on on Wednesday afternoons when it's our cleaning day. If we had more 'elp from t'nurses, we'd be that much faster.'

'I'll see what I can do,' I say.

One afternoon a week, the domestic staff push all the beds into the centre of the ward, splat polish over the wooden floor, spread it with a special mop and buffer it with a heavy, padded polisher. Nurses hate cleaning after-noons. They can't reach the patients without stepping in polish or climbing over chairs. Although it is not a nursing duty to help with the cleaning, if everyone pitches in, it is over quickly. If nurses do not help, the domestic staff take all afternoon, making it impossible to proceed. I know that some sisters take a two-five on cleaning day. I intend to be one of them. After all, there has to be some advantage to being a sister. But I will make sure the nurses help.

I go back into the ward where many curtains are closed because a bedpan round is in progress. I start my round with Dr Hartman's patients who are in beds 1–13. The first patient is a lively woman with silver hair and severe rheumatoid arthritis, particularly of her hands. I introduce myself.

'So you're the new Sister, are you? Well, you're a bonny lass but you don't look old enough to be a sister.' She leans forward to look across to the next bed. 'Mabel, this is t'new Sister. Better looking than the last one, eh?'

A weak voice comes from Mabel's bed. 'Aye, she is that. But she's awful young. Does tha' think she knows owt?'

'Time will tell, time will tell.' The silver head shakes from side to side.

I read Mrs Deakin's notes and then pull the curtains so I can examine her joints. 'How are you, Mrs Deakin?' I ask as I bend her fingers backwards and forwards.

'Pain's less, Sister, but I wish I could move more. I'm not used to doing nowt.'

Her poor hands are gnarled and bent, the joints swollen and shiny, and she has very little motion in them. She is on gold sodium thiomalate so she is in hospital for the supervision of this toxic treatment.

'T'doctor says I never will be able to move my fingers so I must make t'best of it. I'll have to learn to use my toes.' She gives me a wan smile.

'Have you seen the physiotherapist?' I ask.

'Not yet, but I've only been in two days.'

I make a note in my book to refer her to physio. The TPR book is an essential working document. Patients' names are listed on the left page and columns are drawn for recording temperature, pulse and respiration twice a day. There's a space to note whether there has been a bowel movement and what laxatives or enemas are given. The right-hand page records all tests to be ordered or other tasks to be done. These are ticked when finished. A glance at this page, and previous pages, tells us what requisitions to send, what phone calls to make and, where there are no ticks, what to follow up. I write 'Ref. physio.' beside Mrs Deakin's name and move on.

At nine o'clock half the student nurses leave for a half-hour break while Joan, Brenda and I go into the sideward to enjoy the coffee and biscuits that Eva has set out for us. I note with satisfaction that the coffee is good and there is a decent selection of biscuits. I must make sure that Eva is content.

We pour our coffee and then sit down. We look at each other, waiting for someone to speak. I know that my two staff nurses will be wondering what I am like and will be cautious until they do. I suddenly feel nervous and don't know what to say. I wonder what they have heard about me. The previous sister had a reputation for being inconsistent but they could have got on well with her and may be missing her.

'Look.' I speak first. 'I know you may not want to work with me and if you want to move, I shall understand and speak to the office for you.'

'What do you think of that, Brenda?' Joan says. 'She's only been here an hour and she's telling us we can leave.'

'Maybe it's the way we said prayers.'

'Or it's the way you wear your cap.'

'Or it's the way you made out the work list.'

'Or it's…'

'Alright you two,' I say, laughing. 'I was only giving you a chance because I know you got landed with me.'

'Oh I think we can put up with you. We'll let you know if you become impossible,' Joan says. 'Anyway, Eva seems to like you. We've never had such good coffee.'

'I took the advice of Sister Busby and introduced myself to them as soon as possible.' I say. 'I asked if there's anything they need. They said they wanted help on cleaning day. Haven't they been getting it?'

'No. Sister was one of those who didn't think nurses should help with cleaning. So it took all afternoon.' Joan's expression is blank.

'Well I would like everyone to pitch in but I have to warn you – I intend to have a two-five.'

'You rotter,' Brenda says and then adds, 'But I don't blame you; I would be off if I could.'

'When do you go into purple?' I ask her.

'December the first. In two months.'

'Where do you want to perm?'

Brenda grins at me and says, 'If I can put up with you, here.'

'What makes you think I'll have you?'

The atmosphere has become light-hearted and I know we are all going to get along. It is so important that the trained staff works well together. Friction affects the performance of the students and thus, the care of the patients. Besides the work is hard enough without sideward fights.

The door opens and Dr Hartman's registrar, Stewart

Walker, and his houseman, Dave Ullman, walk in. I know Dave from nights but have had no dealings with Stewart.

'Hello, Jen.' Dave says. 'Nice to see you on days. Stewart, this is Jenny Ross. She's just come off nights.'

A voice with a Scottish accent greets me and then says, 'Can we do a round after coffee?'

'I'd be grateful,' I say. 'It will help me get to know your patients.'

Stewart trained in Edinburgh and I have not yet met an Edinburgh-trained physician who is anything but excellent. Our round reinforces my view. Stewart is thorough but gentle and the patients clearly worship him. He answers their questions with an air that he has as much time to spend with them as they need.

Back in the sideward we discuss his patients further, saying things we would not want them to hear, such as pros and cons of treatments or their prognosis. Most of the ward business is conducted in the sideward and we frequently sit over a cup of tea or coffee exchanging information, asking advice or just chatting.

Stewart talks about a study he wants to undertake. 'Jenny, we give our rheumatology patients so much aspirin that I'm concerned about the state of their stomach walls. I would like to pass Ryle's tubes into them and take specimens every morning. Is that possible?'

'You mean you would like us to pass the Ryle's tubes, not come here yourself?'

'Aye. That's what I was thinking.'

'Will we get credit in the research write-up?'

'Of course, of course,' he says, but I know that nurses rarely receive acknowledgement for their part in medical studies.

I manage to finish going round all the patients just as the dinner trolley is pushed into the centre of the ward and plugged into the floor. I roll down my sleeves, put on my hard cuffs and prepare to serve 34 meals. Joan helps me. She knows how much each patient can eat better than I do. Those on special diets are served first, then we dole out lamb stew, mashed potatoes and brussel sprouts. There is mince and mashed carrots for those who need a light diet.

Joan is looking round the ward saying, 'Mrs Deakin. Not much of an appetite, so give her a small helping. Mrs Jones. Her teeth don't fit so give her mince. Miss Twaites, huge appetite. Mrs Tetley needs feeding, Nurse Harrop. And Mrs Black, Nurse Yardley.'

We serve the pudding from a regular trolley that we push round the ward, closely followed by Eva with a trolley of tea. A third trolley holds the dirty plates. Then it is time for a bedpan round and my dinner.

After nights it is strange to see so many in the sister's dining room even though it is the weekend and half of them are off including Sandy. When I have settled down I will make my off duty the same as hers.

I spend the afternoon exploring the cupboards under the

stairs that hold clean linen and equipment such as lumbar puncture sets. I am responsible for the ward inventory that includes sheets, towels, equipment, plates, cutlery, curtains, beds – everything in fact. Each ward closes for one week a year to allow the inventory to be checked and missing items replaced. It is also a time for repairs and painting and I have to see that these are ordered ahead of time or they won't get done.

Because it is easy to lose equipment if another ward borrows it, some sisters lock their cupboards at night. This practice infuriated me when I was a night sister and needed a lumbar puncture set for example, as I had to run round the hospital to find one. I left rude messages for the offending sisters but they did not alter their ways. I intend to leave my cupboards open. After all, I don't own the equipment even though I am responsible for it. Obtaining new supplies is a simple matter of filling out a requisition.

I go home tired but happy. I think my first day went well. I really like Joan and Brenda and I feel fortunate to have inherited such good staff nurses. Perhaps I won't have to wait long to make changes after all.

Chapter 27

Rules for the Administration of Medicines:

1. *Never give a medicine from an unmarked bottle or from one on which the label is illegible.*

2. *Read the label before and after pouring a dose.*

3. *Check up with the patient's Front Sheet.*

4. *Shake the bottle by turning it upside down with the finger on the cork.*

5. *Hold the cork in the bent little finger while pouring the dose.*

6. *Hold the glass with the mark denoting the quantity to be given on eye level and marked by the thumb.*

7. *Pour out the dose with the label uppermost.*

8. *Never speak, or allow anyone to speak to you, while measuring the dose.*

9. *See that the patient drinks the medicine at once, never leaving it at the bedside for him to take later.*

10. *Give iron mixtures with a straw, or allow the patient to brush the teeth immediately afterwards, as they blacken the teeth.*

11. *Never give two medicines at the same time without definite orders, as they may react with one another.*

12. *When the drug given is included in the schedule of 'Dangerous Drugs' it must be checked by a State Registered Nurse and entered in the poisons register.*

13. *After a drug has been given, watch carefully its effect on the patient.*

ALTHOUGH CONSULTANTS ARE informed of the appointment of a new ward sister on their wards, they have no say in the selection. Theoretically they could object to the choice but I have never heard of this happening. I am greeted politely by each of my five consultants, who then carry on as usual. I spend most of every morning accompanying one or other of them on their rounds and must be prepared for these by acquiring outstanding lab reports or X-rays, and by thoroughly knowing the patients.

Each consultant has an entourage comprising a registrar, a houseman and medical students. Collectively they are known as a 'firm'. Early on Monday morning, Jack Hartman, the rheumatologist, and his firm arrive. He introduces

himself and welcomes me before we move to his first bed.
He is a courteous man and seems bent on having the
medical students learn to respect nurses.

'What is the normal ESR?' he asks them. They look
blank and shake their heads. 'In fact, what does ESR mean?'
Still no response.

'Sister?'

'It's the Erythrocyte Sedimentation Rate,' I say. 'Normal
values vary with age and sex but the upper limit of normal
is 15mm for a man and 20mm for a woman. It rises in the
acute stage of rheumatoid arthritis, which is why it is being
checked on this patient.'

He turns to the students. 'Never forget how much you
can learn from nurses. When in doubt, ask them.'

I feel like hugging him and bless his wife who used to
be a nurse here.

Because Stewart Walker is so competent, there is little
Jack adds to the treatment plans so he spends most of his
round teaching the students and supervising their examination techniques.

The first time I see Hugh Dingwall, the neurologist, I
want to laugh. I know he is nicknamed Pansy Dingwall and
when he appears, I can see why. He wears a morning suit
of pinstriped trousers, a grey waistcoat and a black jacket
sporting a carnation. His appearance defies his reputation
of being a brilliant diagnostician and I have to resist the
urge to sing 'Burlington Bertie from Bow'.

I had also heard that he has an eye for the girls. As we stand at the foot of a bed listening to the houseman report on the patient, his eyes are focused on the legs of every nurse who walks by. He looks as though he isn't listening but I soon find out that he doesn't miss a trick. Many of his patients are suffering from the neurological aftermath of syphilis that they usually acquired in their youth and which has lain dormant all their lives. It is tragic to see these women with paralysis of their limbs or with locomotor ataxia in which there is pain and loss of position sense. Once the diagnosis has been made from a positive Wasserman test, there is little treatment to offer except penicillin, which has a minimal effect at this stage.

Sideward life becomes more and more lively as Joan, Brenda and I get to know each other better and to appreciate each other's humour. Joan is very Yorkshire with her direct, down-to-earth approach. 'Bluddy 'ell,' she'll say, 'that Potts woman is chuntering on about her bowels again. It's driving me spare.'

Brenda is energetic and enthusiastic. It is to her that I first mention that I want to initiate daily teaching sessions, and instead of 'We don't have enough time,' or 'Do you really think you'll get the housemen to teach?' she says, 'Wonderful. When do we start?'

'Let's talk it over with Joan,' I say.

The three of us discuss how the morning routine can be changed so that the nurses finish at 11.30 instead of 12 noon, leaving half an hour to sit down for a talk.

'I'll teach them about some of the medicines that patients are on,' Brenda says. 'In fact, I'll start a Materia Medica.'

'I can yak about neurological stuff,' Joan says.

'I know more about medical conditions so I'll prepare a session on chronic bronchitis,' I say. 'And we'll rope in the housemen,' Brenda says. 'When shall we start? Tomorrow?'

'Why not?' I am so pleased at their response and I can feel my own enthusiasm rise with theirs.

The next day I explain to the nurses what we are going to do. Despite cutting out the round of lockers it is difficult for them to finish earlier than usual but we do manage to gather round the table at 11.40 and I give a talk on chronic bronchitis, a condition that brings in perennial patients at the first November fog.

Even though the session may be for only ten minutes, we manage to hold one every day. The housemen are keen to join in and I am delighted with the eagerness shown by everyone. The student nurses seem more energetic and I remember how I felt after a teaching session with Busby.

I order a supply of folders and paper. When they arrive, I make up a folder for each student nurse and assign each a patient. I explain that they are to write up the condition, medical treatment and nursing care of the patient and to make daily progress notes. They are to go to the library to read about the disease and they are to find out about the action and toxic symptoms of each medicine their patient is on. Their notes will be kept in the box that hangs from the end of the bed to hold Front Sheets for doctor's prescriptions, intake and output records and other notes.

Once the nurses have become accustomed to the task, I make a point of reading the notes when I do a round and I try to remember to comment on them. We have the nurses present their cases at some of the teaching sessions. Although they are nervous at first, they are stimulated by the experience.

One afternoon when the ward is quiet and there is an extra nurse on duty, I assign a first-year student to give out medicines under my supervision. A metal cupboard on legs tall enough to bring the cupboard to eye level is wheeled to the foot of the bed and the medicine is dispensed there. The prescription is checked against the Front Sheet, the medicine is poured and a record is made on the chart. Nurse Carter is clearly anxious.

'You have plenty of time,' I say. 'Don't worry if you're slow. There's such an array of bottles it is difficult to find the right one at first.'

She settles down and begins to enjoy herself as she shakes out pills on to a teaspoon and measures liquid medicines into small, glass measuring cups. I explain the action of the medicines and have her refer to the Materia Medica that Brenda started in a hard-covered notebook with an alphabet index.

I read out, 'Sulphonamides. Salts of sulphonic acid. Action is to inhibit the growth of certain bacteria but does not kill them. Bacteria sensitive to sulphonamides are streptococci, staphylococci, pneumococci and meningococci. The sulphonamides are excreted rapidly so they should be given at frequent intervals. Their action is assisted by alkalis. They should be given with plenty of fluids (4–6 pints) to prevent crystallisation in the kidneys.'

I stop reading to say, 'That's why Mrs Hall is on I & O.' I pick up the book again. 'A course of treatment should not exceed six days. Administration is usually by mouth in the form of half-gram tablets. Toxic effects can be nausea, vomiting, cyanosis, skin rashes (like measles), suppression of urine, fever, agranulocytosis and haemolytic anaemia.'

Although it has taken three times as long as usual to give out the medicines and I am behind in my work, I am pleased with my effort. I realise how much I like teaching. It thrills me to see how earnest these young women are when they are learning something new and how they carry on with their work with renewed vigour.

'There's something else I want to try,' I say to Joan and Brenda one day.

'Oh cor strewth, what now?' Joan asks.

'Well you don't have to do it but when I'm on tonight I'm going to reverse the work list and do kitchen and bedpans.'

'I thought she was barmy when she first showed up and

now I know she is.' Joan says. At five o'clock, when I come on duty, I write the work list:

Sister	Kitchen, bedpans, lockers
Nurse Tindale	In charge, medicines
Nurse Harrop }	Beds and backs, treatments, hourly
Nurse Yardley }	fluids to 7, 10, 14, 19 and 23

As the nurses come on and read the work list, I watch their reactions. Nurse Tindale says, 'I think there must be some mistake, Sister. You're down to do kitchen and I'm down to be in charge.'

'There's no mistake Nurse Tindale. You take finals soon and I want you to know what it's like being in charge before you are suddenly a staff nurse.'

'But Sister, I don't know what to do!'

'Of course you do. You've been in charge on nights and it's much the same. Anyway, I'm here if you need me. When the Ass. Mat. comes I will tell her you are in charge and ask her to take the report from you. You just take her to the sickest patients who are on this list. I'll give you the report now.'

I give the report and then I go out into the foyer, plug in the food trolley and stack it with plates. I set a trolley with cutlery and water jugs and I am just about to wheel it into the ward when an Assistant Matron comes in. She is here to collect the report of the sickest patients. I tell her that Nurse

Tindale is in charge this evening and would she receive the report from her. She seems surprised but nods in agreement.

I start to set bed trays with knives and forks, fill water glasses and retrieve napkins from lockers. It is surprisingly relaxing to do these chores that I once hated. I check a couple of Dangerous Drugs and some insulin with Tindale but otherwise she is managing splendidly.

At suppertime, Tindale serves and I feed patients. Then I put on a pink gown and do a bedpan round.

I am thoroughly enjoying myself. When that is finished, I go into the bathroom to wash rubber draw sheets with carbolic. While I am there, Nurse Yardley comes to tell me that we are getting an acute, a patient in status epilepticus, which means that the patient is having a continuous epileptic fit. It is a medical emergency and requires immediate attention or the patient will collapse.

I watch through the bathroom door window to make sure that Tindale knows what to do. She is pushing over an oxygen cylinder to the bed and Nurse Yardley is setting up a tray with a wooden wedge to hold the mouth open. The houseman is there. Tindale gets an injection tray and prepares a syringe, of paraldehyde I expect.

I wander into the ward and can smell the sickly, sweet aroma of paraldehyde before I reach the bed. 'You seem to be coping beautifully,' I say to Tindale. If she was on nights, she'd be doing just what she is doing with only a visiting night sister.

'I saw you hovering behind the door,' she says accusingly.

'I would have come out if I thought you needed help or weren't managing but you were. I'll wait until this patient stops fitting and then I'm going for supper,' I say.

Tindale gives the report to the night staff while I listen and interject only when it's information she couldn't know. As we both go off duty, she turns to me. 'That was a really good experience. Thank you so much for your trust.'

On 1 December Brenda comes on duty at 8am in her new purple uniform. I now have two perms. I wonder how long I will be allowed to keep them before the office intervenes. Normally, a ward has one perm and one or two staff nurses. We have a little party for her in the sideward. I brought in some cakes and the men, who have been forewarned, show up all at once, Stewart with a bunch of flowers for Brenda.

'Congratulations,' I say. 'Let us raise our coffee cups to toast my new perm.'

Dave says, 'What are you keeping all these boxes of chocolates for? Can't we open one?'

He is referring to a pile of 10 or 20 pound chocolate boxes that is growing as Christmas approaches. It is a Yorkshire custom for patients and ex-patients to express their thanks with chocolates, especially at Christmas.

'They're for Christmas but we could open one as part of Brenda's celebration.' I open a box of Black Magic and pass it round. 'You know, it's not fair, none of the other departments get chocolates and they do as much for patients as we do. I'm going to send them around.'

I write little cards saying, 'With many thanks for your services from Ward 1', attach one to a box of chocolates and send a box to the porters, kitchen, dispensary, physio and the Lady Almoner's office, which, among other duties, assigns convalescent beds at the Ida. Little do I realise at the time the effect this gesture will have.

Whenever we need a porter, one appears in an instant; we receive special extras with the food, like apples; when we need an Ida bed for a patient we are allocated one faster than any other ward; and I'm invited to the pharmacy Christmas party.

'I have discovered what an expression of appreciation can do,' I say to Joan. 'I must try to do it more often. I'll start by saying how glad I am that you're on my ward.'

'I like working with you too,' she says. 'Even though you're as daft as a brush.'

She and I spend an afternoon shopping for toiletries for our patients' Christmas presents. We use a fund of donations from patients over the year and supplement it with our own money. The chemist across the road from the hospital gives us a discount so we are able to buy some really nice gifts.

We decide to decorate the ward as a circus. Joan brings in her bike, which we stand on the central table, and above it we suspend a stuffed figure with its arms on the handle-

314

bars and its legs in the air. Brenda is surprisingly artistic and she and some patients paint clown faces on large pieces of cardboard. We attach these to each junction of the curtain rails so the effect is that of a row of clowns looking down on us.

We remove a bed and its curtains and enclose the space with half-inch wide strips of aluminium foil so that it resembles a cage. Dave fashions two extraordinary bird-like creatures from plaster of Paris, one larger than the other. We sit these in straw behind the foil with a big label, 'Pneumosaurus and chick.'

Leeds City supplies each ward with a 15-foot tree and porters set these up in the middle of the ward. Needless to say, our ward is the first. Porters also hang decorations near the top of the tree while the step-ladder is available.

Many patients go home for Christmas but we are left with about 12. We bring their beds up to the front of the ward. We leave one really sick woman further down where it is more peaceful.

I am expecting the Salvation Army band to play carols on Christmas Eve but I am not prepared for so many musicians with their silver instruments. I fear that they will deafen the patients but when they raise their trumpets, trombones and tubas to their mouths, the sound is so sweet that it brings tears to everyone's eyes.

Although I am exhausted from staying up late every night for pantomime rehearsals, I eagerly go on duty on

Christmas Day. The patients have opened their stockings and are ready for a special breakfast of bacon, eggs, mushrooms and black pudding. Visitors are welcome from 10am on and in the afternoon we serve them tea and fruit cake. The highlight of the day is the carving of the turkey by Dr Hartman in a white chef's hat. He makes quite a display of sharpening the knife before he carves with a flourish, giving a running commentary on the anatomy of a bird. His family is also here to help serve the meal.

After we have cleared up and the patients settle down for a nap, I go to the dining room where I wait on the student nurses. Then it is the sisters' turn and the housemen wait on us. Matron and her assistants eat with us. After the Christmas pudding Matron stands up to present the cup for the best decorated ward.

'We had a hard time deciding this year as there are so many clever and original themes. I must say that my sisters take a great deal of trouble with their decorations and you are all to be congratulated. After much deliberation we decided to award the cup to Ward 1. Sister Ross, would you come up please.'

To the sound of applause, I go up to the head table to receive the silver cup, which I will display in the ward until next Christmas. I return with it and jubilantly carry it round to show the patients. Then I place it on top of the DDA cupboard. Joan and Brenda are as thrilled as I am and we do a little dance in the sideward.

We have been rehearsing for the pantomime every night after nine o'clock and those of us who live out are allowed to stay in the Nurses' Home during this time. Sandy and I are in the sisters' wing. I am enjoying being woken with a cup of tea each morning and putting my shoes outside my door to be cleaned. Despite these luxuries, I would not want to live in permanently as one never seems to be off duty.

We put on two performances of the pantomime, which, as usual, goes down a treat. We have collected anecdotes over the year and these have been translated into the script or a song. One registrar, Michael Todd, was running a rectal outpatient clinic one day. He went out to the waiting room to call for his next patient, a Mrs Murphy, who dutifully entered his examining room. He asked her to take off everything below the waist and lie on the table. She looked puzzled but didn't say anything until he had gloves on and was ready to examine her rectum prior to doing a sigmoidoscopy.

At this point she sat up and said, 'But Doctor, it's me ears I've come with.' It seems there were two Mrs Murphys in outpatients that day. Michael was not allowed to forget it though, as our verse in the registrar's song, to the tune of 'John Brown's Body' was:

You must all beware when Michael Todd is on the prowl,
His faux pas down in Outpatient's Department was a howl,
For in the rectal clinic they've a brand new therapy,
For pains in the ears, it's sigmoidoscopy.

A new decade. 1960 dawns. Every day I wake up eager to go to work. When I get there, I am soon buoyed up by the enthusiasm of my staff nurses and students who are all so willing to work hard and stay late if necessary. On my weekends off I enjoy walking in the Dales with Sandy. We frequently take two days over a hike and stay the night in a youth hostel.

Yes, my life is good.

Chapter 28

MY RELATIONS WITH Matron and her office are not always cordial. I think they believe that if there is nothing negative to say, then all is well. Whenever the tall, thin figure of Ann Wilks appears, my stomach knots and I feel as though I am a schoolgirl instead of a State Registered Nurse in charge of a ward of 34 patients.

One day she appears as we are serving dinner. I leave the trolley and greet her at the door. She stands at the foot of each bed while I recite the patient's name, diagnosis, treatment and progress. She makes no comment to me but asks each patient how she is. 'Nicely thank you,' or 'A bit poorly today,' are the regular answers. In a bed at the end of the ward is a lively, toothless octogenarian, Mrs Daley, and I see, to my horror, that she is trying to eat a slice of roast beef. In the next bed, a patient on a normal diet is eating mince. Clearly the trays have been mixed up.

'Why is this patient sucking on a slice of beef, Sister, when she obviously cannot chew?'

I know that Mrs Daley is stone deaf so I say to Matron,

'She is so tired of mince that she asked for roast beef today so she could suck on it. Isn't that right, Mrs Daley?' I say, nodding at her.

'Aye, aye,' she says, nodding back, and I bless her cotton socks.

On a fairly regular basis, the office sends for me, sometimes to see Matron and sometimes to see Miss Darcy, her deputy. We are expected to stand in front of Matron's desk as she sits and I wish I had BB's courage to pull up a chair and sit down. I don't, so I stand there like a naughty schoolgirl.

A PTS nurse is on the ward one morning for a few hours experience. Shortly after the patient's dinner we have a blood transfusion to start. I ask her if she'd like to watch and help. 'Ooh yes, Sister' she says, her eyes lighting up. I can remember how I felt at that stage when everything is so new and exciting. Dave is starting the transfusion and I prepare the trolley.

'While the doctor is washing his hands,' I say firmly, looking at Dave, 'We check that the blood is the right type.'

As there is no movement of Dave towards the sink, I say again, 'While the doctor is washing his hands…'

'Oh right,' Dave says and moves to the sink.

I supervise the procedure for a while and then leave them. At 1.30 I go behind the curtains and say to the PTS nurse, 'It's time you went for your dinner. Thank you. I'll take over now.'

'Oh Sister' she says. 'We've nearly finished and I don't mind being late for dinner.'

'We'll be about five minutes,' Dave says.

'Alright then,' I say. I forget about the incident until the call to Matron's office.

'Sister Ross,' she says as I stand before her. 'I understand a PTS nurse came in late for her dinner the other day. I must point out that these probationers are sent to the wards for very basic experience and are NOT to be used as staff.'

I imagine that the nurse had gone to the dining room to crow to her friends about helping with a blood transfusion. Her story must have reached the ears of Up and Down, who reported the event to Matron.

'I wished to excite her by letting her attend the start of a blood transfusion.' I say. 'I asked her to go to her dinner but she chose to stay until the procedure was finished.'

'Well Sister, this must not happen again. As I said, PTS nurses are not there to replace staff.'

I am furious and stomp back to my ward. Despite all that I have initiated, there has been no word of encouragement and now I'm told off for making a student late.

An ex-LGI nurse is admitted as a patient for neurological tests. One morning she has to go across the road to the School of Dentistry. We are extremely busy, as we are one nurse short, so I send for a porter with a wheelchair to transport her there. I make sure she is well wrapped up before sending her on her way. After she is discharged, I am summoned to the office.

'I have had a letter from Miss Gold,' Matron says. 'She complains that she was sent over to the School of Dentistry without a nurse accompanying her.'

'She didn't need a nurse to accompany her. She was up and about, not ill, and we were extremely busy.'

'She is an ex-LGI nurse, Sister, as I think you know.'

'Does that mean I was supposed to neglect 33 other patients by losing a nurse for the whole morning?'

'No, but…'

'You are calling my judgement into question. I'm sorry but I think the welfare of 33 patients takes precedence over one, even if she is an ex-nurse.' I turn on my heel and march out.

I notice one day that Ward 11 has new ward doors with an attractive stained-glass declaration that this is Ward 11. My doors do not close properly. They swing on their hinges smoothly but when they close, there is a gap between them. I write a requisition: 'One pair of new ward doors.'

Miss Darcy sends for me, shows me the requisition and says, 'You can't just order a pair of doors!'

'Why not?' I say. 'Mine don't close properly.'

'Yes, but although you can order supplies, you can't order things like doors.'

'Why not?' I say again. 'Ward 11 has just got new doors.'

'So that's it. Doors are extremely expensive. The House Committee must order that sort of thing. Ward 11's doors were rotten, had come off their hinges and were completely dysfunctional. Yours are not. She laughs. 'You must learn to live with them, Sister Ross.'

Although Sundays are quiet, we have all the student nurses on duty. The next time I work out the off duty, I give a student a Saturday afternoon and Sunday off. She is delighted as students only get weekends off during block. After that I make a habit of giving each student, in turn, a weekend. Not for long.

Miss Darcy says, 'Matron has asked me to talk to you about your off duty allocation. We have learned that you are giving students weekends off.'

'Yes,' I say. 'It doesn't make sense to have everyone working on a Sunday when the ward is quieter than any other day.'

'Well, I'm afraid this practice must stop. Students may not be off on the weekend.'

'Why not?'

'You are creating a precedent. If they get weekends on your ward, they'll want to know why they can't have the same on every ward.'

'Well, why shouldn't they? Why can't I be the one to set an example?' I try not to sound as frustrated as I feel.

'Other sisters have complained.' Miss Darcy looks embarrassed.

'So even if it doesn't suit my ward work and I am short on a Tuesday, for example, I can't give a student a Saturday afternoon and Sunday off?'

'I'm afraid not.'

I tell Joan and Brenda about this latest edict. 'It's ridiculous. I expect it's the Dragon. She'd rather be short all week than allow a student to be off at the weekend.' I show my annoyance by stabbing the TPR book with my pen. 'All right, I'll give them a half-day on Friday, Saturday and a morning till one on Sunday. Not as good, but at least they get a Saturday night and a lie-in the next day.'

I do get a compliment eventually, back-handed though it is. Miss Darcy comes on the ward to see me, rather than summoning me to the office.

'I am sending you a Nurse Sinclair,' she says. 'She's in second year and wants to hand in her notice. She's fed up she says. She has agreed to a trial of three months so I have decided to put her here so you can inspire her. I know how much the nurses love working here.'

After that I regularly get disaffected nurses on my roster. All they need is encouragement and some effort to make the work interesting for them, especially in second year when they seem to hit a period of disenchantment.

In addition to rounds by the office, Sister Tutors occasionally visit. One day, much to my surprise, AJ appears. She stands at the door smiling and asks me if she may do a round. 'Don't bother to put on your cuffs, Sister.'

We walk slowly round the ward but AJ does not seem interested in the patients as she does not want to hear their diagnoses. 'I hear your students each have a case to study and write up. May I see one of them?' Ah, so that's why she's here.

I proudly show her a student's notes about a patient with leukaemia. The student has taken great pains to investigate the condition and even quotes the latest research reported in *The Lancet*.

'Hmm,' is all AJ says.

'Can't you think of anything positive to say,' I think. I suddenly feel disheartened and carry on with the round in a dispirited way. We reach a patient with a Ryle's tube.

AJ looks at me and starts to laugh. 'Do you remember when you put one of those down yourself? I don't know how I kept a straight face! That was one of the funniest sights I'd seen for a long time.' Her laughter turns to wheezing so she has to take out a handkerchief to wipe her eyes.

I do win a major battle with the office, largely because Hugh Dingwall takes a stand. A third-year nurse, close to finals, is admitted because she has had several episodes of brief periods of unconsciousness. After a number of tests she is told she has Petit Mal and is given a drug to control it.

When the office finds out, she is told she cannot continue her training and that she may not be a nurse. I make an appointment to see Matron.

'Nurse Weller, as you know, has been diagnosed with Petit Mal. As you also know, there is a great deal of ignorance about epilepsy. The sufferers can live a normal life; they just have to be careful doing certain things, like driving a car.'

'It is impossible for an epileptic to be a nurse, Sister. We must think of the patients.'

'Yes, I know, but there are many places she could work where she does not put patients in danger. Out-patients for example.' I am trying to keep calm.

'It is out of the question, Sister. Nurse Weller will have to find another, more suitable career.' Matron turns to her paper work in a dismissive gesture.

Next time Dr Dingwall comes on the ward, I tell him about the incident.

'We'll see about that,' he says. 'It's appalling the way epileptics are treated. I don't know why we don't lock them behind bars and have Sunday outings to go and stare at them.'

I hear nothing more until Nurse Weller visits the ward, in uniform.

'I am to finish my training after all. I only have three months to go and I'm spending it in out-patients.' She looks as if she wants to give me a hug. 'I'm so grateful that

you went to bat for me. I can't see any reason why I can't
go on. After all I've been like this for two years and I didn't
harm anyone. Now I'm on drugs, my fits are controlled, so
I shall be even less of a danger.'

Chapter 29

EACH YEAR, TO inform us of new developments in nursing, the sisters are taken off their wards for two 'study days'. These days give us a chance to sit back and reflect on what we are doing. They are held in the Nurses' Home in the same room where the Sod first addressed us. We wear mufti. There is a general carnival atmosphere until the topic of the day is explained: we are to know what to do in the event of a nuclear war.

Sandy and I sit next to each other to hear about how we are to move our patients, beds and bedding to tents beside the River Wharfe. We are to spend part of this day making a list of everything we will need.

'What makes them think we will survive a nuclear bomb?' Sandy says.

'And what makes them think that the water in the Wharfe won't be radioactive?' We queue for a cup of coffee before sitting down again.

'How on earth can we move a ward full of patients anyway? What in, for starters?' Sandy says.

'And there aren't tents big enough.'

We are shown slides of nuclear bombs going off including pictures of survivors of Hiroshima. By the end of the day we are all thoroughly depressed.

'Let's go to the Golden Lion,' someone suggests. Most of us go to the hospital's local pub where, after a couple of beers, we cheer up as we begin to see the inanity of the day's exercise.

'Oh, we'll all go together when we go, all suffused in an incandescent glow,' we sing from one of Tom Lehrer's songs.

The next day is better. One of the sisters describes her tour of hospitals in the United States and Canada where she learned how they organise nursing care. In addition to her technical descriptions, she shows slides of the places she visited. Sandy and I are particularly impressed with those of Vancouver in British Columbia.

'Hey look at those mountains, Sandy. We could ski on our days off if we lived there,' I say.

'Even better, look at the sea. Isn't it beautiful? We could sunbathe on the beach.'

'It looks cleaner than grotty old Leeds.' I think about the times when the patients' counterpanes are covered in soot after being out on the balcony for a couple of hours.

'That hospital looks nice. What's it called? St Paul's?' Sandy leans forward trying to read the name on the building.

'Maybe we should think about emigrating, Sandy. There's lots of advertisements for nurses to come to Canada.'

'Not just yet, Jen. We've only been ward sisters for a few months and I'm not tired of it yet, are you?'

I don't answer but I think about her question. No, I'm not tired of my ward, but I can foresee the day when I will be. Now that I have made the changes I had imagined, now that I am confident about what I am doing, the routine is becoming just that, routine.

One morning while doing my usual round, I go into the sterilizing room. The night staff boils up the long forceps with their container. Once sterilized, carbolic is poured into the container to keep the forceps sterile. For some reason, nurses are loath to fill the container, but put about one inch of carbolic in the bottom, which means that the shaft of the forceps is unsterile. I have mentioned this so often that it is known as one of my quirks, along with opening the windows in the morning to air the ward. Today there is an inch of carbolic. I lose my temper and give Joan a histrionic display of fury.

'Look at this! How many times have I gone on about this before? It simply shows no concept of sterility. I feel like bringing back the night staff.' As I say the words I remember the Dragon summoning a night nurse from her bed to clean a trolley. Am I becoming like her? I am mortified. 'Oh my god, I'm getting like the Dragon. Sorry, Joan.'

I remember Judith saying that power tends to corrupt and absolute power corrupts absolutely. Is the power I hold as a ward sister going to my head? I wish Judith were around to discuss these issues with. I talk to Sandy of course, but she is a cheerful soul who dismisses anything philosophical with, 'Don't worry about it.'

Stewart is doing a round. We come to a large woman who is recovering from pneumonia. 'How are you, Mrs Bradley?' Stewart asks.

'Ah feel a bit poorly, Doctor.'

Stewart listens to her chest. 'Your chest is clear now. Do you have pain anywhere?'

'Nay.'

'How much are you getting up?'

Mrs Bradley shakes her head. 'Ah don't feel like getting up, Doctor. Ah feel better in't bed.'

'You must get up more, Mrs Bradley. I know it's hard but it's time to get going.'

As we move to the next bed, Stewart says to me, 'Get her going Jen or she'll be here for ever. There's nothing wrong with her now.'

After Stewart has left, I go to Mrs Bradley and say, 'Right, let's have you up to walk to the bathroom.'

'Ah don't feel like it, Sister.'

'The doctor says you have to be up. Where are your slippers?' I help her out of bed then hold her arm as she reluctantly walks down the ward to the toilet.

'Come along, Mrs. Bradley, you have to do better than this or you'll never go home. You just need to make more effort.' My voice is sharp.

I leave her in the toilet and ask a nurse to keep an eye on her. A few minutes later the nurse comes to me in alarm. 'Sister, come quick. Mrs Bradley has collapsed.'

I rush to the bathroom. I can hardly get into the toilet as Mrs Bradley is lying against the door. 'Go and phone a porter urgently to bring tools to take the door off,' I order the nurse. I climb over the partition from the next toilet but there is nothing I can do. Mrs Bradley is dead.

I sit in the sideward all day, crying. Brenda says, 'There's nothing you could have done, Jen. She had a pulmonary embolism. She would have died anyway.'

'That's not the point.' How could I tell her how officious I'd been, how I had used my authority to make the poor woman get up when she knew she wasn't up to it, how I had listened to Stewart instead of her. 'Dressed in a little brief authority' – the words haunt me.

I arrange to go to Cambridge on my next weekend off. I ask Judith if she could take some time off as I simply have to talk to her. She meets me at the station.

'I am so pleased to see you,' I say. We hug each other. 'You look really well. The academic life seems to suit you.' Judith is dressed in tartan slacks and a big sweater with a Cambridge University scarf wound round her neck.

'Alan is away on a course so we have the weekend to

ourselves and I have one or two small things to do but, otherwise, I'm all yours,' Judith says as we walk out of the station to the bus stop. 'Whatever is the matter? You sounded quite distraught on the phone. Let's go and talk over a pub lunch before we go to the flat.'

In the pub we order cider and pork pies. Once settled, I tell Judith about the incident with Mrs Bradley.

'You always were oversensitive, Jen. You were only doing what a physician asked you to do.'

'Yes, but it was the way I did it. I'm turning into a bitch. It seems to be an occupational hazard for sisters.' I hastily drink some cider to stop myself from bursting into tears.

'How long have you been a ward sister now?' Judith asks with her mouth full.

'Eighteen months.'

'And how old are you?'

'Twenty-seven.'

Judith leans back to look at me. 'Do you really want to spend your entire youth at LGI? I know you always wanted to be a ward sister and now you have. It's time to move on and find out what a young person's life is really like.'

'I don't want to swoon over the Beatles, if that's what you mean.'

Judith laughs. 'No you're too sensible. But there's a life out here. You should he joining clubs, going to parties, taking classes, playing games. Be a 20-year-old before you're 30 and over the hill.'

'I've been thinking of going to Canada. They're advertising for nurses like mad. The pay as a staff nurse is three times what I'm getting as a sister and they only work eight-hour shifts.' I am beginning to feel more cheerful. 'Trouble is, Sandy doesn't want to leave Leeds and I don't want to go on my own.'

'Why not? You'd soon make friends. Come on Jen, start applying for a visa or whatever you have to do.'

I return home with a sense of relief. Yes, it is time to leave. The housemen are not only looking younger but they seem more serious. I remember Howe saying that it was time to move on when they did.

'Sandy,' I say when she comes in. 'I've decided to leave and go to Canada. To Vancouver with those wonderful mountains.'

'When?'

I thought Sandy would scoff at the idea but she looks interested. 'As soon as I get my immigration stuff sorted out and have a job to go to.'

'I'm coming too. I've been thinking about moving on ever since we saw those slides of Canada. I don't know what my father will say but I can't live my life around him.'

We stare at one another in excitement. Over the next few weeks we gather information about visas, travel, Canada, Vancouver and choices of hospital. In record time we have landed immigrant status and can apply for a job. We write to Vancouver General Hospital requesting a position. A letter, by return mail, tells us they will be happy to see us at any time, the sooner the better.

I write to Matron giving her my notice. She sends for me. I enter the inner sanctum, draw up a chair, and sit down.

She says, 'I have received your letter of resignation. You are certain about this, Sister?'

'Definitely. I have a job, a visa and a boat ticket.'

'I am very sorry to lose one of my best sisters, but I wish you every happiness.'

Good grief, she gave me some praise. Isn't it typical that one only hears that one has done a good job when it is time to leave?

Time flies by as we pack our trunks and clean out the flat. The final day arrives. With mixed emotions I walk on to Ward 1 for the last time. After prayers the nurses present me with a case for carrying gramophone records. Buzz stays up to attend a coffee party for me in the sideward. BB calls by later in the day to give me a giant hug. There is so much warmth and friendliness, I almost change my mind, but after dinner I take my clean uniform to the sewing room, pull the thread out of my bonnet and deposit it and my dirty uniform into a bin for the last time.

Instead of going straight home, I ride my scooter all around the smoke-grimed hospital, coming to a halt where I can sit and gaze at Ward 1. For a while I am overcome with nostalgia. I can hear the clatter in the main corridor;

I can smell the fish for dinner; I can see the beds in my ward stretching down its length filled with women in varying degrees of discomfort, but all grateful to be waited on for once in their lives. My mind is in the sideward discussing patients with Stewart and his houseman. I smile as I recall the laughter I have shared with Joan and Brenda. I can almost hear Joan saying to me, 'You daft bugger, what will you do next?'

Although the work is exhausting, I only remember the fun we have: the jokes that sweep through the hospital like a bush fire; the antics of the housemen; the earthy Yorkshire humour of our patients, their stoicism, their generosity; the pantomimes with their amiable ribbing of consultants; the delight in making sick people feel better; the pride in one's competence; the affection of Leeds' people.

I kick start my scooter and roar away. Look out Canada, here I come.

Afterword

O NE OF THE pleasures I enjoyed after the publication of the first edition was the letters I received. They came from New Zealand, Canada, France and the UK and were from nurses I had known, nurses who trained in hospitals other than LGI, physicians of that era and even one from a man who had been a patient in LGI in the fifties. It was heart-warming to know that the book stirred up so many happy memories – even from the patient.

One ex-nurse told me, quite rightly, that I had omitted the Ritual of the Hot Water Bottle. Although patients routinely rebounded off the floors, burned holes in their sheets with cigarettes (and on one memorable occasion, nearly lit up in an oxygen tent), or went AWOL, the administration was intimidated by the fear that they might burn themselves with a hot water bottle. Consequently, the temperature of the water had to be measured before filling. I can't remember what that temperature was but I do know the result would be classified as 'tepid'. The bottle was filled two-thirds full and the empty part squeezed before the plug was inserted. Check the plug was tight; turn bottle upside-down and shake; dress it in a flannel cover; take to patient. The expression on their faces when presented with this 'hot' comfort can only be described as 'resigned'.

As the book began on my first day I didn't deal with the admission interview with Matron, but one reader recollects hers vividly. Like me she was required to respond to, 'Convince me you will not leave training after three months'. Matron was the sole judge of whether you would be admitted to her school or not. Although she submitted a list of suitable candidates to the Board of Governors for official approval it would have taken a brave, perhaps foolhardy, board member to challenge her selection.

Some people wrote asking if such and such character was so and so. No, I really did try not to use real people; with one exception – Amy Squibbs. Squibby was far too colourful a character to hide under another guise. I named her Agatha Japp in the book but otherwise I have described her as I remember her. And she really did catch me with a rubber tube down my nose!

A researcher from the BBC wrote saying that the book was an immense help in planning a programme where a few of today's student nurses would be put in a fifties setup. Unfortunately, because I live in Canada, I was unable to participate, but I was able to give them contacts. The programme, *Thoroughly Modern Matron,* was aired in November 2005. Two Scottish nurses, Sandra McQuat and Pat Johnson, played the parts of Matron and Sister as they initiated six students, mostly from universities, into Preliminary Training School. Funnily enough, the six young women liked their uniforms; they said they made them feel professional and feminine. They had trouble with the discipline, imposed by Matron. Although Matron did not take part in the daily activities of PTS, for this programme she did. The students were lined up daily and inspected like military recruits. One student was told to remove her tongue bar and they were all warned, as we were, not to wear jewellery. In our day, it didn't occur to us to stick metal into man-made orifices so that problem did not arise.

When talking to the BBC researcher I urged her not to portray the matron as some sort of comic ogre. I don't think Hattie Jacques did the nursing profession any good in her portrayal in *Carry On Doctor*. Neither did 'Hot Lips' in *MASH*. The matrons who ran the hospitals for so many decades were well-educated, dedicated and highly responsible. They deserve respect, not ridicule.

My 'set' (students who began training at the same time), was unusual in that we were small to start with and the attrition rate was exceptional. As far as I know the remnant that finished has made no effort to get together again, unlike other sets that have reunions every few years. The set of September 1953, for example, nine months after mine, had their 50th reunion in Leeds. Fifty years! Where did they go? The funny thing is that we are just the same despite the obvious change in body mass – same smiles, same mannerisms, same voices and same personalities

I sometimes wonder if my memories of my twenties are too golden, if I've forgotten the unpleasant parts and if I've developed the mind set that things were better in my young day. Many things have not changed: there is still a shortage of beds, for example. Remember when we had extra beds down the centre of those long wards? The poor patients had no privacy at all. And the work is still hard, both physically and emotionally. The young women and men who enter nursing today are more sophisticated than we were but, judging from my recent hospital experiences, are equally kind and caring. I salute them ... the lamp burns on.

Jennifer Craig, 2010

Acknowledgements

I am deeply grateful to my old buddies who went through this experience with me, and who so generously shared their memories. To:

My long-standing friend, Isobel Foggitt, who came to Canada with me but who is not 'Sandy.'

Margaret Thompson (Tommy) and Margaret Smith, ex-Theatre Sisters who provided me with the stories about theatre.

Betty MacArthur, Pat Jessop and Margaret Ball for reminiscing about night duty and the housemen with me.

I was helped in the writing of this book by the encouragement of:

Caroline Woodward, Vi Plotnikoff and Verna Relkoff, who are teachers of writing at the Kootenay School of the Arts.

Dale Walker, who heartened me by her chuckles as she read the first drafts.

Wendy Grayburn, my aunt, who also trained at Leeds General Infirmary.

My writing group: Jana Daniels, Bill Metcalfe, Vika Lamborne and Ann Alma, for their invaluable critiques.

Thanks are also due to Christine Budd, Wendy Lyall and Dorothy Brown for providing pictures.

Thank you everyone.

About the Author

Jennifer Craig trained at Leeds General Infirmary and rose to become Ward Sister. She emigrated to Canada in 1961, where she married and had two children. Later she studied for a Bachelor's degree in nursing, followed by a Masters degree in education and finally a Ph.D. Ten years as an educational consultant in a medical school preceded semi-retirement when she became a student of homeopathy and obtained her diploma. She now lives in the mountains of British Columbia with a dog and a cat. She is also the author of *Jabs, Jenner and Juggernauts*, a look at vaccination from 1746 to the present day, which might be particularly useful to parents who are facing the decision of whether to vaccinate their children.